D0929780

Native Americans
as Shown
on the Stage
1753-1916

by
EUGENE H. JONES

The Scarecrow Press, Inc.
Metuchen, N.J., & London
1988

Library of Congress Cataloging-in-Publication Data

Jones, Eugene H., 1928-
    Native Americans as shown on the stage, 1753-1916 / by
Eugene H. Jones.
        p.   cm.
    Bibliography: p.
    Includes index.
    ISBN 0-8108-2040-4
    1. American drama--History and criticism. 2. Indians in
literature. 3. Racism in literature. I. Title.
PS338.I53J66 1988
812'.009'3520397--dc19   87-16121

CONTENTS •

Acknowledgments

Introduction

ACKNOWLEDGMENTS •

For their generous aid in the research and preparation of this
book, I would like to thank, in particular, the staffs of the
Lincoln Center Library for the Performing Arts and the Li-
brary of the United States Military Academy at West Point;
most of the plays examined herein were read at those insti-
tutions. Special thanks are also due to Mary Cope, Cohen
Library, City College of New York; Claire Bowie and Helga
Feder at the City University of New York Graduate Center
Library; Cynthia English, Library of the Boston Athenaeum;
Velma Cunningham, The Butterfield Memorial Library, Cold
Spring, New York; Richard Brower, New York Public Library
Microfilm Division; John Lancaster, Amherst College Library;
and the staffs of the Columbia University Library and the
Harvard Theatre Collection.

In addition, valuable information and advice were given
me by the Institute of Outdoor Drama, University of North
Carolina, Chapel Hill; Annie Chadwick Hardin, artistic direc-
tor, and Clif Dowell, publicist, of The Aracoma Story, Inc.,
Logan, West Virginia; Professor Robert Spence, Southern
West Virginia Community College at Logan; Andrea Smith,
MTV Legal Department, New York; Kae Koger, Ann Arbor,
Michigan; and Hanay Geigomah, Indian Art Center, New York.

All other aid would have been in vain, however, if I
had not had the wise counsel of Dr. Vera Mowry Roberts, Dr.
Stanley Waren, and Professor Stanley Kauffmann at City University of New York. Their interest in the subject helped to
direct my lifelong fascination with Native Americans into a
focus on Indians as characters in American plays. Some in-
spiring consultations with each of them when the project was
forming, and their sensitive editorial guidance as it progressed,
helped to make it a pleasure to work on and far easier to complete than it would otherwise have been.

The final work is dedicated to Laura S. Jones, without

whose continuing encouragement and support it would not have been completed at all.

E. H. J.

When Lynn Riggs' play <u>The Cherokee Night</u> was performed at
the Hedgerow Theatre in 1930, it was the first time a stage
work by a full-blooded Native American had ever been produced. Plays about Indians had held the stage for over two
hundred years in England and on the Continent, and in America from the middle of the eighteenth century, and closet
dramas with Indian characters were avidly read, but all of
them were written by white playwrights. The characterizations of Indians in their plays, sympathetic or otherwise, was
biased by the writers' education, racial background, and set
of mind based on current social and political thinking.

The purpose of this study is to examine the attitudes
toward Native Americans as demonstrated in the ways they
were characterized by white playwrights, and to show how
these characterizations apparently masked white people's fear
of Indians as obstacles to the fulfillment of their desire to
settle in the New World. The desire was complicated by the
Europeans' assumption of racial superiority and by fear that
the Indian might be equal or even, in some ways, superior.
Plays about Indians, as seen and read by white Americans
from 1753 to 1916, gave promise of supporting this conclusion
with their dramatization of emotional and moral conflicts between whites and natives.

All the plays examined for this project were written in
English and performed in American theatres or read by American audiences. The study was conducted by, first, documenting the titles and production or publication dates and circumstances of all plays known to include Native American characters; second, reading the extant plays for examination of their
content and attitudes; third, identifying lost scripts through
playbills and newspaper or other records of them and, if possible, ascertaining their point of view; and, fourth, analyzing
the attitudes they displayed over the period of approximately
one hundred and sixty years during which the American theatre grew from an occasional diversion to a full-scale industry,

concomitant with the United States' growth from a colonial appendage to an independent world power.

Some of the plays to be studied made reference to historical incidents and characters; it seemed logical, therefore, that an extended study of other plays with a more fictional basis might also reveal the influence of white American political and social thinking on the lives of the aboriginal population and its portrayal on the stage. Several trends, practices, and turning points might profitably be studied in conjunction with the plays: exploitation of the Indians by the Puritan settlers and British military forces in the colonies, for example, was known to have changed Indian social patterns enormously. Then, after the Revolutionary War, and particularly after the Louisiana Purchase, the acquisition of Indian lands for white settlers, either by removal of the tribes or by their actual extirpation, became a serious consideration for the young federal government. This resulted finally in the Indian Removal Bill of 1830, followed by the ugly episodes of the "Trail of Tears" in the ten years afterward, when whole communities were uprooted and displaced for the benefit of white settlers.

The failure of the removal policy was soon stressed by discovery, during the great migration beginning in the 1830s, that another whole population of Indians on the Plains had to be overcome before settlement, or even adequate traveling conditions, could begin. Completion of the transcontinental railroad in 1869 solved some of this dilemma, but the Indian was viewed increasingly as a pestilential obstacle to the self-righteous claims of the white man's "Manifest Destiny." As the juggernaut of the Westward Movement rolled on, the Indian enemy was finally crushed. The new reservation policy of the post-Civil War years limited the Indians' movement and action, but it turned out to be no more effective as a solution of the Indian problems than removal had been. But in time the Plains and the entire West were settled, and as Indian-white conflicts decreased and as white Americans found their world-view broadened, newer, more clear-sighted and more sympathetic attitudes toward Native Americans came into being.

Since each of the plays examined is based on some facet of these events, it was decided to study them in this historical context for their indications of the varied and changing attitudes of the white public and playwrights toward the

Indians. A surprising variety of theatre pieces proved to be available for consideration, and they have made it a revealing and rewarding study.

Chapter I

THE FIRST FIRST AMERICANS
ON THE AMERICAN STAGE

From the time the native people of the American continents
were first depicted on a European stage in two Jacobean
masques[1] and mentioned in a European play, Ben Jonson's
The Staple of News,[2] and for almost three hundred years
thereafter, playwrights and all other purveyors of theatrical
entertainments most often considered Indians with awe and
wonder as creatures of exotic fantasy. For audiences of
Jacobean, Caroline, and Georgian England and their counterparts in Continental theatre centers, theatre, though a treasured experience, displayed a world of the unreal, of the
fantastic imaginary, but not a depiction of their daily lives.
In plays the sounds, the smells, the unacceptable mores known
to exist among savage men could be ignored. The real experience of dealing with Native Americans on their own far-off
ground was left to those colonizers who cared to take on so
arduous and threatening a task. Theatre craftsmen in Europe
saw native people according to the most prevalent view of
primitives in the seventeenth and eighteenth centuries--as
Noble Savages. Leaving any actual savage beings entirely
unexamined, they made the Indian useful as a dramatic presence in several ways.

First it was sensibly observed that Indians were a
sure-fire audience lure in any spectacle piece: in masques
such as those at the court of James I, in public theatres in
the newly developing form that would come to be called pantomime,[3] and eventually in theatrical dancing when it began
to be formalized into story ballet presentations.[4] Images of
Indians suggested to creators of such entertainments colorful
new themes and decorations that would enhance the hardest-
worn dramatic clichés.

Secondly, any playwright with a satirical or a moralistic

1

bent could use the Noble Savage as a righteous cudgel to beat the writer's fellow Europeans for their foibles and sins. The first play in which North American Indians appear as characters is a delightful comedy, The Widow Ranter; or, The History of Bacon in Virginia (1689), and the writer, Aphra Behn, was only the first of many to demonstrate how "savages" could be more honorable, more reliable, and in every way more attractive than the Europeans in her plot. Satirical variants are found in the many versions of the Inkle and Yarico story[5] and in farces based on the tale of Tombo Chiqui, a real Indian who visited London during the reign of George I,[6] and more heroic ones occur among the honor-bound cardboard figures of heroic tragedy. Dryden established Indians in that genre with The Indian Queen in 1664, and his emulators continued it for the next hundred years and more. Their influence is strongly evident in important early American works such as Robert Rogers' Ponteach; or, The Savages of America. At the turn of the nineteenth century another new form, the melodrama, continued to be peopled with characters no less moralistic and one-dimensional than their Restoration and Georgian progenitors.

A third use of Native Americans in drama was as a propaganda device at times when national unity was stressed in the theatre--during the French and Indian Wars, for example, when the British found it expedient to claim that their relations with New World natives were better than those of the French. In 1759, a news-of-the-day farce called The French Flogged; or, English Sailors in America was a success at a Bartholomew Fair booth theatre, where it was preceded by a rousing "Indian"-garbed parade to draw in patriotic audiences who would huzzah as British tars and friendly Indians put down the hated French.

With such examples before them, it is hardly unexpected that the earliest American plays to show Indians should present them in no more realistic a guise than their European models. But whatever the dramatic form, Native American characters in any theatrical entertainment were fancifully idealized and overdrawn, even in an age of unusually bombastic theatrical writing. Without exception they were no more than disguised white men painted and costumed to look like Indians according to poorly informed European concepts of them.

The first play about Native Americans written and performed in America is known to us only from the sketchiest
written records. No copy of the text has survived. This
was Le Père Indien, apparently a sentimental tragedy typical
of its kind and period, composed in French in 1753 by an
otherwise unknown writer, Le Blanc de Villeneuve, an officer
stationed in the colony of Louisiana. The scanty records of
its production appeared long after the fact, the most extensive being a half-page description in James Rees' Dramatic
Authors of America (published in 1845), in which he states
that it was performed by an amateur company at the governor's mansion, no proper theatre having been built at that
time. The plot utilized an actual incident of recent local interest in New Orleans. Rees knew it in an account he had
translated from Gayarré's Histoire de la Louisiane:

> In 1753 a Choctaw and a Calapissa Indian having had
> a quarrel, the former said to the latter that his tribe
> were the humble dogs of the French, who made them
> fetch and carry at will. Irritated by this taunt the
> Calapissa levelled his carbine and killed the Choctaw,
> and then fled to Orleans. [The Choctaws petitioned
> the French to let them have the murderer, and the
> French,] having made vain efforts to inspire them
> with other feelings than those of vengeance, gave
> orders for the arrest of the assassin; but he escaped.
> In the mean time the father of him whose blood was
> sought for, delivered himself up to the Choctaws, to
> be sacrificed for his son. His proposition was ac-
> cepted, and the old man stretched himself upon the
> trunk of a fallen tree, and offered his neck to the
> axe, and the next moment was a corpse! The deed,
> which none but the heart of a father could have dic-
> tated, furnished the plot for a tragedy, written by
> ... Le Blanc de Villeneuve.[7]

Another, perhaps similar, play is also mentioned by
Rees as of this period, but even less is known about it.
"The Last of the Serpent Tribe," he writes, "was played at
the French Street Theatre by a regular company. This was
the second original drama played in New Orleans."[8] To our
frustration, no place of entertainment called the French Street
Theatre has been documented, and no "regular company" is
known to have existed in New Orleans before the 1790s.[9] The
title of the play hints at a romantic tragedy of honor in the

vein of Le Père Indien; whether it was such we are unlikely
ever to know. The fact that Rees thought it the "second
original drama played in New Orleans" implies a performance
date earlier than the last decade of the century, but again,
no documentation has been found that can give us that date.

Although Ponteach; or, The Savages of America has
one of the most extraordinary--not to say perverse--histories
of any American dramatic work, we are on surer ground with
this, the first play about Native Americans by an American-
born author--though even his authorship has been ques-
tioned.[10] Major Robert Rogers, the playwright, was a New
Hampshireman famous in his own time as a brilliant but mer-
curial military leader of a band of Indian-fighting rangers
who aided in subduing a rebellion in the Old Northwest in
1763-1764 led by, among others, the Ottawa chief Pontiac.
Immediately after this adventure, Rogers went to England,
hoping for political preferment, which he succeeded in getting, and also to publish his Journals and Concise Account
of North America (both 1765). While in London he apparently
also wrote Ponteach. Never produced in its own time,[11] Ponteach was brutally attacked in the press on its publication
in 1766. The objections in the press seem contradictory,
since the idea of a play on the subject had been suggested
to Rogers by a line in a magazine review of his Concise Account. The modern historian Allan Nevins, in the introduction to his edition of the play, wrote:

> A seemingly trivial circumstance determined the na-
> ture of his third and last publication. That part
> of the Concise Account which had most struck the
> fancy of several reviewers was the description ...
> of the chief Pontiac, widely famed in England for
> his recent rebellion. Rogers had drawn him with a
> taciturn dignity which fired the imagination of the
> writer for the Critical Review [who] made a sugges-
> tion upon which the major hastily acted. "The pic-
> ture exhibited of the Emperor Pontiac," he said, "is
> novel and interesting, and would appear to vast
> advantage in the hands of a great dramatic genius."[12]

The reviewers soon made clear that Rogers himself was
not a dramatic genius capable of handling such material, although it now seems more than likely that his treatment of
Englishmen as the villains of the piece biased their views.
Nevins continues:

It closed disastrously Rogers' career as an author,
for the press united in condemnation of it. "One
of the most absurd productions we have ever seen,"
was the verdict of the Monthly Review. "It is a
great pity that so brave and judicious an officer
should thus run the hazard of exposing himself to
ridicule by an unsuccessful attempt to enliven the
poet's bays with the soldier's laurels. In turning
bard and writing a tragedy Rogers makes just as
good a figure as would a Grub-street rhymester at
the head of our author's corps of North American
rangers." Even the Critical Review, which had suggested the topic, admitted it could bestow no en-
comiums upon Rogers as a poet, and pronounced
the drama unprecedentedly insipid and flat. The
Gentleman's Magazine alone gave the play more than
a few lines, and it did so only to point out the
flimsiness of its plot and the "disgusting familiarity
of its language."[13]

As to the question of Rogers' authorship of Ponteach,
it is known that at this time he had hired in New Hampshire
a man called Nathaniel Potter, an Englishman, educated but
of doubtful character, as a kind of amanuensis, who may
have gone with him to England. With this conjecture in mind,
perhaps, as Nevins writes, Potter "may be partially deserv-
ing of credit for the Concise Account and Ponteach which
represent a greater literary facility than do the Journals or
Rogers' ordinary letters and reports; although the content
of both is by internal evidence largely Rogers.'"[14]

As for the material Rogers utilized in Ponteach:

Participation in the suppression of Pontiac's rebellion in 1763 finally equipped him with the adequate
knowledge of the chief and his conspiracy which the
tragedy manifests. Indeed, Rogers' informing historical accuracy is beyond many definite parallels
between the language of the play and that of the
Concise Account--one of the surest establishments
of the authorship which he never formally claimed.
No other hand in London could have written with
such directness and truth to fact the two first and
expository acts of the drama.[15]

Ponteach is a five-act play employing the conventions of heroic tragedy established by Restoration dramatists almost a hundred years before. It is remarkable, however, less for the turgid verse style it emulates from other eighteenth century plays than for the directness and truth to fact Allan Nevins describes, which are typified by this conversation between two conniving British traders in the first scene:

M'Dole: But now the Thing's to make a profit from them,
Worth all your Toil and Pains of coming hither.
One fundamental Maxim is this,
That it's no Crime to cheat and gull an Indian.

Murphey: How! Not a Sin to cheat an Indian, say you?
Are they not Men? haven't they a Right to Justice
As well as we, though savage in their Manners?

M'Dole: Ah! If you boggle here, I say no more.
This is the very Quintessence of Trade,
And ev'ry Hope of Gain depends upon it;
None who neglect it ever did grow rich,
Or Ever will, or can by Indian Commerce.
By this old Ogden built his stately House,
Purchas'd Estates, and grew a little King.
He, like an honest man, bought all by Weight,
And made the ign'rant Savages believe
That his Right Foot exactly weigh'd a pound!
By this for many Years he bought their Furs,
And died in Quiet like an honest Dealer.

Murphey: Well, I'll not stick at what is necessary:
But his Device is now grown old and stale,
Nor could I manage such a barefac'd Fraud.

M'Dole: A thousand Opportunities present
To take advantage of their Ignorance;
But the great Engine I employ is Rum,
More pow'rful made by certain strength'ning Drugs.
This I distribute with a lib'ral Hand,
Urge them to drink till they grow mad and valiant;
Which makes them think me generous and just,
And gives full Scope to practise all my Art.[16]

The play opens with a series of such scenes as this, showing Ponteach's tribesmen being cheated, first by British traders, then by government military agents, and murdered by English hunters who steal the furs they are bringing to trade. Making an impressive appearance, Ponteach objects to these practices, but the British officers discount his objections and blatantly continue their illicit operations. Ponteach sees this as sound reason to forward his people's revolt, which includes the siege of Detroit. In a subplot, persecution of the Indians is further illustrated by the aggressively attempted seduction of an Indian girl, Monelia, first by an obnoxious British officer, then by a drunken French priest. This girl, the daughter of one of Ponteach's chief allies, has two rival suitors, the two sons of Ponteach. All three of these young people die in the course of the conflict. In the face of all his adversities, Ponteach, in the grand tradition of heroic tragedy, rises nobly to the occasion and continues his defence and protection of his people, hopeless as he knows it to be.

Fustian and overblown as much of the writing is, yet an attempt is made with some success to give the role of the old chief a clear-cut, noble ring. These qualities are illustrated by lines from his speeches in the concluding scene of the tragedy:

> The Torrent rises, and the Tempest blows;
> Where will this rough, rude Storm of Ruin end?
> . . .
> This is too much, and my griev'd Spirit sinks
> Beneath the Weight of such gigantic Woe.
> Ye that would see a piteous, wretched King,
> Look on a Father griev'd and curs'd like me;
> Look on a King whose Sons have died like mine!
> . . .
> Were I alone the boist'rous Tempest's Sport,
> I'd quickly move my shatter'd, trembling Bark,
> And follow my departed Sons to Rest.
> But my brave Countrymen, my Friends, my Subjects,
> Demand my care: I'll not desert the Helm,
> Nor leave a dang'rous Station in Distress.
> . . .
> And though I fly, 'tis on the Wings of Hope.
> Yes, I will hence where there's no British Foe,
> And wait a Respite from this Storm of Woe;

> Beget more Sons, fresh Troops collect and arm
> And other Schemes of future Greatness form;
> Britons may boast, the Gods may have their Will,
> Ponteach I am, and shall be Ponteach still. (Exit)

Finis[17]

Rogers' acceptance and use of this worn-out style of false and shallow verse writing seems surprising in view of the fact that he had grown up on a frontier where he knew and lived with Indians--one of the only two American playwrights who ever did (the other being Mary Austin)--and heard their earthy and vigorous speech from earliest childhood. No doubt Nathaniel Potter or some other literary advisor persuaded him that the conventions of eighteenth-century playwriting were logical and necessary. As we have seen, the reviewers apparently felt that Rogers had gone too far toward everyday realism in his treatment of the subject matter. In any case, no more realistic treatment of Indians and their speech would be attempted again for another hundred years or more. But despite its flaws and failures, Ponteach; or, The Savages of America has great vitality in its straightforward melodramatic development and neatly defined characters, marred as they may seem to twentieth-century sensibilities by the conventions of what was then thought to be proper stage diction and acceptable stage action.

Native American characters appear in few serious plays written from the time Ponteach was published to the end of the century. In these few, the Indians of South America are featured more frequently than their northern counterparts. An outstanding piece popular in America was Columbus; or, The Discoverie of America by the Britisher Thomas Morton, performed at Covent Garden in 1792 and two years later in Philadelphia. Its fantasticated story, suggested by an incident in the discoverer's career, shows him landing in Peru and being aided in a struggle against his mutineering sailors by a young Spaniard, Alonzo, and a gratuitously introduced British tar, Harry Herbert. Much of the charm of the play lies in its logic-be-damned attitude toward history and geography and a naive jingoism, perhaps typical of popular British playwriting in that troubled era after the French Revolution. Early in the play, the notably democratic Columbus takes time out (for no very sound dramatic reason) for a conversation with the lowly English sailor and praises Britain for helping him to conquer South America. In keeping with this sentiment, the work is brought to a final conclusion with this speech of Columbus:

> Had I earlier known that England's monarch would have graced my fortunes with his victorious banner, then would your freedom been firmly fixed.--They only, who themselves are free, give liberty to others.
>
> BRITONS again behold Columbus sue
> To have his fortunes patronised by you;
> to your support alone he trusts his cause,
> And rests his fame, on Englishmen's applause.[18]

Morton's Columbus is also notable for two other reasons. First it is one of the few plays in which European men are allowed to form apparently permanent mating alliances with Indian women, a practice increasingly rare in plays by Americans as our drama developed. Alonzo marries the Indian priestess Cora, with whom he has fallen in love while saving her from a temple during an earthquake, and Harry Herbert marries a girl called Nelti (a version of the comic-relief character of the Romp, so popular in eighteenth century comedy, the ancestress of all Soubrettes). Secondly, it includes the first use in English of one of the most popular dramatic stories of its time, originated by the German playwright August von Kotzebue.

Kotzebue's Die Sonnenjungfrau (1791) and Die Spanier in Peru; oder, Rollas Tod (1795) together tell the triangle story of the priestess Cora and her two suitors, the noble Spaniard Alonzo and the noble Peruvian Rolla, blending it (somewhat more logically than Thomas Morton allowed) with the narrative of Pizarro's failures among the Inca Indians of Peru. Cora, Alonzo, and Rolla were among the most popular and desirable roles for two generations of actors in at least eight versions of The Virgin of the Sun and no fewer than eleven adaptations of The Spaniards of Peru. (The latter is best known in the versions by Richard Brinsley Sheridan of 1799 and the American William Dunlap of 1800, both called simply Pizarro.) In America, Rolla's self-sacrificing death and the rarefied charms of Alonzo and Cora attracted major stars from the time of the first production of Dunlap's play at the new Park Theatre in New York in March 1800. John Hodgkinson, Mrs. Hodgkinson, Mrs. Melmoth, Lewis Hallam

and other important early American actors played prinicipal
roles.[19] Lesser performers and touring stars carried the
tragedies all across the country. By the 1830s they were
familiar in the playhouses of the Ohio and Mississippi Valley
circuits, as we know from Noah Ludlow's amusing descriptions
of makeshift performances with the unlikeliest of Inca priests
and virgins skimpily draped in borrowed costumes.[20] It was
such tragedies as these that set the tone for many or most
serious plays seen on the American stage from the turn of
the century to the time of the Civil War.

The multi-play programs that became the norm in eighteenth century theatres were filled out with musical acts and
shorter pieces usually called farces. These were generally
one-act or two-act plays, frequently containing songs or other
musical specialty acts, dramatizing and commenting on current
events of general interest to the audience. They might, however, also include or be entirely composed of some special
kind of performance--for example, the appearance of actual
Indians in native dances and archery exhibitions.

One American-written farce produced in the colonial
theatre refers to Indian news of the time. This anonymous
work of 1764 is called The Paxton Boys, and its title describes
an unruly mob of backwoodsmen who murdered fourteen
Conestoga Indian men, women, and children sheltered in a
jail at Lancaster, Pennsylvania, on December 17, 1763. This
self-appointed posse then terrorized Philadelphia's citizens,
by marching on that city, intending to take over the colony's
government. The Paxton Boys does not bring this intensely
dramatic situation to the stage. It is instead a discussion
piece in which neither the Indians nor the Paxton mob appear.
Two Artillerymen, a Citizen, two Presbyterians, and a Quaker
carry on discussions, treated satirically, as to whether towns-
men or frontiersmen are the better governors for a state.
The religious men, particularly the Quaker, are treated in a
less than friendly manner throughout, although the Quaker
is allowed to make reference to the murdered Indians in a
single sympathetic line: "Oh! Lancaster, Lancaster, the
blood of murder'd Innocents cry out for vengeance" [sic].[21]

The real issue of burgeoning conflict between whites
and Indians on the frontier, illustrated by the cowardly action of the Paxton Boys against the Indians they wished to
remove, is entirely disregarded by the playwright. His

attitude toward the Paxton mob seems to be positive, implying that the backwoodsmen were unequivocally right in their
murderous action and in their move on Philadelphia to justify
their claims. He shows all the townsmen-talkers in the piece
to be foolish and wrong-headed in their scared-rabbit attitude
toward civil defense. The Paxton Boys is not, then, a real
news-of-the-day play, but fits rather that category of occasional pieces for which the writer jumped at a catch phrase
like "The Paxton Boys," or a current newsy idea, in this
case the permanently controversial subject of Indian-white
relations, and made them fit into a popular form of the time--
a farce filler for a theatre evening--without exploring their
meaning or implication.

The first instance of an approach to literal realism on
the American stage may have been the actual appearances of
Indian tribesmen. This was hardly a new phenomenon--
Columbus' presentation of several Carib Indians at the court
of Isabella in April 1493 was a theatrical coup of some note,
and Indians had been shown on British and Continental stages
not infrequently since then[22]--but it became a more frequent
one by the end of the eighteenth century. A group of "Indian Chiefs ... drest in the character of warriors" performed
on horseback at Ricketts' Circus on Greenwich Street in New
York on March 7, 1795.[23] Their tribe was not identified in
the playbill quoted by Odell, but presumably, being horse-
men, they were from the South or West and not the North-
eastern woodlands. On the more legitimate stage, "a party
of Shawnee and Delaware Chiefs" was brought in to perform
dances at the Chestnut Street Theatre in Philadelphia by its
manager, Thomas Wignell, in 1802,[24] and "Five celebrated
Wyandott Chiefs" played an engagement at the same theatre
in 1818.[25] The entertainment provided by the visiting Indians was often made up not only of "war-songs" and dances
(all Indian music and movement being construed as aggressively warlike) but also of exhibitions of their dexterity with
the tomahawk and bow and arrows. The convention of describing any native visitors in public appearances as chiefs,
kings, or emperors was presumably thought to be more likely
to attract larger audiences, and of course persists into our
own time.

Yet despite these occasional appearances of actual Indians on the stage and their not infrequent presence in most
towns and cities in public places, audiences nevertheless

continued to accept a dramatic image that totally misrepresented them. In time, as the frontier receded westward, these stage exhibitions of genuine tribesmen set a precedent that would culminate in such vaudeville-like presentations as the appearance of Sitting Bull and other famous figures with Buffalo Bill's wild west circus in the 1880s and 1890s.

In the variety-show format of an eighteenth-century theatre evening, the topical farce was not the only kind of piece that lightened the tone of the show. Before or after a full-length tragedy or comedy, a ballet or pantomime was often featured, particularly on artists' benefit nights if such a piece contained a role that showed off some aspect of a performer's talent not otherwise often displayed. The actor John Hodgkinson, for example, often appeared in pantomimes or comic-opera singing roles, though he was best known in Shakespearean or other serious parts.

Material for a pantomime might be entirely original, or adapted from some familiar source. It was inevitable that so familiar and beloved a work as Defoe's Robinson Crusoe would be dramatized in some form. The first known stage version, called Robinson Crusoe; or, Harlequin Friday (attributed, incidentally, to Richard Brinsley Sheridan) was seen at the John Street Theatre on December 12, 1785. The foremost American actor of the day, Lewis Hallam, played Crusoe, and the Friday was our first important male dancer, John Durang; Thomas Wignell played Pantaloon, and other parts included a Captain, Petit Maître, Pierrot, Pantalina, and Pantaloon's Daughter.26 Clearly, any representation of the Carib Indian Friday and his cannibal pursuers was foregone and all were transmuted and prettified into latter-day Commedia dell' Arte figures.

However, Robinson Crusoe was a very successful pantomime. It was still being played as late as 1798 and seems to have gone through considerable modification--specifically, it would seem, Indianization--since it was retitled for a later production and billed as Robinson Crusoe; or, The Genius of Columbia, "with a solemn Indian Incantation ... And an Allegorical Finale."27

Another familiar dramatic story of this period was that of Inkle and Yarico, which had been a great success in various versions and languages since the 1740s. It was most popular in the operatic treatment by the younger Colman in 1787. Inkle is a young British businessman shipwrecked on a West Indian island, where he is saved by the native girl Yarico. A passionate affair develops, but the heartless young man later tries to sell her as a slave. He is shamed by his business associates, made to see the error of his ways, and marries Yarico. The American pantomime version, called The American Heroine, was performed in 1792 at the John Street Theatre, with Madame Gardie, a principal dancer of the company there, as Yarico. It was described as a "grand Historic and Military Pantomime," including in its cast a "King of Savages" and several other "Savages."[28] An elaborate revival was presented five years later at Ricketts' Circus in Greenwich Street at a performance attended by President John Adams. This time it was advertised as "an Heroic Pantomime, in 3 Acts," with "grand military evolutions, single combats, new decorations, etc.," and the addition of several "Indian Chiefs" to the cast, "the whole to be concluded with a Grand Indian Dance."[29]

From the point of view of Native American history, the most interesting pantomime of the decade was Nootka Sound; or, The Adventures of Captain Douglas. It had only one performance, at a benefit night on June 5, 1794, for an actor called Mr. Prigmore, who may also have been its author. The subject, of course, was connected with the controversy between Great Britain, Spain, and the United States over trading rights on the northwest coast of the continent and their rival dealings with the Indians of Nootka Sound for sea otter skins and other treasures of the region.

No script or scenario of Nootka Sound has survived, so we must make conjecture of its qualities from three archivists' descriptions. Seilhamer, in his history, mentions it briefly:

> Prigmore's afterpiece, "Nootka Sound," was a pantomimic trifle whose only merit was in the fact that it was new. There was a more genuine dramatic purpose in the other new pieces presented at benefits during the season.[30]

Odell, in his Annals, comments tartly:

> Prigmore, as usual with him, prepared a tremendously

long bill, for his night ... June 5th.... He offered
as the main piece, The Patriot, or Liberty Asserted....
Mrs. Pownall, at the end of the play, sang A Soldier
For Me.... After a hornpipe by a Young Gentleman (for that night only), Prigmore proceeded to a
repetition of A Bold Stroke For a Wife, and ended
with a pantomime, "never acted here," entitled Nootka Sound, or the Adventures of Captain Douglas.[31]

The cast from the original playbill is given without
comment by Ireland in his Records of the New York Stage.
It includes Captain Douglas (the name of the actual comman-
der of the American ship involved in the scuffle); two
Spaniards; two sailors given conventional joke names, Sam
Stern and Tom Grog; and two Indians, Wampumpoo and Alknomook.[32] Of the latter pair, the absurdity of a name like
Wampumpoo speaks for itself, and Alknomook implies a character of greater dignity because of its origin in a popular
song of the day called "Alknomook's Death Song" (familiar to
audiences of the time from Royall Tyler's use of it in The
Contrast, as well as its inclusion only a few months before
the Nootka Sound performance in Mrs. Hatton's Tammany at
the same theatre)--although the use of it in a farcial pantomime hints that it may have had a kind of ethnic-slur quality,
like later usages such as "Sambo" or "Chief." None of the
records indicate what music was used in the piece, but it
would not be surprising if a version of this "Death Song"
had been included since there were no scruples about borrowing it, as Mrs. Hatton had done. The two Indian roles
were performed by Mr. West and Mr. Miller, members of the
John Street company we would describe as character dancers
or eccentric dancers.

Other than Nootka Sound, pantomime and dance entertainments of the day with Indian references or characters
were less current-events oriented. Works described as ballets included another single-performance item, The Huntress;
or, Tammany's Frolics, given at the John Street Theatre in
June 1794 on a benefit program that included a tragedy about
William Tell and a comic opera.[33] The dancers Miller and West,
again billed as "Indians," were among the group of artists
benefited.

Another pantomime, probably inspired by dance exhibitions of real Indians, was The Indian War Feast (1797).[34]

The implication from such titles is that American theatre managers and creators of entertainments for them at least occasionally opted for local material, however fantastically it was treated. British harlequinade pantomime first showed Native Americans in 1738 as the aforementioned Art and Nature and later in Harlequin and Quixotte; or, The Magic Arm (Covent Garden, 1797). But this style of pantomime never gained the favor with American audiences it has always had with the British, although this was not for lack of trying on managers' parts--Harlequin Fisherman and Columbine Invisible; or, Harlequin Junior (both of 1792) are typical titles. But only one American harlequinade which introduces Indian characters (other than the first Robinson Crusoe) is known. It has, however, one of the most delightfully absurd titles in all the history of the theatre: Harlequin Panattatah; or, The Genii of the Algonquins. It was performed at the Park Theatre on January 9, 1809.

Already, by the time Harlequin Panattatah was produced, some of its elements, such as the use of music accompanying spoken dialogue, songs apart from the action, and mimic action itself, began to fade into melodrama and later into burlesque entertainments. An interest in Indians as speaking characters took precedence over their role as pantomime figures, although they did continue to appear in ballets at least into the 1820s. Among dance works recorded are The Rival Indians and La Belle Peruvienne (both 1822, the latter performed at the Park Theatre),[35] and The Indian Heroine, "A Grand Ballet of Action" featuring two principal Indian characters, Miami and Mina, which was played at Vauxhall Gardens in New York on June 16, 1823.[36]

Moving from ballet and pantomime to larger-scale works, we are confronted with a kind of hybrid curiosity called Tammany; or, The Indian Chief. The operatic historian Oscar Sonneck describes it as "a serious opera with its libretto by Mrs. Anne Julia Hatton and music by James Hewitt," and goes on to establish its importance in our theatrical history. It was "probably the most earnest effort of its time. In fact it came quite near qualifying as our first native real opera; and it certainly was the earliest of American operas on Indian subjects."[37] In connection with this work and other so-called "operas" of this period, we should clearly understand how the term was used. Opera, serious or comic, in the theatres of England and America was not always a musical

work for the theatre such as those of Handel, Haydn, or Mo-
zart that we still listen to, structured around an overture
and a series of set pieces in a unified musical style, connected
by patches of dialogue which told the story being illustrated
by the musically related arias, duets, and ensembles. Tammany was more typical of the less specialized "operatic"
pieces of the day in having, like any other eighteenth-century
play, a spoken prologue and epilogue and elaborate speaking
roles for the actors--who also occasionally sang a musical
number. The composer, James Hewitt, is credited with the
overture and "accompanyments," but some of the songs were
not even composed by him, a case in point being the popular
number "Alkmonook's Death Song."[38] Hewitt's abilities must
have left something to be desired, if we are to believe Sonneck's comment: "Musically, the most interesting number is
'The sun sets in night,' which is an adaptation of the Alkmonook, or Death Song of the Cherokee Indians."[39] In any
case, this kind of theatre piece is what we now think of as
a play with music, and not at all an opera, operetta, or musical comedy.

Apart from Tammany's musical qualities, or lack of
them, its greatest interest for us is in the libretto and its
treatment of Native Americans, and in the audiences' reactions to it. The script itself is long lost, but, as Sonneck
comments, "The surviving lyrics indicate a libretto characterized by 'impossible flights of poetic imagination.'"[40] The
story, which seems to have been set in Pennsylvania, tells
of a noble chief of no identifiable tribe called Tammany, whose
ladylove, Manana, is threatened with abduction by one Ferdinand, a ruffian member of Christopher Columbus' band of
explorers, who have just landed. When Tammany rescues
Manana, Ferdinand vengefully sets fire to their wigwam and
destroys them. The local Indians sing a dirge for their noble
leader and his lady.[41]

Tammany's creator, Mrs. Hatton, was a member of the
Kemble theatrical family (Sarah Siddons was her older sister)
and apparently a lady of considerable enterprise. She determined, when her play was not accepted for production by
the managers of the John Street Theatre, to get other support which would persuade them to change their minds. This
she did by enlisting the aid of the newly formed Tammany
Society. She also seems to have been a fast worker. Having arrived in New York late in 1793, she had already supplied

the plot and one song lyric to a "musical trifle" called <u>Needs Must, or the Ballad Singer</u>, and, as Seilhamer put it,

> [she] at once became the bard of the American democracy. When the Democratic Society of New York celebrated the recapture of Toulon, she furnished the ode for the occasion for which she was voted the thanks of the Society. She also succeeded in interesting the Tammany Society in her opera, the wish of this powerful organization for its production being equal to a command.[42]

The John Street managers succumbed to the political clout and money supplied by the Society and gave the work an elaborate production in new scenery on March 3, 1794.

The documenting of audience reaction to <u>Tammany</u> reflects--perhaps more than records of any other American theatrical production of the 1790s--the political climate prevailing in the two or three decades following the Revolutionary War. Odell points to a direct influence with his comment:

> Tammany, we observe, was produced in 1794, only shortly after the high crest of the wave of Liberty, Fraternity and Equality in France, which, indeed, broke rather violently on our shores. The piece was consequently turned into a symbol of republicanism, and as such was patronised by the hot-heads of New York, to the utter rout of the aristocrats.[43]

"Utter rout" is, perhaps, an exaggerated term, although one of <u>Tammany</u>'s few performances did begin with action approaching a riot when members of the audience loudly and rudely demanded of Hewitt that he begin with a familiar popular song rather than his overture. (He complied with the demand.) Most newspaper writers of 1794 saw theatre as at least a demi-aristocratic pastime, so it is not surprising that a letter published in the <u>Daily Advertiser</u> on March 7, 1794, speaks in slightly barbed tones of the audience.

> I would endeavour to give you my opinion on this Opera;--but after the rout which has been made and the threats given out, I am almost deterred from it tho' under this disguise, and with the Liberty of the Press on my side!

> There was a great deal of liberty and equality
> in it--Tammany received much applause for his in-
> dependent and noble spirit.... The Prologue and
> Epilogue were brim full of the present popular no-
> tions of liberty; and of course went down with great
> eclat.... The audience was of one complexion in
> point of sentiment. In the Pit, and several of the
> Boxes, I saw a considerable number of respectable
> mechanics, and other industrious members of society,
> who with honest (some with misguided) sentiments
> are always inclined to applaud every expression
> that has the semblance of patriotic principles.... I
> saw persons there ... who ... cannot well afford
> the expence of public amusements....
>   I saw poorer classes of mechanics and clerks,
> who would be much better employed on any other
> occasion than disturbing a theatre.--Others I saw,
> who, generally follow no useful occupation, what-
> ever, and who exists [sic] only in a riot or a frolic.
>   These remarks, I am aware, will be termed aris-
> tocratic--be it so. 44

For Mrs. Hatton and the Tammany Society, Tammany;
or, The Indian Chief was a succes d'èstime. It had only
four performances in its first New York run, a couple more
in a revival a year later; one in Philadelphia in the autumn
of 1794; and one in Boston in January 1796, when John Hodgkinson, the original performer of Tammany, revived it once
more. The first New York revival was at the behest of the
Tammany Society, but, regardless of their growing power,
they could after all supply only a limited audience. It would
be more than a generation later before "mechanic" audiences
would fill great theatres like the Bowery to see such works
and found a tradition that would one day make the success
of vaudeville, ten-twent'-thirt' melodrama, nickelodeons, and
commercial television.

We have seen that in the earliest years of the American
theatre the Native American, when shown at all as a stage
character, was shown in a fantastic guise entirely falsifying
his life, his character, and his relations with the European-
Americans who had come to displace him. The colonial policy
of Great Britain and of France in America was exploitative.
Native Americans were considered as occasional suppliers of
commodities such as furs but more commonly as no more than

obstacles to colonial expansion. This fact of colonial life is dramatized in only one known play, Robert Rogers' Ponteach; or, The Savages of America, and Rogers' use of it is probably the reason the play was never produced in its own day. Not only the government but theatre managers and their public rejected the concept of responsibility for native peoples they were exploiting in their colonies.

This attitude was supported by philosophical views of the Enlightenment and the developing Romantic Movement, which chose to see Indians either as amusing exotics or as Noble Savages, excellent types for representing ideas in literature or on the stage, but never more than white characters with cliché comic or noble personalities disguised with red skins and feathered costumes. Indian people were never considered as real human beings whose lives might be dramatically interesting.

For the Native Americans themselves the realities of eighteenth-century history in America were neither amusing nor noble. Their experience was one of almost continual loss of their homelands and resources for living, from the early seventeenth century onward. None of that series of devastating "wars" throughout the colonies--the Pequot War in New England, the Yemassee War in the South, the conflicts that made up Queen Anne's War or the French and Indian Wars-- in any way benefited the Indians. But as subject matter for a great variety of plays, incidents of these wars were to be blended with the ready conventions of stage Indians for many years to come. As the nineteenth century began and the American theatre expanded into a commercial entertainment industry, the Indians, while in reality being destroyed or removed from white-dominated areas that included theatrical centers, were increasing in an inverse ratio in those centers as stage presences.

NOTES

1. For the marriage of James I's daughter Elizabeth to the Prince Palatine in 1613, one by Sir Francis Bacon, the other by George Chapman, both in splendid productions by Inigo Jones. See Frances Mossiker, Pocahontas, The Life and the Legend (New York: Alfred A. Knopf, 1976), p. 221.

2. Act II, scene 1, lines 119-124.

3. The French pantomime Arlequin Sauvage (1721) was adapted for an English version as Art and Nature (1738).

4. The first such work recorded in which Indians appear was an American product, The Huntress; or, Tammany's Frolics, performed at the John Street Theatre, New York, on May 21, 1794. G. C. D. Odell, Annals of the New York Stage, 15 vols. (New York: Columbia University Press, 1929-1949), vol. I, p. 358.

5. Both preceding and following the most familiar version, the "opera" by George Colman the Younger, first performed at the Haymarket Theatre, London, on August 11, 1786.

6. The earliest being John Cleland's Tombo Chiqui (1758). The plot was borrowed from the already familiar Arlequin Sauvage.

7. James Rees, Dramatic Authors of America (Philadelphia: G. B. Zieber & Co., 1845), p. 20.

8. Ibid.

9. William C. Young, Documents of American Theater History: Famous Playhouses 1716-1899, 2 vols. (Chicago: American Library Association, 1973), vol. 1, p. 39 and p. 132.

10. By the historian Francis Parkman, in The Conspiracy of Pontiac (New York: Collier Books, 1962), p. 140, fn.2, and Appendix B.

11. The first known performance took place in New York City, of the first act only, at Alice's Studio in April 1970, and of the entire work by the American Theatre Company on January 20, 1975.

12. Robert Rogers, Ponteach. With an Introduction and Biography of the Author by Allan Nevins (Chicago: Caxton Club, 1917), p. 101.

13. Ibid.

14. Ibid.

15. Ibid., p. 12.

16. Montrose J. Moses, Representative Plays by American Dramatists, 3 vols. (New York: E. P. Dutton & Co., Inc., 1918; reprint ed., New York: Benjamin Blom, Inc., 1964), vol. 1, pp. 118-119.

17. Ibid., pp. 206-208.

18. Thomas Morton, Columbus; or, The Discoverie of America (Boston: William Spotswood, 1794), pp. 51-52.

19. Odell, Annals, vol. II, pp. 84-85.

20. Noah Ludlow, Dramatic Life As I Found It (St. Louis, 1880; reprint ed., New York: Benjamin Blom, Inc., 1966), pp. 65-68.

21. Anonymous, The Paxton Boys ([Philadelphia]: n.p., 1764), p. 12. A detailed discussion of the Paxton Boys episode and its outcome is given in Parkman, Conspiracy, pp. 350-375.

22. Carolyn Thomas Foreman, Indians Abroad (Norman: University of Oklahoma Press, 1943), pp. 4-5.

23. Odell, Annals, vol. I, p. 396.

24. William B. Wood, Personal Recollections of the Stage (Philadelphia: Henry Carey Baird, 1855), p. 86.

25. Ibid., p. 231.

26. George O. Seilhamer, History of the American Theatre Before the Revolution, 3 vols. (Reprint ed., New York: Greenwood Press, 1968), vol. II, p. 186.

27. Odell, Annals, vol. I, p. 275. Odell notes that it was billed as a "pantomimical romance."

28. Ibid., vol. I, p. 410.

29. Ibid., vol. I, p. 473.

30. Seilhamer, History, vol. II, p. 19.

31. Odell, Annals, vol. I, p. 357.

32. Joseph N. Ireland, Records of the New York Stage from 1750 to 1860 (New York, 1866; reprint ed., New York: Benjamin Blom, Inc., 1966), vol. I, p. 115.

33. Odell, Annals, vol. I, p. 358. He refers to it as a "pantomime ballet."

34. Seilhamer, History, vol. II, p. 367.

35. Ireland, Records, vol. I, p. 399.

36. Odell, Annals, vol. IV, p. 80.

37. Oscar Sonneck, Early Opera in America (New York: G. Schirmer, 1915), p. 24.

38. The name was variously spelled Alknomook, Alkmonook, and Alkmonoak.

39. Sonneck, Early Opera, pp. 24-25. The song had already been used in a British "opera" on Indian themes called New Spain; or, Love in Mexico, performed at the Haymarket Theatre in London on July 16, 1790, in which Alkmonook is the noble young hero of the piece.

40. Ibid., p. 24. The lyrics are available in the Readex Microprint Collection, American Plays, 1714-1830.

41. Ibid.

42. Seilhamer, History, vol. III, p. 85.

43. Odell, Annals, vol. II, pp. 346-347.

44. Quoted by Odell, op. cit., vol. II, pp. 347-348.

Chapter II

NATIVE AMERICAN NOBLE SAVAGES
ON THE STAGE

Suitably enough for our purposes, the term "Noble Savage" seems to have had a theatrical origin. It first occurred in John Dryden's Conquest of Granada (1670), and it was Dryden who had already set the precedent for the use of this concept when he wrote The Indian Emperour, a play purportedly about Aztec Indians, in 1665. In heroic tragedies like these, exoticism was the keynote, love and valor were the subjects, and the characters were no more than illustrations of abstract ideas. The exotic combined with love, honor, valor--all were burgeoning seeds that would blossom in the great Romantic Age a century later, after gathering to themselves a complementary burden of sentimentalism from the eighteenth-century drama. As Hoxie Fairchild has pointed out in his study of the Noble Savage:

> Provided the author set his fable in a vaguely foreign land, he was permitted to "let himself go" a little. It was in drama, especially during the ascendancy of the heroic play, that exoticism reached its greatest vogue.... On the whole, our Incas and Aztecs are used, just as the Moors and Persians and Siamese are, to satisfy a demand for more violent action, more ranting, more elaborate scenic effects and richer costumes, than would be decorous in plays with Greek or Roman characters.[1]

Furthermore:

> Though Dryden declares in his preface [to The Indian Emperour] that he has "traced the Native Simplicity and Ignorance of the Indians, in relation to European customs," he has done nothing but write a play of court intrigue and warfare.[2]

With this background, it is easy to see how the idea of the Noble Savage would be perpetuated through the eighteenth century and into the time of the Romantic Movement. By 1800 some of the nobility ascribed to the savage gentleman was watered down by his appearance in farce, pantomime, ballet, and the sentimental play (with or without "operatic" enhancement), but in the American theatre the phrase continued to have strong meaning: the Noble Savage was an admirable Native American of heroic honor, profound sentiments, and the expectation of a dark future, whose virtue could be used to contrast dramatically with the uglier qualities of European-born white men. In the first third of the nineteenth century there was a movement toward a more realistic presentation of Native Americans on the stage, but only in that it was a movement away from his appearance in farce or musical productions toward that in the newly developing melodrama. In that new genre, the Noble Savage continued to be a stage favorite, particularly when he was a dramatization of an Indian well known in history (such as Pontiac or Osceola) and wherein villainous, ignoble Indians were few. This pattern has been continued in theatrical presentations of Native American characters ever since, with variations such as those shown in American plays written between 1800 and 1830.

A choice of three plays of this period shows typical variants of the Noble Savage stereotype character as they were seen by American audiences. The first of these is a shallow amateur work which was published by its author, Joseph Croswell, in Boston in 1802. His play, A New World Planted; or, The Adventures of the Forefathers of New England, is one of the few to deal with the Puritan colonists and their relations with New England Indians. It is about the settlers and not about the Indians, but included among the list of white historical figures--Bradford, Brewster, and others--are several Indian names known from history: Massasoit (described as "An Indian King friendly to the Settlers"), Tisquanto, and Samosett. To these are added the fictitious "Hobomac and Natives, faithful to the Emigrants" and "Pocahonte, a native beauty, daughter to Massasoit." The far-fetched plot has to do with Popish intriguers infiltrating the Puritan community and arousing the neighboring Indians against them. Early in the play, a ceremonial scene shows the Puritans making a treaty of peace with Massasoit, but thereafter he, Tisquanto, and Samosett appear only as not very noble

errand-boy characters whose principal action in the play is
to make repeated entrances to report an offstage battle (in
which they are fighting). They are no more believable than
the fancifully named Pocahonte. For this playwright, any
nobility in the savage character is supplied by the execrable
blank verse they speak and by their usefulness as fighters
for the Puritans against bad Indians, who cannot be noble
since they have not become servant-like friends to the whites.
Pocahonte is acceptable because a Puritan officer, Hampden,
finds her so desirable that a possible connection with her is
suggested. He accepts the possibility with an apologetic comment, "I know she's browner than European dames, but
whiter far, than other natives are."[3]

A remarkable difference of attitude is notable in Mordecai Manuel Noah's comedy She Would Be A Soldier; or, The
Plains of Chippewa, first performed at the Park Theatre, New
York, on June 21, 1819. It is as if the fading tradition of
the Noble Savage had been revived and restored in the seventeen years since Croswell's play was written. One of the
featured characters in this comedy about American successes
in the War of 1812 is an Indian chief who is persuaded to
change his allegiance from the British to the American side
before the final curtain. (Note that he is a chief, as all
Noble Savages should be; the highly touted democracy of the
new nation could not destroy its citizens' faith in the value
of class differences.) From this chief's first entrance, he is
shown to have dignity and humor, wit and perception, to an
unusual degree. In coping with a foppish English officer,
not only does his dialogue make clear that he is the nobler
of the two, it also utilizes speech constructions and phraseology that seriously attempt to sound like Indian speech:

Pendragon: (Examining him with his glass.) Where the
            devil did this character come from? he's one
            of the fancy, I suppose.

Indian: Who and what are you?

Pendragon: Who am I? Why, sir, I am the honourable
            captain Pendragon, of his majesty's guards,
            formerly of the buffs.

Indian: (Aside.) The officer who is to be under my
            command. Well sir, you have lately arrived

from across the great waters: How did you leave my father, the King of England?

Pendragon: How! call my most gracious sovereign your father? Why, sir, you are the most familiar --impertinent--'sdeath! I shall choke--What the devil do you mean?

Indian: (Coolly.) What should I mean, young man, but to inquire after the health of my father, who commands my respect, who has honoured me with his favors, and in whose cause I am now fighting.

Pendragon: Well, sir, if you have the honour to hold a commission from his majesty, I desire that you will speak of him with proper awe, and not call him your father, but your most gracious master.

Indian: Young man, the Indian warrior knows no master but the Great Spirit, whose voice is heard in thunder, the whose eye is seen in the lightning's flash; free as air, we bow the knee to no man; our forests are our home, our defence is our arms, our sustenance the deer and the elk, which we run down. White men encroach upon our borders, and drive us into war; we raise the tomahawk against your enemies, because your king has promised us protection and supplies. We fight for freedom, and in that cause, the great king and the poor Indian start upon equal terms.

Pendragon: A very clever spoken fellow, pon honour; I'll patronise him.4

The implication in Noah's play is that this agreeable Indian and his people have only to join with the Americans to be able to contemplate the rosiest of futures. In Nathaniel Deering's five-act tragedy Carabasset; or, The Last of the Norridgewocks, the titular hero's death, as the natural conclusion of a true Noble Savage's career, precludes any future at all. Deering wrote Carabasset in 1830 for performance at a theatre in Portland, Maine, where it was first seen on February 22, 1831. The Norridgwocks had been a local tribe wiped out in the eighteenth-century frontier wars, so the subject must have elicited special interest from the Portland audience. If inherited antagonisms were brought to the theatre, they may well have been stilled by the stereotypical nobility of the dying hero.

Carabasset is drawn as even nobler than most of his kind. He has never killed a man except in battle, he is so kindhearted that he will send a captured child back to its mother, and his eventual suicide is brought on by his remorse at having been drawn (by a villainous Frenchman) into joining ignoble Indians in an anti-white rampage.

These three works illustrated aspects of the shifting outlook on Native Americans that was the unfortunate inheritance to the young country's administrators of British colonial policy (dramatized with considerable accuracy, as we have already seen, by Robert Rogers in Ponteach). The English colonists, secure in the idea that their military power could keep the Indians under their control and arrogantly bigoted against the "lesser" race, persistently pushed the natives off their lands with no thought of their place as subjects of the British Empire or of any future problems the usurpation of American lands might cause. After the Revolutionary War, George Washington gave the situation some consideration:

> I am clear in my opinion, that policy and economy point very strongly to the expediency of being upon good terms with the Indians, and the propriety of purchasing their lands in preference to attempting to drive them by force of arms out of their Country; which ... is like driving the wild Beasts of ye forest ... when the gradual extension of our settlements will as certainly cause the savage, as the wolf, to retire; both being beasts of prey, tho' they differ in shape.[5]

Thomas Jefferson seems to have been of two minds about the problem, and much less direct in letting his thoughts be known. Publicly, up to the time of the Louisiana Purchase in 1803, he advocated the intermixture of Indians and whites and the hope that the natives would give up their hunting lands, which they would no longer need since they were to become farmers like the white settlers. The fact that most of the Indians in the colonies lived in settled farming communities was disregarded in favor of the fantasy that all "savages" were hunters. Jefferson's idealistic view, however, was not to be maintained. In July 1803 he drafted a constitutional amendment for the removal of eastern Indians to Upper Louisiana on the far side of the Mississippi River. For several months before this he had been proposing to various key figures a number of devious ways to gain this end should the amendment not be accepted. He had submitted a confidential paper to Congress in January 1803 based on a working paper, "Hints on the Subject of Indian Boundaries," which suggested several ways of tricking tribal leaders into ceding lands. These included outright bribery and encouraging them to incur large debts to traders which could then be cleared by signing over title to tracts of tribal land. In case of resistance to these means of relieving them of their real estate, Jefferson proposed sterner measures in a confidential letter to William Henry Harrison, then governor of Indiana Territory and one of the men who was to implement such measures:

> As to their fear, we presume that our strength and their weakness is now so visible that they must see we have only to shut our hand to crush them, and that all our liberalities to them proceed from motives of pure humanity only. Should any tribe be foolhardy enough to take up the hatchet at any time, the seizing of the whole country of that tribe, and driving them across the Mississippi, as the only condition of peace, would be an example to others, and a furtherance of our final consolidation.[6]

The blatant hypocrisy of such attitudes and the techniques of land acquisition they engendered were of course not new, and as administration followed administration and their methods became less covert in use, they also became accepted precedents for all white administrators and citizens of the young nation to follow. The thinking of founding fathers such as Washington and Jefferson on Native Americans, as on any other subject of public concern, came to be revered. As the nation expanded and more populist attitudes developed, the concept of removal grew increasingly attractive. When Andrew Jackson set up his Indian Removal Bill of 1830, resistance to it--except from the Indians--was hardly a factor to be considered.

The theatre of these years was ambivalent in the face of the known approaches to the Indian problem. Publicly, at the turn of the century, government saw Native Americans much as theatre did, as the Noble Savage that seventeenth- and eighteenth-century philosophy had found him to be. As the country prospered and spread, however, and government found him less and less noble, theatre audiences continued to find his romantic nobility attractive and entertaining.

In Joseph Croswell's A New World Planted, the Native American was rather a second-rate Noble Savage, at a time when he was not yet seen to be a major obstacle to westward expansion. By 1819, an ironic and flattering portrait of a noble native seemed in order, as in Mordecai Noah's She Would Be a Soldier; his people might still be conned, as Jefferson had originally hoped, into giving up their lands to white settlers. Ten years later, when Nathaniel Deering wrote Carabasset, and when booming immigration and industrial growth already made the country seem to be bursting at its seams, it was devoutly to be wished that all Indians were the last of their tribes and would soon leave the land to noble white farmers and town planners.

There had been in this period, however, some few stage Indians who were not Noble Savages at all. In 1803, a dramatic curiosity based on a famous captivity story of the eighteenth century, and apparently done up in sensational form as a pantomime, was played at the Park Theatre in New York. Odell describes it thus:

> The sad story of Miss McCrea, once familiar to all school children, was turned into pantomime, under the title of Indian Cruelty, The Death of Miss McCrea, and played by Hallam jun. as Captain Jones, Prigmore as McCrea, Shepter as a Sergeant, Mrs. Jefferson as the unfortunate lady, and Jefferson and Martin as the terrible Indians.[7]

The implication in Odell's notice is that children of the time were brought up on this kind of grisly tale of a frontier woman captured and killed by Indians, and that there was still audience interest in a stage realization of the story in 1803. He might have added that a year later it was given strong graphic form in one of the best known American paintings of the time, John Vanderlyn's slightly erotic canvas

called The Death of Jane McCrea, in which the terrified "unfortunate lady" is forced to the ground by two muscular and
determinedly evil-looking men who threaten her with toma-
hawks. The death scene in the pantomime was likely to have
been staged in a similarly exaggerated pictorial manner.

Another work of the period depicting ignoble savages,
The Armourer's Escape; or, Three Years at Nootka Sound
(1817), was a melodrama of current political interest, since
the dispute with Great Britain over the Northwest boundary
between Canada and the United States remained unsettled.
(It will be remembered that the original incidents in the controversy had inspired a pantomime of 1794, Nootka Sound.)
The occasion for the production was the appearance in Philadelphia of John Jewitt, the actual armourer on the ship Boston which had figured largely in the controversy. Jewitt
was one of its few survivors when it was blown up in Nootka
Sound. At that time, he and a shipmate called Thompson
were made captives by the Nootka Indians. The script, which
has not survived, was written by Philadelphia playwright
James Nelson Barker as a kind of benefit for Jewitt, who appeared as himself in the production at the Chestnut Street
Theatre on March 21, 22, and 24, 1817.

The villain of the piece, one Maquina, chief of the
Nootka Indians, is so ignoble and unfriendly as to direct the
explosion destroying the ship and then to cause some unpleasant moments for captives Jewitt and Thompson. But
the two men are saved by the friendly Klaissat tribe and
eventually rescued when an American brig sails into the Sound.
The audience found this slender plot filled out with spectacular effects, including the firing of the Boston and an eclipse
of the moon. But to us the most interesting scenes are those
presumably based on details supplied by John Jewitt. (His
three-year captivity must have been a memorable experience,
not unlike that of Melville's sailor-hero in Typee.) These
scenes in the pantomime included funeral ceremonies over the
body of a chief, a passage described as "ludicrous ceremonies
of the Bear," a war dance and Indian attack, and a dramatic
dance of young girls carried off by male dancers wearing
animal masks.[8] It is unlikely that the masks and choreography
were at all authentic, but if the reconstruction of dances and
ceremonies even remotely resembled the real thing this production was the first that attempted to show the customs and
manners of Indians of specific tribes as they actually were.

Also, character and tribal names seem to have been attempts at recreating sounds Jewitt had heard--characters called Mac-hee Utilla and Yuqua, for example, and tribes such as the Wykinnish, Esquates, and Cayuquits.

The most heroic of Noble Savages in early nineteenth-century drama were characters based on actual historical personages. Whether living in the distant past or in recent years, Native American heroes were found to suit very well as Noble Savage characters. Once safely dead, they could be romanticized on the stage, although a rare exception might be made in the case of a hero still living. Such was the Sauk Chief Black Hawk, who was brought to the Bowery Theatre in New York in 1834 to see himself portrayed in a current sensation drama occasioned by his visit to the city.9

The impetus for a biographical play was often something more than the hero's life story. In the case of Joseph Dodd-ridge's Logan, The Last of the Race of Shikellemus, Chief of the Cauyga Nation (1821), the playwright, a country doc-tor and literary amateur, made a statement about the futility of war as well as providing a setting for a much-admired ora-tion made in the 1770s by the Mingo chief Logan. Thomas Jefferson thought so highly of the speech that he compared Logan to Demosthenes and Cicero and had it printed in his Notes on the State of Virginia (1785). It was still a schoolboy-recitation favorite in Doddridge's time, and it is still spoken by a theatricalized Chief Logan in an annually produced out-door drama, The Aracoma Story, at Logan, West Virginia.

Logan had been a famous peacemaker between Indians and whites, but in the spring of 1774 many of his tribe, in-cluding his entire family, were murdered by frontier Indian-haters. Logan joined in a retaliatory action sometimes called the Earl of Dunmore's War. Doddridge's "Dramatic Piece" (which, according to its title page, was "Recited at the Buf-faloe Seminary, July the 1st, 1821") covers the period of this action without including any of it. The entire first act (of five) consists of a debate between "Captain Furioso" and "Captain Pacificus," each with his supporting lieutenant, about whether to make friends with the Indians or try to destroy them. Much of the second act is a parallel discussion among the Indians about whether to start a war for revenge of their losses, and the third contains their prolonged argu-ment about the abuse of prisoners and making war more humane. Logan has promised a white prisoner his life rather than death by burning at the stake according to Indian tradition, and his promise is kept. Never really characterized, Logan is shown throughout as an earnest peacemaker, turning the other cheek even after the whites have killed his family.

These long discussion scenes do not make a play. There is no development and no climax, and the work simply stops after a long conversation in the last act about the probability of a peace treaty and after Logan has delivered his famous speech beginning, "I appeal to any white man to say, if ever he entered Logan's cabin hungry, and he gave him not meat: if ever he came cold and naked and he clothed him not...."10 The work's most interesting element is Dr. Doddridge's dialogue written for his Indian characters. It is quite speakable and realistic-sounding for its time. Although he was not so successful with the highflown artificial speech of his white characters, he seems to have been sincerely interested in making his stage Indians talk like real Native Americans. False notes do appear, as in a hymn-like, neatly rhymed "War Song of the Chiefs," but more typical is this passage in which a contentious chieftain speaks:

> Tawatwees: I am for revenge at once. The bones of my people must be covered. I am not afraid to die. I can die but once, and no matter how soon if I have made satisfaction to the spirits of my murdered friends. The large snake rattles, and bites, altho' he knows he is to be killed the next moment; but he dies contentedly, because he has struck his enemy the first blow, so says Tawatwees if the great spirit says it shall be so.11

A more professionally written, though far more pretentious, Noble Savage is the product of George Washington Parke Custis in The Indian Prophecy (1825), popularly performed in Philadelphia, Baltimore, and Washington. Custis was the first President's step-grandson and a preserver of legendary memories about him, including a famous one that Indian marksmen found their bullets could not kill the young Colonel Washington when he was Braddock's second-in-command in the campaign against Pittsburgh in 1755. An old chief, claiming to have been a participant, is said to have repeated the story many times, particularly after Washington became

President. In Custis' play he is called Menawa, and one reason for his remarkable nobleness is his conformity with Jefferson's stereotype of a good Indian:

> Menawa no more sheds blood. Long Knife, brother, here is my hand; it has often been red with the Long Knives' blood, but Menawa is changed; good man has been here, (pointing to his heart,) good man has changed Menawa.[12]

The slight plot of The Indian Prophecy is concerned with a crusty old settler and his wife who are bringing up Manetta, the daughter of Menawa, with firm instruction in good white Christian ways. They think they are in for a bad time when Menawa appears and seems to menace them. But he quickly lets them know that he is a champion of peace between the races. He tells the story of Washington's infallibility, and dies, showing that Indians can benefit society both white and red either by integrating or by removing themselves. His story of the prophecy is the final scene and speech of the piece:

> Our rifles were levelled, rifles which but for him, knew not how to miss; 'twas all in vain, a power mightier than we, shielded him from harm. He cannot die in battle. Menawa is old and soon will be gathered to the Great Council fire of his Fathers in the land of the shades; but ere he goes, there is something here which bids him speak in the voice of Prophecy. Listen! The great Spirit protects that man, and guides his destiny. He will become the chief of Nations, and a people yet unborn, hail him as the Founder of a mighty Empire! (After a pause, his arms outstretched to Heaven,) Fathers! Menawa comes. Menawa sinks slowly in the arms of his attendants, strain of music, curtain falls.)[13]

Another eighteenth-century hero was Pontiac, the Huron chief known to us from Robert Rogers' Ponteach. He appeared on stage again in a later work written, appropriately enough, in Detroit when its author, General Alexander Macomb, was stationed there in the 1820s. Robert Rogers also appears in this version as a wise officer who saves defeated British troops after a brush with the Indians. General Macomb probably wrote Pontiac; or, The Siege of Detroit for his officers and men to perform in their off-hours entertainments (which thus constituted the first known dramatic activity in the city of Detroit). The play was best remembered, however, for a production at the National Theatre in Washington in 1838 in which the United States Marines took part in the processional and battle scenes. 14

Macomb saw the Indians from a positive point of view-- surprising in an officer of Jackson's day--and showed them sympathetically as honorable opponents of the British. In his Prologue he comments:

> The savage native of this blessed land
> Will now in character before you stand,
> Revengeful, cruel,--not by nature so,
> But 'tis because depressed by us so low. 15

The character of Pontiac is strongly drawn and, like his counterpart in Ponteach, he is very much the Noble Savage in his (historically accurate) expounding of nationalism for his people and his rejection of treaties with the whites. In his first scene he makes his reasons clear:

> Against the enemies of our race it is our duty as
> well as our pride to contend. How comes it that
> you should invade these distant regions, and leave
> a country and a King you delight so much to praise?
> Is war the trade of the British King? What brings
> him here to destroy our friends and allies and to
> ruin us? From the day that the British King sought
> conquest and dominion in these distant parts--these
> plains and forests, these rivers and these lakes have
> been the scenes of nought but dismay, rapine, deso-
> lation, and murder. 16

The other two Indian characters are less clearly drawn. Augushaway is a chieftain who, unable to persuade Pontiac to give in to the whites' negotiations, stabs him to death in the climactic scene. Ultina is an uncertainly motivated girl who is used to start the play's action by informing the British officers of Pontiac's plans for attack. In the final scene she is overcome by remorse and cannot bring herself to accept the soldiers' invitation to go away with them.

Next in the line of Indian heroes dramatized is another

nationalist leader, the Shawnee Tecumseh. Together with
his brother Tenskwatawa, called the Prophet, Tecumseh not
only envisioned but attempted to organize and set up a pan-
Indian nation with its center in the old Northwest (Indiana
Territory)--exactly the kind of arrangement Thomas Jefferson had originally proposed to keep the Indians centered and
out of the way of the westward-moving whites.

Richard Emmons' Tecumseh; or, The Battle of the
Thames, first played at the Walnut Street Theatre in Philadelphia on October 3, 1836, is an uneven melodramatic work
which centers, with considerable sympathy, on the Shawnees'
downfall at the hands of William Henry Harrison's forces in
1813. This playwright, less successful than either Custis or
Macomb in depth of characterization, did, however, make some
attempt to write the broken English of Indian speech, possibly as he had heard it. But in his hands it only comes
out as over-theatricalized and pompous, giving the Indians a
false nobility to contrast them with the white characters.
When Tecumseh is enraged at his ally, a cowardly British officer who has ordered a retreat before the American forces,
the chieftain responds:

> Retreat! who--what tongue dare speak that coward
> language? Lisp it no more! Here fixed Tecumseh,
> like a planted oak, stands, till thunder smites his
> breast!
> . . .
> (Tecumseh raises his war club.)
> Die! no me will not do it. Some raw, green boy,
> for pastime, may aim his arrow at thee. Tecumseh
> never yet put forth his might to slay a timid hare.
> Say, did you not at Raisin pledge your faith to cap-
> tives, then betray them? (Proctor trembles.) Why
> shake you like the poplar thus? Has not Tecumseh
> said he would not kill a hare? Then, much less thee,
> a creeping thing, beneath it far in courage. The
> Red man keeps his promise--'tis here--here in his
> heart! (Proctor attempts to withdraw.) Stand or
> die beneath the thunder of my voice.[17]

For character names, Emmons transliterated actual Indian names with some accuracy: Maypock, Tuscarora, Kus-
Kerkoo, and Ohpothleholo are included in the cast list. Tenskwatawa's name is not used; he is only listed as the Prophet.

The variable quality of this script may be due to Emmons' working in a form new to him, the drama, and adapting material he had already treated in a pretentiously heavyweight epic poem.

Emmons' non-Indians are typified by an unlikely trio of "Kentucky Backwoodsmen," as he describes them in the character list, put in for comic relief. Their purported rough-tough personalities are belied by their almost painfully nice, formal conversation and the gratuitous interpolation into one of their scenes of a popular song of the day, "The Hunters of Kentucky." In a very few years this character type would come to the fore in anti-Indian plays (as we shall see in Chapter IV), in far less attractive representations. Tecumseh is further theatricalized by a tableau finale of a kind still popular in the 1830s in which, after the Indians' death scenes, the Goddess of Liberty descends from a bank of clouds with a huge stars-and-stripes banner.

In number of dramatic appearances Tecumseh was perhaps the most popular historical Indian hero of that time and since. He had been seen in William H. C. Hosmer's The Fall of Tecumseh in 1830, and turned up again in Joseph Stevens Jones' The Hunter in the Far West at Boston's National Theatre on November 14, 1836 (although the principal character is not Tecumseh but "Earthquake the Kentuckian," the hunter of the title and probably a backwoodsman like the those of Emmons). He was on stage again in an anonymous Tippecanoe of 1840, as well as on the page in the only extant works of this group, two particularly inept closet dramas. The first is "an Original Historical Israel-Indian Tragedy, in Five Acts" by George Jones called Tecumseh and the Prophet of the West, published in 1844 with an elaborate paraphernalia of historical notes, quotations, and letters on the subject. The second, still another Tecumseh, is a 185-page script in declamatory blank verse by Charles Mair, published in 1886. He is still an audience favorite, as noble a savage as any audience could wish for, at an outdoor summer tourist attraction called Tecumseh! by Allan W. Eckert, performed yearly since 1974 at Chillicothe, Ohio.

Playwrights in the 1830s also dramatized such contemporary Noble Savages as Osceola, the great warrior of the Seminoles. This tribe had been victimized and harassed by United States forces in a drawn-out series of conflicts, not

unlike the Vietnam War,[18] called the First and Second Seminole Wars (1817-1842). In October 1837 Osceola tried to open
peace negotiations and was treacherously captured while approaching American troops under a white flag of truce. His
wife was sold into slavery and Osceola was confined in a dun-
geon at Fort Moultrie, South Carolina, where he died in January 1838.

There were at least three plays (all of them now lost)
about the Seminole troubles dramatizing different aspects of
these petty wars. The earliest was a news-of-the-day piece
by Joseph Stevens Jones called The Fire Warror, "A National
Drama, founded on events in the Seminole War," performed
at the Warren Theatre in Boston on March 29, 1834, while
the Second Seminole War was actively in progress. "The Fire
Warrior" is listed as the principal character, and several
fanciful "Indian" names are included in the dramatis personae,
but not Osceola's--J. S. Jones was not a playwright who
documented history in straightforward illustrative fashion in
any of his works.[19]

Another play called Osceola, by Lewis F. Thomas, a
Cincinnati playwright, was played in that city and in Louis-
ville and New Orleans in 1837. The third, still another Osceola, "an Indian drama of much interest" as James Rees
described it, "founded upon events startling in their character, which occurred during the Florida war,"[20] by J. H.
Sherbourne, was played at the National Theatre in New York
on October 15, 1841. Since Sherbourne's play postdates the
war's conclusion and the famous warrior's death, it seems
likely that he treated Osceola in dignified romantic style as
a true Noble Savage; a dead hero, after all, is no longer a
threat to his opponents or their dramatic spokesmen.

Current as the topic may have been, however, any
political leanings the playwright may have had were not often
stressed in these history-based plays. Instead, the staunch
tradition of sympathy with the Noble Savage was the soundly
entrenched, crowd-pleasing emotional element playwrights
strove to purvey. Besides, it was always possible for an
author to avoid recently controversial personalities by choos-
ing a subject from the distant past. The Aztecs, for instance,
never failed to provide interesting material to dramatize. They
were among the first Native Americans shown on the stage in
the seventeenth century, and a recent opera on Montezuma

by Roger Sessions and G. A. Borgese (1981) indicates that they have not lost their attractions for playmakers.

On December 24, 1846, there was played at the Arch Street Theatre in Philadelphia a work called Montezuma; or, The Conquest of Mexico by George Hielge (again, since the script no longer exists, one of those enduring mysteries as to style, quality, and treatment of Native American characters). Perhaps its appearance at this time was influenced by William Hickling Prescott's balanced view of Cortez and and Montezuma in his then recently published and widely popular Conquest of Mexico (Boston, 1843). A later work by Lewis F. Thomas, Cortez the Conqueror, dated 1857 but apparently not produced, is said to have been based on that work.21 In any case, Montezuma was traditionally treated as a heroic and nobly suffering personality from the time of Dryden's honor-bound cardboard figure in The Indian Queen in 1664 through the Aztec emperor's eighteenth-century incarnations and on to Sessions' recent operatic version of his life.

In contrast, lesser known heroes and incidents of the early conquest of American natives were not frequently treated on the stage. One of the few was seen in George H. Miles' drama De Soto; or, The Hero of the Mississippi, which he wrote for the popular tragedian James E. Murdoch. First played on April 19, 1852, at the Chestnut Street Theatre in Philadelphia, it gave Murdoch a considerable success, and it was revived in 1857 in New York with a greater star, Edward L. Davenport, in the title role.

Conflict between Indians and explorers, as usual, makes up the story of De Soto, which of course centers on the career and death of the Spanish explorer Hernando De Soto. It is a romantic play with tragic complications provided by Ulah, apparently an Indian girl and the daughter of Tuscaluza, chief of the Floridas. A passionate affair develops between Ulah and De Soto and, even though she turns out to be a white girl, the child of a Spaniard from an exploring expedition which had preceded De Soto's, she is put to death by Tuscaluza for her transgression of native law, in what A. H. Quinn described as an "effective scene." Quinn also commented that among the Indian plays of the time, this is "one of the most appealing from the literary point of view."22 The nobility of character seems to have been mostly De Soto's, in contrast with the sternly Mosaic letter-of-the-law figure of Tuscaluza.

In surveying this group of plays written between 1800 and 1850 in which the Noble Savage character type from seventeenth- and eighteenth-century literature is utilized as a central figure, it becomes clear that a metamorphosis has taken place. At first there was a fanciful, aloof, and quite unrealistic character who might be shown as admirable but naturally subservient to white men exemplified by the markedly nobler Puritan emigrants who settled New England in Joseph Croswell's A New World Planted. Thereafter, the Indian learned to emulate the Americans in the War of 1812 and then became witty and sensible men of great dignity, like Mordecai Noah's chief in She Would Be a Soldier, entirely at one with the Americans against foreign intervention. Finally, he became a great romantic hero who, because he and his people were an obstacle to the progress of white civilization, would pass away, as demonstrated by Nathaniel Deering's Carabasset, Custis' Menawa, and the many other real Native American men romanticized on the stage throughout the 1830s, 1840s, and 1850s. This latter development, a kind of national wish-fulfillment realized only on the stage, became so prominent that it will require a separate chapter to examine these "Last Indians" (see Chapter IV).

Early in the nineteenth century--but rarely--a darker side of relations with Native Americans was sometimes shown in plays, as in Indian Cruelty, dramatizing a remnant of eighteenth-century Indian-hating folklore, and a few years later in Barker's The Armourer's Escape, which propagandized the purported rightness of the United States' boundary claims against England in the Northwest. A still stronger negative view of Indians was to be reserved for quite another kind of play developing in the late 1830s and 1840s, as we shall see, a kind more directly concerned with expansionism and the great Westward Movement then beginning.

Thus, as styles in playwrighting changed, the usefulness of Native American characters as dramatic tools shifted greatly in a fifty-year span. Even more evident was the change in playwrights' observation and characterization of Indians. The fanciful aloofness of earlier Indian characters was due most often to the arch and pompous prose or verse they spoke, but by the 1830s attempts were being made to put into actors' mouths the speech rhythms and phraseology, the kind of real talk, that an audience might hear from actual Indians. Also, specific environments were used more often, with pleasing effect. No longer was a name like "Cherokee" used to denote any Indian, as eighteenth-century British playwrights had done; no longer was an endless vista of American forests an acceptable general setting for any Indian action. Barker's Armourer's Escape indicates particular tribes, places, and times--whether accurate or not, at least the attempt was made to be specific and truthful. In Emmons' Tecumseh, the hero and his fellow tribesmen are correctly named and personified. In Macomb's Pontiac, the distortions of historical fact are used as much to stress varying degrees of nobility and savagery in Native American characters as for dramatic convenience.

The American theatre audience continued to enjoy these admirable heroes on the stage and did not allow their enjoyment to be marred by what they knew about the natives they were displacing or the increasingly more stern and repressive government policies toward them. Plays were yet to come, and would be received by this audience, with equal enthusiasm or neglect, that would reflect with greater truthfulness the facts of their relations with Native Americans.

NOTES

1. Hoxie Neale Fairchild, The Noble Savage, A Study in Romantic Naturalism (New York: Russell & Russell, 1969), p. 33.

2. Ibid., p. 29.

3. Joseph Croswell, A New World Planted; or, The Adventures of the Forefathers of New England (Boston: n.p., 1802), p. 20.

4. Mordecai Noah, She Would Be a Soldier; or, The Plains of Chippewa, in Montrose J. Moses, ed., Representative Plays by American Dramatists, 3 vols., (reprint edition, New York: Benjamin Blom, 1964), vol. I, p. 660. Since this role was first performed by Edwin Forrest, it is interesting to compare this scene, particularly the last speech, with the passage from Metamora, written for Forrest ten years later, on page 67.

5. In a latter of September 7, 1783, quoted in Richard Drinnon, Facing West: The Metaphysics of Indian-Hating and

Empire-Building (Minneapolis: University of Minnesota Press, 1980), p. 65.

6. Letter of February 17, 1803, quoted in Drinnon, op. cit., p. 89.

7. George C. D. Odell, Annals of the New York Stage, 15 vols. (New York: Columbia University Press, 1929-1945), vol. II, p. 185.

8. Scenario reconstructed by Arthur Hobson Quinn from a playbill, in his History of the American Drama From the Beginnings to the Civil War (New York: Appleton-Century-Crofts, 1951), vol I, p. 145.

9. Odell, Annals, vol. III, p. 680.

10. Joseph Doddridge, Logan, The Last of the Race of Shikellemus, Chief of the Cayuga Nation, A Dramatic Piece (Buffaloe Creek, Va.: Buffaloe Printing Office, 1823), p. 34.

11. Ibid., p. 18.

12. G. W. P. Custis, The Indian Prophecy, A National Drama in Two Acts (Georgetown, D.C.: James Thomas, 1828), p. 34.

13. Ibid., p. 35.

14. Quinn, History of the American Drama, p. 274.

15. Alexander Macomb, Pontiac; or, The Siege of Detroit (Boston: Samuel Colman, 1835), p. 9.

16. Ibid., p. 19.

17. Ralph Leslie Rusk, The Literature of the Middle Western Frontier, 2 vols. (New York: Columbia University Press, 1925), vol. 1, p. 424.

18. Drinnon, Facing West, pp. 200-201.

19. From a playbill supplied through the courtesy of the Boston Athenaeum Library.

20. James Rees, The Dramatic Authors of America (Philadelphia: G. B. Zieber & Co., 1845), p. 126. Rees gives the author as Colonel John E. Sherburne.

21. Fred Sitton, "The Indian Play in American Drama, 1750-1900" (Ph.D. dissertation, Northwestern University, 1962), p. 122.

22. Quinn, History of the American Drama, pp. 274-275. Quinn had read a manuscript of the play, now apparently lost.

Chapter III

THE INDIAN WOMAN AS AN
AMERICAN STAGE CHARACTER

If the Native American man was viewed by European
thinkers of the eighteenth century as the newly discovered
Adam of the time, his female counterpart was considered no
less to be a perfect dusky Eve. The innocence of these idyllic primitives was short-lived, of course, as their idealization
into the Noble Savage and his equally noble and virtuous mate
came more and more to be recognized for the philosophical
fiction it was. Adam persisted in refusing the gifts of "civilization" as white settlers encroached on his native homelands,
and Eve--considering the white men's libidinous urges and
the natural generosity of the Indians (for many of whose
women were little more than tradeable chattel)--was so easily
smirched that it was difficult to keep a healthy European respect for her.

But in theatrical terms, playwrights could gloss over
the terrifying reality of confrontation with actual Indians on
the rugged American frontier and continue to portray the
new Adam as the ever-popular Noble Savage who would ultimately give in to the settlers' desire for his land, and to
show the exotic heroine as a romantic dark lady not unlike
her Caucasian sisters. Sometimes she was the more sympathetic, even tragic, due to the stigma of her skin color and
could therefore more be fitted into stereotypical character
patterns old and new. This new type, feminine counterpart
of the Noble Savage, may be called the Pathetic Dusky Heroine.

As the nineteenth century began, older patterns were
still featured in many plays. Those of August von Kotzebue,
for example, were as popular in England and America as in
their native Germany, with their tearful heroines drawn from
the drame bourgeoise and the comédie larmoyante of earlier

days. Newer characterizations of women arose with the developing Romantic Movement in the arts, whose writers discovered in women greater capabilities and stronger personalities than had been created since Shakespeare's time. Women in public life--Mary Wollstonecraft, Madame de Staël, Sarah Siddons--made valid careers for themselves. In fiction and drama, determined and intellectually competent heroines--Beaumarchais' Rosine, Goethe's Charlotte, Austen's Elizabeth Bennett--were coming to be the accepted norm. Why, then, should not Native American heroines be created who had similar characteristics?

Playwrights, finding the new Romantic woman of action one of the most popular characters of their time, tended to blend her with the pathetic maiden, victim of fatal circumstances, for greater sensational effect. The two lines, though in some plays quite distinct, were often joined, and the stories of such women characters provided basic plots for numerous Indian plays mounted in the first half of the century.

The ancestral Pathetic Dusky Heroine first appeared in 1689 in Aphra Behn's tragicomedy The Widow Ranter; or, The History of Bacon in Virginia. She was an Indian "Queen" who, disguised as a boy in a climactic battle scene, is killed by a mistaken blow from her white lover. Other writers were to follow this pattern in English plays, but the earliest Indian heroine of an American dramatist is Monelia, the only female figure in Robert Rogers' Ponteach; or, The Savages of America, published in 1766. In Monelia we can see many standard elements of the stereotype that would become a popular one throughout most of our theatrical history. Monelia is the spirited daughter of a chief (or "King"), and therefore a respectable and admired "Princess"; she is the beloved of the young hero (in this play an Indian); she is plagued by several villainous characters and situations; and she is dead by the end of the play. This pattern, with certain variations which became equally standard, would serve for almost all Indian women characters seen on the American stage in the next two hundred years.

An excellent example of the type in full flowering is found in Lewis Deffebach's melodrama Oolaita, or the Indian Heroine (1821). The plot concerns a daring and noble-hearted "young chief," Tullula, and the great love between him and Oolaita, daughter of Machiwita, "King of the Sioux Nation."

Tullula is threatened with a mysterious menace of death from
unknown assailants. Machiwita, for reasons of policy, wants
his daughter to marry a vain old chieftain called Monoma.
But Tullula has done some detective work and, as the wed-
ding day arrives, exposes Monoma with his discovery that
the older man not only has a cowardly past but is also the
"treach'rous fiend" who is trying to have him murdered.
Monoma, who assumes that his hit man has succeeded, spreads
news of Tullula's death. When Oolaita hears the news, she
commits suicide by jumping from a high rock rather than
marry the loathsome Monoma. Tullula, too late to save her,
stabs himself.

Much of Oolaita's goodness of heart and nobility of
character are shown in a subplot in which she saves the lives
of three young white people (an eloping couple and their
comic male friend) lost on the prairie. Happening upon them
as they are captured by a party of murderous manhunters
of her own tribe, she snatches away the dagger of a threatening warrior, saying:

> Stay, stay that murderous weapon in its course,
> lest death and infamy await you all.... What; mur-
> der beauty, innocence, and truth? What[,] kill
> thus fiend-like a defenceless woman, and bring dis-
> grace upon the Sioux nation? Away, be gone, or
> fear the power of Machiwita's daughter.[1]

Yet assertive as she is with her own people, Oolaita is
constantly demeaning of her personal situation in scenes with
the whites--obviously to satisfy white audiences who, ever
fearful of male savages, wanted to believe that at least an
Indian woman would succor them and prove that under her
darker skin she was as Christian as they thought themselves
to be.

Oolaita never hesitates to demean herself with speeches
like this:

> As for me, a poor unhappy Sioux, I was nursed in
> this savage wild, and taught no other lesson by my
> father than war, the chase, peril and toil, and dan-
> ger. But the Great Spirit, who loves the Indian as
> he loves the whiteman, gave me a feeling heart as
> well as you. Little, perhaps, did you suppose to

find, in this uncultivated wild, a form like thine, a
savage form that own'd a Christian soul.[2]

When her three young white friends are ordered before her
father to learn their fate, she assures them she will make a
sort of prairie-Pocahontas gesture:

> ... fear no danger. Oolaita can calm the turbu-
> lence of aged hatred, and quell the rising passion
> of the soul. I will be with you--I will intercede;
> and if a daughter can mould a father to her pur-
> pose, your lives are safe, your liberty secure.[3]

The playwright makes her conclude this scene with: "Though
Oolaita's skin were black as night, her soul is pure and spot-
less as the snow."[4]

Throughout the early history of these Indian plays--
certainly up to the time the great Westward Movement began
at the end of the 1840s--we will find strong veins of wishful-
fillment expressed by white playwrights: the desire that
Native Americans will admit an inferiority the white people
wanted to see in them (dark of skin, unhappy in their savagery); that they will protect white people from fearful elements both natural and human (pure of soul, interceding to
secure life and liberty for their conquerors); and--the ultimate relief--that they will finally leave the land to the whites
and vanish over a distant horizon. These wishes are divided
among the characters deemed to be the appropriate expres-
sers of them. The desired admissions of inferiority and offers of protection for white people, who sometimes feel like
children lost in the wilderness, are usually spoken by women
characters such as Oolaita, while agreements to stop resisting white encroachment and to move westward are most often
given to male characters, as in G. W. P. Custis' play Pocahontas (see page 53) or as we saw in Custis' earlier play,
The Indian Prophecy.

The theatrical usefulness of a popular character in
maintaining white people's faith in their superiority is not to
be underestimated, nor is the whites' need to find the Indians
--if only stage Indians--forgiving and supportive. Certain
popular heroines reappeared (as did much-admired male characters) in numerous plays of this period. The dramatic story
of Oucanasta, heroine of the several Wacousta plays, combines

an appealingly bright and able young woman, seduced and deceived by white characters, led into a pathetic career of misguided beliefs and final downfall. The story was first presented in a melodrama by Louisa Medina (one of her earliest plays) at the Bowery Theatre in New York in 1833. It was reworked in 1850 by another skilled melodramatist, Nathaniel Bannister, as Oua Cousta; or, The Lion of the Forest, and again in 1851, in the only extant play version, by an otherwise unknown playwright identified as R. Jones, under the title Wacousta; or, The Curse.[5]

Jones' version is a rousing melodrama involving the familiar story of the rebellion of Pontiac and the siege of Fort Detroit in 1763. Amid the loosely-handled historical materials, the writer has placed an Indian girl, Oucanasta, in love with a British officer, Captain De Waldemar. She betrays her own people by informing the British of the preparations for the rebellion. In a taut love scene (Act I, scene 2) before leading her lover to observe the Indians' preparations, she explains her reasons:

De Waldemar: But is there no danger to yourself?

Oucanasta: Danger! Have you forgotten when you dashed death aside in the angry waters of the lake, and[,] horror around you[,] saved Oucanasta from its wild depths. I tell thee in that hour I swore an oath of gratitude, which is recorded in the stars --and until the great spirit shall quench their fires that oath will be remembered.

De Waldemar: How can I thank thee?

Oucanasta: The skin of the Ottawa is not white like the snows of Canada, nor her cheek blooming like the flowers of the red bush but her heart is warm. You held me to your heart amid the wild waters, and Oucanasta loved you. Let her be your slave.

De Waldemar: This generous confidence, Oucanasta--I will not deceive thee, there is a pale girl whom I love better than my life. I can love no other.

Oucanasta: Ha--(<u>screams</u>) ... For this have I been false to my people--the great spirit has frozen the fountain of my life, but the love of the Indian girl will not change like the flowers of the forest. She will save thy pale love, and when that fair head like the willow with its long curls shall pillow on thy breast, then Oucanasta can die.

Oucanasta is rejected by the Indians, including Wacousta, the warrior chieftain of the title, and the historical figure Pontiac. The latter appears only in one long scene, first negotiating with the British and then denouncing Oucanasta for her treachery. In a later scene the whites betray her trust, and Oucanasta dies cursing them (hence the title).

The emotional reaction of white audiences to such a play as Jones' is easily imagined. Oucansata is an attractively fiery young woman whose decision to perform an act useful and desirable to the white conquerors could only have been accepted by viewers with approval. She was perceived as sweetly pathetic in her hopeless love for an upper-class white officer (who, naturally, would not wish to pursue more than a momentary dalliance with her) and in the rejection she suffers both from her own people and from those she wishes to adopt. She is admirable for her strength of character, shown in aiding the British with useful information and later in the passionate delivery of her curse on them when they betray and desert her in her hour of need--a fine climactic scene for the white actress who played Oucanasta.

A later version of the Oucanasta character, but only lightly sketched in, is Ultina, the only female character in Alexander Macomb's <u>Pontiac; or, The Siege of Detroit</u> (1838). General Macomb's limitations as a playwright and his naturally greater interest in the military aspects of the material he dramatized surely had much to do with Ultina's thinnesss of character. She appears only in two scenes in the play, in one of which she informs the British officers of the Indians' plans for rebellion and in the other laments that she has done so. Thereafter she simply drifts away, a pathetic but unresolved character.

The oddly named "Pocahante" of the much earlier <u>A New World Planted</u> (1802) (not a dramatization of the

Pocahontas of Virginia legend) is an equally shadowy character, a giamorous dark lady who appears briefly and is later
described by the officer, Hampden, who wants to marry her.
Her story is left even more unfinished than Ultina's (See page
46).

For greater pathos, the playwright sometimes employed
the device of making his heroine either half white or, in some
plays, a white girl living as an Indian.

In Henry J. Finn's Montgomery; or, The Falls of Montmorency (1825) (revised in 1830 by Finn and the actor James
H. Hackett as The Indian Wife; or, The Falls of Montmorency),
the wife of the title is Altamah, daughter of a Frenchwoman
and an Indian. Altamah is married to a Frenchman called La
Valle, and when her husband goes off to war she is hounded
by the villainous L'Araignée. This determined rogue, frustrated at Altamah's equally determined conjugal fidelity, re-
venges himself by putting her baby in a canoe which is about
to shoot over the falls of Montmorency. But Altamah's tribula-
tions end happily when her baby is saved and the escaping
villain is overtaken.

Instances of white women living as Indians are dramatized
more as stories of Arcadia gone wrong. Naramattah, for example, in the several dramatizations of James Fenimore Cooper's
novel The Wept of Wish-Ton-Wish (1830), is happy to be abducted by the handsome young Indian she loves and lives an
idyllic life as wife and mother until she and her husband are
captured by her own people. She sees him murdered by
them and then dies of a broken heart.

An equally pathetic but even more violent fate over-
takes Ulah in George Henry Miles' De Soto; or, The Hero of
the Mississippi (1852). Ulah's story is somewhat more fanciful than Naramattah's. The daughter of white parents (her
father an early conquistador-explorer), Ulah has been left
with the Indians on her father's death in the wilderness, and
has taken on all the attributes of an Indian woman and a de-
vout faith in the Indian gods. Therefore she must suffer
death at the hands of her Indian adopters when she breaks
that faith by what they construe as her "unholy" love for the
titular hero. Naramattah's story was probably based on some
true incident Cooper had heard; Ulah's tale is cut out of a
whole piece of melodramatic cloth.

Numerous situations involving actual white women who went or were taken to live with Indians are recorded and seem not to have been quite so sad and theatrical as these two. Most often, the change from the harsh difficulties of frontier pioneer existence to the more established comforts of Indian life was apparently a less than traumatic adjustment.[7] But for romantic theatrical purposes, a white woman who has taken on a dark-skinned persona must suffer for her defection; she is seen as a kind of pathetic traitor to her race, regardless of how honorable she is in her fidelity to her adopted way of life.

Most play titles of the period, however, indicate specifically Indian and not half-breed characters. As usual in the pre-copyright era, we have the titles of numbers of plays which were produced but whose texts have long since been lost. Many of the playwrights' names are unknown, as, for example, those who wrote The Indian Heroine of 1821, The Indian Girl of 1838, Ontiata; or, The Indian Heroine, produced some time in the 1830s, The Indian Queen of 1851, and Magnolia; or, The Child of the Flower in 1855. Of works by known playwrights, Joseph Stevens Jones' The Indian Mother was played in Boston in 1832, Sassacus; or, The Indian Wife by William Wheatley came out in 1836, Onylda, The Pequot Maid by F. H. Duffee was performed on some unlocatable date in the 1830s, and Prairie Bird; or, A Child of the Delawares by the actor-playwright Walter M. Leman in 1846.

The portrayal of Indian women as the unhappy victims of white progress across the continent was then neglected for many years until Mrs. Jackson's Ramona came to the stage in 1887, followed ten years later by the noble martyr Maria Candelaria, and the suicidal wife of The Squaw Man in 1905. Thereafter the tradition not only continued but expanded in the twentieth century through additional pseudo-tragic stories both dramatic and operatic, including, for example, highly publicized works such as Victor Herbert's Natoma. Such stories continue to be popular, as with a sorely-used Shawnee heroine of West Virginia legend in an outdoor spectacle-pageant, The Aracoma Story, to name only one example.

*   *   *

Returning to the flowering of the stereotypical Indian woman character, we come upon an unusually interesting script which shows a transitional character, based on a real woman then still living. It makes a bridge between the pathetic heroine and the more positive Pocahontas type. This odd work is a long one-act play in four or five scenes called Catherine Brown, The Converted Cherokee.[8] It is the naive and amateur product of an unidentified lady, written to be performed by church missionary groups. The playwright seems neither to have known the real Catherine Brown's story except in simplest outline nor to have been remotely conversant with life at frontier missionary stations. Only the author's faith in the goodness of the missionaries' attempts to Christianize Indians keeps these scattered scenes going.

In the opening scene, Catherine (her Cherokee name is never given) is a vain, overdressed, and impertinent teenaged girl--virtually an epitome, if rather a pale shadow, of the eighteenth-century Romp character type. Her parents have brought her to the Brainerd Mission school (in the old Southwest territory, near modern Chattanooga, Tennessee) to be educated in white ways, their despairing attitude implying that the missionaries can deal with this difficult child better than they. In the next two scenes, Catherine is entirely changed, having learned English perfectly and become a saintly young woman who teaches and acts as a sort or surrogate mother to the Cherokee children at the school. The missionaries have succeeded in turning her nearly "white."

Catherine and all the characters are no more than one-dimensional cutouts and author's mouthpieces, and there is no other action, only discussions of how the mission teachers have turned Catherine into a good and intensely religious girl--until the last scene, in which her parents return and arbitrarily insist that she return to her old Indian life with them. This, we are allowed to understand, would be an indescribable horror to her after her indoctrination into a "higher" form of life at Brainerd. She makes no decision in the dialogue of the play, which thus ends inconclusively. But it is known that Catherine Brown, a true convert, continued at Brainerd for another year or so until she could establish a school and an independent life of her own.[9]

Catherine Brown, the Converted Cherokee was not, of course, intended as a commercial play; its author's slender creative gifts would have precluded any such competition in any case. It is a simple propaganda piece meant to attract

attention to the highly successful activities of the Presby-
terian missionaries in the old Southwest. But its patronizing
attitude toward Native American abilities, its foregone conclusion that whites could show Indians the error of their ways
and turn them into better people, is shared with all the professionally written plays considered in this study.

The religious influence as a dramatic element is also
apparent in what seems to have been a similar work, Lamorah;
or, The Western Wild, by Caroline Lee Hentz of Cincinnati,
where it was first performed in 1832. The text, published
in 1833 (though now lost), was subtitled "DRAMA in five
acts, written in the West, and the scene laid on the banks
of the Ohio!" A reviewer in The Western Monthly Magazine
of that year found it to be:

> ... objectionable because of an injudicious mingling
> of serious and farcical characters, among the latter
> being a coward named Gabriel, who wears a wig to
> avoid being scalped. The same critic was pleased,
> however, with the sentimental character of the In-
> dian heroine, Lamorah, who "will not yield the palm
> to Pocahontas" and who was surpassed only by Atala
> "from having early implanted in her bosom, the
> seeds of a christian education." Such was the lack
> of realism in what might have been expected to con-
> tain a genuine picture of Western pioneer life.[10]

This idea that Native Americans were always improved
by white contact, particularly by religious influence and example, is more subtly stressed in the several plays about
Pocahontas written between 1808 and the 1870s. The idea
was supported, of course, by the fact that the historical
Pocahontas, as everyone knew, did become a Christian convert, married a white man, and died (and was buried, by a
twist of fate, in England) in the arms of the church.[11] The
pious reaction to her death was first recorded in Captain
John Smith's Generall Historie of Virginia in 1624:

> ... it pleased God at Gravesend to take this young
> lady to his mercie; where shee made not more sor-
> row for her unexpected death, than joy to the be-
> holders to heare and see her make so religious and
> godly an end.[12]

This latter part of her story, however, is little used in the plays about her. Most are based on the familiar legend drawn from Captain Smith's Generall Historie. It is one of the basic American myths: In a confrontation in which Powhatan's menacing braves are about to execute him, Smith's life is saved by the intervention of Pocahontas. The grateful Captain returns the favor by aiding the budding romance of John Rolfe and the Indian girl, who is so attracted to the white settlers that she has become a liaison between English and Indians--and is soon transformed into the pious Christian lady, Rebecca Rolfe. The standard pattern is laid out for the playwright: an attractive Indian girl becomes more desirable and approvable as a heroine by aiding the whites and giving up her people and customs for theirs.

In the earliest of our Pocahontas plays, James Nelson Barker's The Indian Princess; or, La Belle Sauvage, the lesson of white superiority comes early in the first act when Pocahontas' brother, Prince Nantaquas, meets John Smith:

Prince: Art thou not then a God?

Smith: As thou art, warrior, but a man.

Prince: Then art thou a man like a God; thou shalt be
          the brother of Nantaquas. Stranger, my father
          is king of the country, and many nations obey
          him; will thou be the friend of the great Powhatan?

Smith: Freely, prince; I left my own country to be the
          red man's friend.

Prince: Wonderful man....

Smith: Prince, the Great Spirit is the friend of the white
          men, and they have arts which the red men know
          not.

Prince: My brother, will you teach the red men?

Smith: I came to do it. My king is a king of a mighty
          nation; he is great and good: go, said he, go
          and make the red men wise and happy.[13]

Pocahontas is not slow to pick up such cues, particularly

when her inspiration comes from falling in love with John Rolfe. In the second of her two charming love scenes with him (Act III, scene ii) we learn how she has received instruction:

Pocahontas:

O! 'tis from thee that I have drawn my being;
Thou'st ta'en me from the path of savage error,
Blood-stain'd and rude, where rove my countrymen,
And taught me heavenly truths, and fill'd my heart
With sentiments sublime, and sweet, and social.
Oft has my winged spirit, following thine,
Cours'd the bright day-beam, and the star of night,
And every rolling planet of the sky,
Around their circling orbits. O my love!
Guided by thee, has not my daring soul
O'ertopt the far-off mountains of the east,
Where, as our fathers' fable, shad'wy hunters
Pursue the deer, or clasp the melting maid,
'Mid ever blooming spring? Thence, soaring high
From the deep vale of legendary fiction,
Hast though not heaven-ward turn'd my dazzled sight,
Where sing the spirits of the blessed good
Around the bright throne of the Holy One?
This hast thou done; and ah! what couldst thou more.
Belov'd preceptor, but direct that ray,
Which beams from Heaven to animate existence,
And bid my swelling bosom beat with love! [14]

Barker originally intended The Indian Princess to be a dramatic piece like his other plays, but among his acquaintances at the Philadelphia theatres was the composer John Bray at whose prompting he added several lyrics; the play became, as the title page of the published edition tells us, an "operatic melo-drame." Accompanied by Bray's delightful score, [15] it was first performed at the Chestnut Street Theatre on April 6, 1808, and was a success that would be continued in revivals for years to come. It was not, however, a true melodrama but a comic musical piece, very like a twentieth-century operetta. Serious dramatic moments are few and easily resolved--the capture and near-execution of John Smith; Powhatan's banquet in the last act at which the white guests, intended to be killed, are saved by Pocahontas' arrival with Lord Delaware to rescue them; and the suicide of the villainous

warrior Miami at his final loss of the heroine. The tone
throughout is consistently comic, and the effective musical-
comedy jollity of dialogue and score preclude more profound
observations on questions such as how to become properly
white and Christian. In the final scene, Pocahontas, having
escaped the unwanted advances of her fierce Indian suitor
Miami, is joined to Rolfe in marriage. At the same time four
other pairs of lovers (from the elaborate subplot about the
settlers) are also wedded, and all ends with a happy chorus.

George Washington Parke Custis, in his Pocahontas; or,
The Settlers of Virginia (1830), altered history somewhat
more than Barker did, but in a romantic manner similar to
Barker's and in a more pretentiously serious play. The scene
of Pocahontas saving John Smith from execution, for instance,
is that part of the story with highest dramatic possibilities.
Barker, in creating a sort of American As You Like It with a
serious center and frivolous edges, introduced all his characters in his first act, then placed this focal action at the beginning of his second act (of three), and balanced out his
play by developing the strong relationship of Pocahontas and
Rolfe and the distinctive, charmingly foolish characters of
his settlers. Custis, on the other hand, saves this incident
for the grand climax of his play, establishing Pocahontas'
friendship for the whites and her love affair with Rolfe early
on and making the main action of the play her cooperative
efforts with John Smith to keep the peace between Indians
and whites. They are opposed by a villain called Matacoran
(once again Pocahontas' suitor) who is constantly trying to
stir up an interracial war.

To account for Pocahontas' Christian learning, Custis
has introduced a character called Barclay, a white man who
(rather against historical probability) has been living with
the Indians for years. Carrying out intentions stated by John
Smith in Barker's play (as quoted above), Barclay has de-
voted his life to teaching his Indian wife and her people the
white man's arts and faith. Pocahontas, comparing him with
Matacoran, explains:

> Matacoran is brave, yet he lacks the best attribute
> of courage--mercy. Since the light of the Christian
> doctrine has shone on my before benighted soul, I
> have learn'd that mercy is one of the attributes of
> the divinity I now adore. To good father Barclay

> I owe the knowledge which I have acquired of the
> only true God, whose worship I in secret perform.[16]

The first production of <u>Pocahontas; or, The Settlers
of Virginia</u>, at the Walnut Street Theatre in Philadelphia, seems
to have been a notably spectacular one. Elaborate pre-
production work caused the theatre to be closed for several
days before the play's opening on January 16, 1830. But
the preparations apparently paid off, as it had the unusually
long run of twelve nights in succession, and it was later
played in New York and revived in Philadelphia. Apart from
its physical attractions, however, certain of the play's sentiments must have appealed mightily to the audience. John
Smith, addressing his forces in the play's first scene, indicates there is to be no time wasted in negotiating with Indians:

> 'Tis fitting that we appear in our best harness, and
> that in its best burnish too, that we may strike upon
> the minds of the natives here, fair impressions of
> our might and grandeur.... Allons! we will pitch
> our camp and array our forces, and to-morrow on
> to the savage court, where we will ... demand, in
> behalf of our gracious sovereign, dominion in and
> over the countries from the mountains to the sea,
> and if denied us--why then--<u>Dieu et mon Droit</u>--
> for God and our right.[17]

The satisfactory response to this approach comes in
the last scene when Matacoran, speaking for all Indians who
have made the mistake of resisting the English conquerors,
makes the right decision for his future:

> The fortune of war is on thy side; thy gods are as
> much greater than the gods of the Indian, as thine
> arms are greater than his. but altho' thy gods and
> thine arms have prevail'd, say did not Matacoran
> fight bravely in the last of his country's battles?
> and when his comrades fled, singly did he face the
> thunders of his foe. Now that he can no longer
> combat the invaders he will retire before them, even
> to where tradition says, there rolls a western wave.
> There, on the utmost verge of the land which the
> Manitou gave to his fathers, when grown old by
> time, Matacoran will erect his tumulus, crawl into it
> and die.[18]

These lines were particularly pertinent in light of the fact that the forced removal of the eastern Indians to a territory west of the Mississippi was being widely talked of at this time, and President Andrew Jackson's Indian Removal Bill would be passed into law only four months later, on May 28, 1830.

Perhaps the best dramatization of the story from a literary point of view is Robert Dale Owen's play, Pocahontas, A Historical Drama. It is a play marked by a well-thought-out dramatic plan, affecting characterizations, and a gifted writer's skilled use of language. Owen was a man of many parts, British-born and educated, well-known as a social reformer and writer, who became a staunch American citizen, served as a Congressman who initiated several important bills (including the one that founded the Smithsonian Institution), and was a founder of the famous utopian community at New Harmony, Indiana.

It is not surprising, therefore, to find Owen's only play a dramatic work of some intellectual value. The very long script was severely trimmed at his own suggestion before its first performance at the Park Theatre in New York on February 8, 1838. The performers included the great Charlotte Cushman, in one of her breeches performances, as John Rolfe and the popular ingenue Emma Wheatley as Pocahontas. In reading it today, one can see that judicious cutting must have made it a very playable, attractive piece. Although not a great success in its own time, it is one of the few Indian plays with enough substance to suggest that it might sustain a modern revival.

John Smith implied in his writings that he felt a strong attachment to Pocahontas. Owen has followed this suggestion and shows Smith as sincerely and profoundly in love with her. He is an appealing hero and, through his sacrifice of his own feelings for her so she may be united with Rolfe, he becomes the central figure of the play. Its real focus, however, is far less on this romantic triangle than on the dissension among the English settlers, probably a more historically accurate situation. For once the troublemaking villains are white men and not Indians. Much of the early part of the play dramatizes treacheries among the English themselves, polarized in a desperate character called Archer, and the consequent poor relations with the Indians that result from these problems.

John Smith makes frequent point of praising the Indians, as here, when he is chiding the suspicious troublemaker, Archer:

> Nay, master Archer, there you wrong the Indian.
> His native sense of courtesy is strong;
> Stronger, perchance, if in less courtly garb,
> Than under damasks, taffeties and tissues.[19]

Not only are the Indians naturally courteous, but also they are not easily deceived by the duplicity of the whites, as a young warrior comments:

> When a Redskin says,
> I am thy friend; and smokes the pipe of peace,
> The sun himself is not more sure to rise
> From out the forest at the morning dawn,
> Than he to bide his word. But, for the Longknives,
> They wear two faces.[20]

Pocahontas, though drawn for the most part with the same gentle innocence we have seen in earlier characterications, can show her loyalty to her own in a healthy streak of defiance when--having brought food to the starving settlers and acting as peacemaker between whites and Indians-- they betray her and her people:

> No policy
> Doth Pocahontas know, save justice. She
> Hath succoured ye, for she believed ye friends;
> But if your arms should e'er be levelled 'gainst
> Her race, mark well? Her country's foes are hers.[21]

The point of the play--the need for fair dealings and cooperative relations on both sides--is strongly stated as the drama draws to its close. In the final scene, when John Smith, as heroic father figure of the colony, has united Rolfe and Pocahontas and put the villain Archer in chains, this exchange occurs:

Smith: Old Warrior! Paspaho! Hear my words!--
            The last before I cross the Great Salt
              Lake--
            You seek revenge?--revenge is ta'en al-
              ready:

(Points to Archer)
Your sachem's daughter's freedom?--she
   is free.
What would ye more? Look on that Yen-
   geese chief;
      (Pointing to Rolfe)
His heart and Pocahontas' heart are one.
They have joined hands and hearts. So
   let it be
With Red Men and Yengeese. Let them
   sit down
Within the lodge of peace, and let their
   hearts
Hence forth be one. Old chief, are my
   words good?

Utta Maccomac: Thy words are good.

Smith: Paspaho?

Paspaho: They are good.

Smith: It is enough. My task is done....[22]

An equally serious but far less successful version is
Charlotte Barnes Conner's The Forest Princess; or, Two
Centuries Ago--perhaps the result of the writer's longstand-
ing attraction to the subject. As a child she had seen her
actor-parents, Mr. and Mrs. John Barnes, play Rolfe and
Pocahontas in Custis' Pocahontas; or, The Settlers of Virginia
in its first Philadelphia production eighteen years before.
The Forest Princess was also played in Philadelphia, at the
Arch Street Theatre, on February 16, 1848.[23]

Mrs. Conner attempted to give her audience more history and less romance than previous playwrights had done,
incorporating important details from Pocahontas' last days in
England. She researched her work at the British Museum,
to which she has in part dedicated the play, adding the self-
effacing comment: "It would appear only an affectation of
pedantry to name the works, (at least twenty in number,)
which were consulted previous to the writing of this ephe-
meral production."[24] Neither the impetus of family tradition
nor serious research in "at least twenty" source books, however, aided Mrs. Conner in creating much of a play, although

perhaps a modern critic is a bit harsh in judging it "an example of nineteenth-century theatre at its worst, a pageant rather than a play."[25]

The unlikeliest scenes (despite the writer's insistence in her Appendix that "The incidents of this play are historical in their most minute details") occur toward the end. When her husband is arrested on a trumped-up charge of treason, Pocahontas (now, of course, Rebecca Rolfe), goes to have a chat with "Anne" and "Charles," whom she seems to know well from her presentation at Court (presumably, Mrs. Conner, the staunch republican, would not use the terms "Prince" and "Queen"), and they promise her their aid. She falls ill, and then comes her prolonged death scene, during which we are treated to the "Vision of Pocahontas." The setting, a room at an inn, is described as having a large window Up Center (obviously for a scrim) through which we have seen the George, the ship that was to take Pocahontas back to Virginia, resting at anchor. Now the George is seen to sail away to America; then Powhatan appears, then figures of Time and Peace, and then George Washington with the Genius of Columbia; the British Lion and the American Eagle are also present. "Time hovers near, and Peace encircles with her arms the Lion and the Eagle." And then the vision fades away. John Rolfe comes to his wife's bedside, and her last words, as she points upward, are:

> I hear my father--Husband, fare thee well.
> We part--but we shall meet--above![26]

In spite of the love of sentiment mingled with pageantry among audiences of the time, it is hardly surprising that John Brougham's spoofs of Indian plays would effectively sweep such pieces as The Forest Princess from the stage within the next few years.

Brougham's burlesque masterpiece, Po-Ca-Hon-Tas; or, The Gentle Savage, was brought out in 1857, the last time the heroine would be introduced on the stage before the Civil War. But the subject was magnetic to playwrights, and another rash of Pocahontas plays began to appear in 1875. Most of them, whether intended seriously or not, are little more than travesties of the story, imbued with a very different, quite cynical attitude held by both public and playwrights toward the material, unlike any displayed in the first half of the century. For this reason they will be considered in a later chapter.

We have seen that the Native American woman as a stage character has had two lines of development, first as the Pathetic Dusky Heroine, growing out of the sentimental drama of the eighteenth century; and second as the Pocahontas type, the female Noble Savage of happier fate. The Oolaitas and Oucanastas were made to seem more assertive and flamboyant, perhaps to make their pseudo-tragic endings the more affecting, while the Pocahontases were turned into more sweetly appealing and less tragedy-prone presences. But playwrights showed them to be very much alike in their striving to emulate their white sisters in an assumption of Christian understanding and humility, as well as in their determination to aid white men in the conquest of the continent. These less-than-Indian options are the more stressed by the heriones' manner of speaking and, occasionally, by notably fairer skin than Indians usually had. Whereas male Indian characters were almost always made to talk with an artificial dialect different from that of white characters, Indian women are, without exception, as eloquent in English as any white. The "whiter" their speech and fairer their skin, the less offensive, of course, was the taboo of miscegenation.

The two branches of the stereotype have varied little, either during the heyday of Indian-play production before the Civil War or since. As long as Indian women gave white men aid and comfort in the task of overcoming their people, spurned the supposedly crude, savage manners and mores of their upbringing, and learned to mouth Christian tenets popular at the time, they fit the accepted mold. If they died in the last act, that was all to the good, as it kept audiences coming and paying to shed a tear over their hopeless cause.

Two possible variants were the native woman as a villain and as the Romp character. But there were no women villains in Indian plays of this period; the only two we know of occur in Dryden and Howard's The Indian Queen (the evil Zempoalla) in 1664, and two hundred years later in a Buffalo Bill thriller, The Scouts of the Plains, (a "Princess" who viciously baits white captives) in the 1870s. The Romp first appeared in Indian guise in a British play, the younger Colman's Inkle and Yarico in 1787--a comic-relief girl suitably named Wowski--but was rarely adapted to characters in American plays. The young Catherine Brown has been cited, but in commercially performed plays the Romp only contributed, on occasion, a certain lively outspokenness (as in Oucanasta and sometimes Pocahontas). It is a comedy type not really suitable in Pathetic Dusky Maidens. And no comedies about Indians were written for many years to come, except, of course, John Brougham's burlesque "gentle savage"--a phrase that would always describe the Native American woman as a stage character.

NOTES

1. Lewis Deffebach, Oolaita; or, The Indian Heroine. A Melodrama in Three Acts (Philadelphia: Printed for the Author, 1821), p. 13.
2. Ibid., p. 14
3. Ibid.
4. Ibid.
5. R. Jones, "Wacousta; or, The Curse." Unpublished manuscript promptbook. The New York Public Library, Manuscript Division. Unpaged.
6. Miantonimoh; or, The Wept of Wish-Ton-Wish and Naramattah; or, The Lost Found (both 1830); Miantonimoh (1831), Miantonimoh and Naramattah (1840); and The Wept of The Wish-Ton-Wish (1850). All are by anonymous playwrights. A much later use of the story appeared in a closet drama of 1884, Robert Boody Caverly's Miantonimoh.
7. See Kenneth Roberts' novel Northwest Passage (Boston: Little Brown, 1937), chapters XXX and XLV, for an unusually interesting fictional description of such women, and Gene Jones' Where The Wind Blew Free (New York: W. W. Norton, 1966) for several nonfiction stories of happily Indianized women. Dale Van Every in Disinherited: The Lost Birthright of the American Indian (New York: William Morrow & Co., 1966), p. 74, shows that the 1825 census of the East Cherokee lists 73 white women married into the nation.
8. [Anonymous], Catherine Brown, The Converted Cherokee (New Haven: n.p., 1819). The extant text, though substantially complete, lacks some transitional passages toward the end.
9. In regard to Brainerd and her life there, Dale Van Every in Disinherited: The Lost Birthright of the American Indian, p. 44, describes the school as "... an immediate and

continuing success ... more than a primary school for children or a trade school for boys. On its faculty were graduates of many northern universities. Young women were offered the same courses as young men. The one limit to the school's educational program was Cherokee ability to learn. Once more it was demonstrated that Cherokee aptitude in this respect was prodigious. Catherine Brown, first Cherokee to be baptized at Brainerd on January 25, 1818, was soon teaching in a school of her own. By 1825 her brother, David, had finished translating the New Testament directly from Greek into Cherokee.... The Cherokee people were embracing education with all the excited fervor with which once they had raised the war whoop." For further details, see the story "No-People Boy" in Gene Jones, Where the Wind Blew Free.

10. Ralph Leslie Rusk, The Literature of the Middle Western Frontier, 2 vols. (New York: Columbia University Press, 1925), vol. I, p. 42.

11. Frances Mossiker, Pocahontas, The Life and the Legend (New York: Alfred A. Knopf, 1976), p. 280.

12. Quoted in Mossiker, Pocahontas. Pocahontas died at the age of 22 in the third week of March 1617.

13. James Nelson Barker, The Indian Princess; or, La Belle Sauvage, in Montrose J. Moses, Representative Plays by American Dramatists, 3 vols. (New York: E. P. Dutton & Co., 1918; reprint edition, New York: Benjamin Blom, Inc., 1964), vol. I, pp. 586-587.

14. Ibid., pp. 611-612.

15. Reconstructed in a superb recorded performance by the Federal Music Society Opera Company, John Baldon, conductor, on New World Records #232.

16. G. W. P. Custis, Pocahontas; or, The Settlers of Virginia, in Arthur Hobson Quinn, Representative American Plays (New York: Appleton-Century-Crofts, 1953), p. 175.

17. Ibid.

18. Ibid., p. 192.

19. Robert Dale Owen, Pocahontas, A Historical Drama In Five Acts; With an Introductory Essay and Notes. By a Citizen of the West. (New York: George Dearborn, 1837), p. 54.

20. Ibid., p. 69.

21. Ibid., p. 196.

22. Ibid., p. 220.

23. Although Arthur Hobson Quinn, A History of the American Drama From the Beginnings to the Civil War (New York: F. S. Crofts & Co., Publishers, 1936), vol. 2, p.273, states that it was first performed in Liverpool in 1844.

24. [Charlotte Barnes], The Forest Princess; or, Two Centuries Ago. An Historical Play in Three Parts [n.p.]., 1848), p. [14].

25. Mossiker, Pocahontas, p. 325.

26. [Barnes], The Forest Princess, pp. 262-263, 268.

Chapter IV

THE "LAST INDIAN" SYNDROME

There was no stronger or more timely topic for a well-made American melodrama, none more sadly serious and none more audience-thrilling, than the lost cause of the Noble Savage, the last of his race. The phrase had a nice melancholy ring, making an intriguing romantic title. And it expressed a subdued but long-standing wish recognized by playwrights and public alike: The Last of the Serpent Tribe--Last of the Norridgewocks--Last of the Shikellemus--Last of the Mohicans--Last of the Wampanoags (or, irresistibly, to a wit like John Brougham, The Last of the Pollywogs).

Not all "Last Indians" were so indicated in their drama's titles. Not many had a speech like Chief Logan's, purportedly utilizing the real Logan's actual words, claiming that not one drop of his blood flowed any longer in any living veins. But most Native American heroes of plays written in the 1830s and 1840s were, to the American public's general approval, shown to be on their way to extinction. Some tears might well be shed over the stern necessity of this tragic loss--a good dramatic scene merited a good cry. But there had always been so many more Indians on this "unoccupied" continent than settlers had bargained for. Extirpation of the tribes would be, after all, the most satisfactory solution to the United States' combined problem of Indians and immigrants-- the Indians with their stubborn presence and, as mid-century came on, the endless stream of immigrants in need of all those beautiful stretches of virgin land on which to spread the new American brand of civilization.

So the wish was expressed, in play after play. In political reality, however, an alternative existed. This alternative was simply to remove the Native Americans from lands the whites wanted in the Eastern ststes to some patch of theoretically unoccupied territory west of the Mississippi.

Removal was not a new concept. Jefferson had proposed it
in 1803, as we have seen. It was revived in 1817 while Mon-
roe was president, and in 1825, during John Quincy Adams'
administration, a removal bill actually passed the Senate but
was defeated by the House and by Adams' failure to approve
it.[1]

And, like the slightly covert wish for extirpation, the
desirability of their removal was also often expressed in theatrical terms. We have heard Indian characters agree without
demur to move west and leave their ancestral homelands to
the whites, as in G. W. P. Custis' The Indian Prophecy and
Pocahontas, and we will hear the sentiment again in more
plays to come. This possibility offered on the stage became
reality in the 1830s, after Andrew Jackson's Removal Bill was
passed and the terrible forced migration, the "Trail of Tears,"
was begun. But whether removal was to be achieved willingly
on the natives' part or otherwise, the public devoutly wished
to see the last Indian traveling westward over the horizon,
and it salved uneasy consciences to hear the idea expressed
by stage Indians in positive, attractive terms.

The problem of conscience in relation to the Native
American more and more comes to the fore in the plays we
are now to consider. The "animals, vulgarly called Indians,"
as they had been described by an eighteenth-century observer,[2] had turned out, as more Americans came to know
them, to be human beings after all, with a desire to pre-
serve their culture quite as strong as the desire of European
settlers to displace it with their own imported ones. The
Indian became the symbol of both a free way of life the whites
wanted and could not achieve and at the same time the wall
of human resistance that seemed to prevent the settlers from
achieving it. No more penetrating analysis of the problem
has been made than that by Roy Harvey Pearce in his brilliant study, The Savages of America. "Pity, censure, and
their justification are the qualities we must distinguish in
American thinking about the Indian between the Revolution
and the period of Removal," he writes.

> ... We can say that the American, as the self-
> consciously civilized and civilizing man, could envision
> the possibilities of a life free from what he somehow
> felt to be the complexities of civilization. Envision-
> ing that life, he might very well yearn for it. But

seeing it, as he thought, in disturbing actuality to the west, he hated himself for his yearning. He was tempted, we might say; and he felt driven to destroy the temptation and likewise the tempters. He pitied the tempters, because in his yearning for a simpler life, he could identify with them. He censured them, because he was ashamed to be tempted, and he refused to deny his higher nature.[3]

They were strong and subtle, those tempters. But the "higher nature" of white men was not to be denied. An Indian was an Indian, and everyone knew what kind of men they were--noble, admirable, of course, but also savages. What had come about was

> the development in the American mind of the Indian as a symbol for all that over which civilization must triumph. The Indian who was important to Americans setting out to make their new society was not the person but the type, not the tribesman but the savage, not the individual but the symbol. The American conscience was troubled about the death of the individual. But it could make sense of his death only when it understood it as the death of the symbol.[4]

In John Augustus Stone's play Metamora; or, The Last of the Wampanoags (1829), when the titular hero has made an overwhelming impression on the two younger (non-Indian) principals, this conversation ensues:

Oceana: Teach him, Walter; make him like to us.

Walter: 'Twould cost him half his native virtue. Is justice goodly? Metamora's just. Is bravery virtue? Metamora's brave. If love of country, child and wife and home, be to deserve them all, he merits them.

Oceana: Yet he is a heathen.

Walter: True, Oceana, but his worship though untaught and rude, flows from his heart, and Heaven alone must judge of it.[5]

It should be easy enough to "make him like to us," since Metamora displays all the good traits one may find, according to writers such as Stone, in any Indian and is therefore a near approach to a white man. Yet knowing him to be a heathen--a savage, however noble--one must leave him to Heaven, unreliable, foreign and untrustworthy, and eschew any responsibility for mistakes of birth and faith.

Metamora, perhaps the most famous Last Indian in the nineteenth-century theatre, was based on the character of Metacomet, known to the Puritan settlers as King Philip of Pokanoket, a son of that Massasoit who had befriended the first Pilgrims at Plymouth. When the Puritans took over all the tribal lands, Metacomet and his people defended them to the death, gaining a grudging respect from their oppressors. In later days, the Romantic imagination of course found the tale of the doomed hero and his lost tribe a congenial one, and it was treated as a dramatic subject no fewer than eight times between 1822 and 1894.[6]

The playwright of Metamora, John Augustus Stone, was a young character actor who had been in the Bowery Theatre company in 1819 when Edwin Forrest appeared there as the Indian chief in Mordecai Noah's She Would Be a Soldier. In 1828, Forrest, by then a rising star, advertised a competition for "the best tragedy, in five acts, of which the hero, or principal character, shall be an aboriginal of this country." Stone was wisely observant of Forrest's needs and abilities. He wrote a play and a role perfectly tailored to them and won the prize. First played at the Park Theatre in New York on December 15, 1829, it became a staple in Forrest's repertoire. He performed it more than two hundred times over the next forty years.

Plot and subplot in Metamora are rife with melodramatic devices--disguises, a long-lost son discovered, an aristocrat-villain trying to force the helpless heroine into marriage--all skillfully blended with Metamora's growing concern about keeping his homeland. The Puritans are mostly a devious and grasping lot whose double-dealing, including their use of an Indian traitor, brings on conflict with the Wampanoags. when they have pushed the hero to the wall with demands for his land, he issues a bold warning:

> White man, beware! The mighty spirits of the Wam-
> panoag race are hovering o'er your heads; they

> stretch out their shadowy arms to me and ask for
> vengeance; they shall have it. The wrath of the
> wronged Indian shall fall upon you like a cataract
> that dashed the uprooted oak down the mighty
> chasms. The war whoop shall start you from your
> dreams at night, and the red hatchet gleam in the
> blaze of your burning dwellings! From the east to
> the west, in the north and in the south shall cry
> of vengeance burst, till the lands you have stolen
> groan under your feet no more!... Thus do I smite
> your nation and defy your power.[7]

Yet to his own people he speaks more despairingly:

> Oh my people, the race of the red man has fallen
> away like the trees of the forest before the axes of
> the palefaces. The fair places of his father's tri-
> umphs hear no more the sound of his footsteps. He
> moves in the region his proud fathers bequeathed
> him, not like a lord of the soil, but like a wretch
> who comes for plunder and for prey.[8]

Outspoken passages like this were the cause of the
single recorded objection to this play throughout its successful career. In 1831 Forrest played Metamora in Augusta,
Georgia. The negative reaction described here came when he
reached the climactic council scene ending with the speech
quoted above, "White man, beware! ..."

> Then, dashing down his tomahawk and drawing his
> scalping-knife, he gives the war-whoop and disap-
> pears in the uproar and confusion of the scene.
> Evident dissatisfaction had begun to find expression
> long before this climax was reached, and as the chief
> rushed from the stage he was followed by loud yells
> and a perfect storm of hisses from the excited audi-
> ence, who seemed ready in their fury to tear every-
> thing to pieces. Order was with difficulty restored,
> and the performance continued till the curtain fell
> upon the dying chief amid unqualified evidences of
> disapprobation. Both actor and manager now began
> to realize what had not occurred to them before--
> that the sentiment of the play was a positive protest
> against the policy which had deprived the Indians
> of Georgia of their natural rights and driven them

from their homes. The next day the public mind
was highly excited, and Mr. Forrest openly charged
with insulting the people of Augusta by appearing
in a character which condemned the course of the
State in dealing with the land-claims of the Cherokee
Indians. The citizens were all deeply interested in
this question, and in consequence felt indignant at
any reference to the stealing of Indian property,
and especially so at being menaced with the toma-
hawk and scalping-knife of the red man's vengeance
so bitterly threatened in the language of the play....
An eminent lawyer ... said: "Any actor who could
utter such scathing language, and with such vehe-
mence, must have the whole matter at heart. Why,"
said he, "his eyes shot fire and his breath was hot
with the hissing of his ferocious declamation. I insist upon it, Forrest believes in that d----d Indian
speech, and it is an insult to the whole community."
The next night Metamora was acted to empty benches,
and consequently withdrawn and the remaining nights
of Mr. Forrest's engagement showed, by the returns
at the box-office, that the citizens of Augusta did
not relish any adverse opinions upon the legislative
decisions of the State of Georgia.[9]

Speeches like those quoted multiply as the drama progresses, giving the impression of a remarkably outspoken
and forward-looking play for its early date. But its message
is double, as if Stone had set out first to needle the conscience of the whites but also to show the necessity for the
Indians' demise. For the play ends, of course, with Metamora's defeat and a scene in which he kills his wife rather
than let her become a slave of the English after he is gone.
The curtain falls on his ringing curse on the murderers of
his people as they shoot him down. "Drums and trumpet
sound a retreat till curtain. Slow curtain." Wild cheers for
Edwin Forrest and hardly a dry eye in the house.

There is no mistaking the meaningfulness of these
scenes for their audiences, from the earliest in 1829 to those
of the play's last performances in the 1870s, at the time of
the brutal Plains Indian wars:

What these nineteenth-century Americans were aware
of was degradation and destruction of the Indian,

Removal, desperate drives to Christianize before it
would be too late, abhorrence of the perverse cruel-
ties of white men on the frontier, frightening glimpses
of the Indian as the vanishing American. If they
were to be borne, if men were to live with them, all
these attitudes and impulses had to be shown to be
products of a civilizing process whose good finally
negated the evil in them, even if it did not make
that evil immediately less painful. When this came
to pass, when the destiny of the savage was fully
comprehended in its relationship to the destiny of
the civilized man, the Indian had been mastered not
only as individual but as symbol.10

The progress of civilization, and the process of civilizing, is even more clearly the theme of James Fenimore
Cooper's novels, carried over into their dramatized versions.
Wherever there are Native Americans in his tales--whether or
not they surround Leatherstocking, his symbolic agent who
clears the way for the coming of white civilization--they are
seen to be disappearing Last Indians. One of Cooper's most
interesting but less familiar novels, The Wept of Wish-Ton-
Wish (1830), is a picture of seventeenth-century Puritan life
in Connecticut. A subplot involves Cavaliers hunting a re-
gicide among the Puritans, but the most dramatizable section
of the story is its Indian part. During an Indian attack on
the Heathcote family's farm-compound in the valley of Wish-
Ton-Wish, an imprisoned young Indian escapes, taking with
him Ruth, the Heathcotes' teenage daughter (and thus the
Wept of the curious title) who has fallen in love with him.
Ruth, now called Narramattah, has several happy years as
wife of the young Indian, now a chieftain called Conanchet.
In a later Indian-settler conflict, Narramattah is returned
with her child to her white family, who have been captured
by the Indians. Because Conanchet is too lenient and re-
leases the captives, he is killed by his own men. Narramattah,
maddened by grief, collapses over his body and dies.

Certain points reveal themselves: No white woman is
to have a successful relationship with an Indian man without
paying for it; Indians are savages and will even kill one of
their own if he is so noble as to aid white men; Indians and
any whites they seduce away from civilized ways must be removed for the sake of the white man's progress.

The Wept of Wish-Ton-Wish was dramatized more than once under different titles (Narramattah; or, The Lost Found, among others), but in one or another version the message was appreciated by many audiences, from its first showing in New Orleans in 1831 to the last recorded enactment in New York in 1874.[11] A standard version by an anonymous playwright was published by Samuel French in the 1850s, midway in the work's long career.[12] As a simplified version of the book, it concentrates on the capture and deaths of Conanchet and Narramattah, with some villainous Cavaliers thrown in to set off those incidents. The only Indians in the play are Conanchet and Uncas, the Mohican who kills him, and both are treated in a shallow, conventional fashion. Conanchet, one of the most touching and believable characters in all of Cooper's books, becomes in this play little more than a shadowy "bad Injun" redeemed by the white herione. Narramattah must have been particularly attractive to mid-century audiences, a real wish-fulfillment fantasy; she is seen first as a dusky noble heroine, then in more titillating scenes with her husband as a white girl gone native. But the ultimate trauma of her divided racial allegiance in the novel is reduced to showing her in a conventional melodrama mad scene. The madness, the playwright implies, is brought on by her Indian-life experience. For this reason her husband and her relationship with him are the more unbelievable; Cooper's balanced development of a woman torn between her two families is dramatized in a few lines of melodramatic dialogue. Narramattah was a famous starring role of the day, performed by many nineteenth-century stars including our first great tragic actress, Mrs. Duff; the beloved British pantomime artiste, Mme Celeste; Maggie Mitchell, Mrs. Barney Williams, Helen Western, and others.[13]

The theatrical simplification of The Last of the Mohicans,[14] while adhering more closely to the novel's plot, suffers similar problems of arbitrary scene structure and shallow characterization. Without the values of Cooper's style and language, the characters seem to be pasteboard, even when their dialogue is borrowed from the book. Magua is no more than a sneaky, lurking villain, and Hawkeye, Uncas, and Chingachgook are sweet-talking goody-good characters speaking odd dialects who interrupt the plot action with "philosophical" discussions in lieu of comic relief, until the final scenes when they fight off the enemy Hurons and Uncas dies.

The other novel of the Leatherstocking series trans-
ferred to the boards was The Pioneers (1823), which shows
the aged Natty Bumppo and Chingachgook in a "civilized"
community, the latter's death, and the sure westward progress of pioneer settlements. It is a witty and charming novel,
filled with intriguing incidents and delightful characters. An
adaptation called The Wigwam; or, Templeton Manor, said to
have been written by Cooper himself,[15] was produced at the
Park Theatre on July 3, 1830, and revived in 1833 as The
Pioneers, but it had little success, was not published, and
the manuscript is lost.

The underlying importance of these Leatherstocking
plays is twofold. The Indians, whether good or bad from a
white point of view, continue to be shown as a declining
breed and so are made to fit the "Last Indian" pattern we
have found in so many other plays. But the demise of their
culture is overseen by a new kind of character, the Frontiersman, a white man living often in intimate relationship with
the natives. Sometimes he seems more Indian than the Indians. His activities as explorer, transmitter of Indian ways
to the whites, and enemy of Indians who resist white progress aid in smoothing the way for the white man's expansion
across the continent. Natty Bumppo is James Fenimore Cooper's
version of this figure, bridging the worlds of the white newcomer and the Native American.

Clearly, the new Frontiersman was a man to be considered in some depth. If pioneers coming into an unknown
area to set up farms had some intermediary--some buffer, so
to speak--who could give them advice about the land and its
savage inhabitants, then the whole process of settlement,
frightening and difficult at best, might be made easier. Perhaps in his communication with Indians he would give them
good words about the white newcomers. And if the Indians
made trouble anyway, it was comforting to know there was
someone available who knew best how to fight them. In literary and theatrical guise this frontier leader might be as
gentle-mannered and soft-spoken as Natty Bumppo, who
nevertheless was a man of steel in a supple buckskin covering
--or, in real life, a Davy Crockett. Or he might be as
coarse and rough-tongued, as raucous and dishonest as Ralph
Stackpole in Robert Montgomery Bird's Nick of the Woods--or,
in actuality, the sinister Simon Girty on whom Ralph Stackpole may have been modeled. But there was space and need,

settlers felt, for all such men in the vanguard of white civilization, whatever their personal traits. The circumstances
and the climate of the time--and the men who came behind
them--were bound to turn these Frontiersmen into heroes.

Circumstances and events of the 1830s gave a strong
impetus to frontier leaders and to the idea of national expansion. In the earliest years of the century, Lewis and Clark
had shown that the continent was crossable and suggested
that large tracts of it might be settled productively. But
the naive belief that the Indians would continue to give up
their lands under treaty agreements dictated by whites was
dispelled by extensive Indian involvement in the War of 1812.
The United States developed a new self-image, having established its sovereignty in European eyes and punished the Indians for allying themselves with Britain in futile attempts to
hold onto their lands. The brutal and vicious battles of
Horseshoe Bend in the South and the Thames in the Northwest, both within a six-month period in 1813, effectively
broke the back of Indian resistance in America. Thereafter,
public as well as government thinking focused on either removal or destruction of the tribes. Such thinking culminated
in the implementation of Jackson's Indian Removal Bill in 1830
by which both, to some extent at least, were achieved.

With the Native Americans swept out of the way, in effect, it was easier for the federal government to attend to
more positive projects. Two were of prime importance: handling the growing number of immigrants from Europe and the
sanctioning of a westward movement by the mushrooming population of the country. The sudden vast increase in immigration and the surge of people moving west in the 1830s and
1840s were to become two great social phenomena of the century. In the two decades before 1830 more than a million
white people had settled on former Indian lands north of the
Ohio River and well over a million and a half in the area
south of the Cumberland.[16]

Not surprisingly, the westward flood of new Americans,
most of them fearful of Indians and little educated about
them, many ill-prepared for the rugged pioneer life they had
thrust themselves into, subscribed to a peripheral social
phenomenon, Indian-hating.

After the War of 1812, as territory west of the Appala-

chians was opened up for settlement, white people saw the
Indians not only as a race that they hoped was dying out,
but as an obstacle that took an irritatingly long time to be
removed. The combination of the tempting lands the Indians
were trying to hold on to and white impatience to get control
of them brought on intense resentment against the natives--
and when men find reason to hate something enough, it is
easy to justify destroying it without a bothersome conscience.
With the aid of the new Frontiersmen, many of whom were
only too eager to relate how dangerously villainous Indians
were, Indian-hating actively spread.[17]

Popular thinking on the subject was reflected in publications of various kinds, and in the theatre. Contrasts in attitude seemed to be to some extent regional. In the Northeast, where so many Indians including whole tribes had been
exterminated and settlement had pushed westward many generations earlier, the enormously influential approach of James
Fenimore Cooper--who found many of his idealized Indians
nobler, better men than many whites--was popular. This attitude was contradicted, however, by anti-Indian books of
much-read nonfiction writers, including Francis Parkman's
The Oregon Trail and his great series of histories. Herman
Melville's brilliant satire of Indian-hating in his bitter novel
The Confidence-Man came somewhat later, in 1857[18] (the same
year John Brougham produced his burlesque of Indian plays,
Po-Ca-Hon-Tas; or, The Gentle Savage).

More serious stage works touting Indian-hating seem to
have included the unfortunately lost plays of Joseph Stevens
Jones, the Boston doctor and prolific playwright. One can
only conjecture from their titles and the few available playbills or scant printed references what they may have been
like. The Indian Mother (1832) implies a more tender attitude
toward the natives than, for example, The Indian Horde; or,
The Tiger of War (1840), its very title suggesting a horror
melodrama. The Hunter in the Far West (1836) includes in
its cast the Shawnee chief Tecumseh as an unimportant secondary character, but features Earthquake the Kentuckian,
the title character and apparently a sort of earlier Ralph
Stackpole. The playbill of The Fire Warrior (1834), his play
about the Seminole wars, indicates that it was little more than
a musical farce.[19]

An anonymous work with one of the most intriguing

titles of its time is The Snow Fiend; or, The Far, Far West.
It was produced in New York at the Franklin Theatre on
November 13, 1837, but lacking any record save a slender
reference in Odell indicating that its Indian characters were
of the Nootka tribe,[20] we will probably never know whether
the far western fiend was a white Frontiersman or a scoun-
drelly Indian.

In the South, conflicts with the so-called Five Civilized
Tribes (Cherokee, Creek, Chickasaw, Choctaw, and Seminole)
continued into the 1830s, delaying whites from taking over
lands they felt they deserved to have. Indian-hating was
propagandized by Southern writers such as William Gilmore
Simms in The Yemassee (1835) and Robert Montgomery Bird
in Nick of the Woods (1837), and by literary opportunists
such as the fraudulent "Judge" James Hall (a sort of earlier-
day "Ned Buntline" and perhaps the original of Melville's
Confidence-Man[21]), who republished his article "The Indian
Hater" and related pieces in book after book from 1828 to
1846.

The Frontiersman was the pathfinder the settlers followed, although not always the Indian-hater that the settler
often became. In popular publications like Davy Crockett's
Autobiography (1834) or the periodic almanacs of the time,
he is shown as a sort of jolly superman (Crockett himself or
the fabulous keelboatman Mike Fink, "half horse and half al-
ligator"), while in the more pretentious literary annuals he
might be treated more seriously. (Hall's "Indian Hater" was
first printed in The Western Souvenir ... for 1829.)

This characterization carried over to a great extent in
stage portraits of the type. The Frontiersman (aside from
Natty Bumppo in the Cooper dramatizations) was often a comic
character. For example, he might become Sergeant Welcome
Sobersides, a loquacious Green Mountain Boy from Vermont
who beats off the villain of the piece and saves the heroine
and her baby in Henry J. Finn's Montgomery; or, The Falls
of Montmorency (1825); or Nimrod Wildfire (said to have been
suggested by Davy Crockett) in James Kirke Paulding's The
Lion of the West (1831), a "human cataract for Kentucky."

But more representatives of things to come, both dramatically and historically, are two heroes, Ralph Stackpole and
the title character in play versions of Robert M. Bird's novel,

Nick of the Woods; or, The Jibbenainosay. Dramatized at
least three times,22 we have only one extant version, that
of Louisa Medina written for the company of her husband
Thomas Hamblin at the Bowery Theatre, where it was first
played on February 5, 1838.

Nick of the Woods is a turning-point play because of
the striking change in point of view from earlier Indian palys.
For the first time in plays about Native Americans, there are
no Noble Savages; the Indians here are all villains, worth-
less savages to be exterminated by the superior whites. This
lethal project is undertaken by a "walking spirit" the Indians
call the Jibbenainosay. This mysterious creature stalks and
murders them, cutting a bloody cross on the corpses' naked
chests. Actually he is a mild-mannered Quaker settler,
Reginald Ashburn, familiarly called "Bloody Nathan Slaughter"
as a joke by his white neighbors because he seems such a
peaceful man. But his secret murderous forays as the Jibbenainosay are his vengeance for having seen his family
killed by Indians.

The Jibbenainosay is a sort of protecting angel for the
white settlers, while his more down-to-earth alter ago, Ralph
Stackpole, always claiming more superhuman qualities than
he possesses, is the bold Frontiersman who teaches whites
the ways of the backwoods. "Tarnal death to me!" Ralph
bellows on his first entrance,

> I'm a gentleman, and my name's fight!--foot and
> hand, tooth and nail, claw and mud scraper, knife,
> gun and tomahawk, or any way you choose to take
> me. I'm your man! Cock-a-doodle-doo-o-o.

Interrupting the scene to kill "a furious panther" about to
carry off a straying child, he then continues:

> Who's for a fight? Where's your old coon can claw
> the bark off a gum tree? Where's your wolf of the
> rolling prairies? Here's a man for you.... Ain't
> I the old snag to shake off a saddle, can go down
> old Salt on my back and swim up the Ohio! Hurrah
> for a fight! 23

A newcomer's comment (aside) on this performance is:
"What a strange medley of the bully and the hero is that man!"

The reaction is not surprising, since Ralph's intention is to make a more extreme impression than whites imagine a wild Indian would create in the maddest war dance.

In the final showdown, Ralph is assaulted by this same naive young newcomer, who mistakes him for an Indian. Nathan Slaughter (or Reginald Ashburn) also disguises himself as an Indian to go into the Shawnee camp after the special object of his hatred, Wenonga, "the Black Vulture of the Shawnees." For both white men, the assumption of Indian disguise makes them more savage, and more successful killers, than the red savages. They are characterized by colorful differences of language and speech rhythm, Ralph bold and loose as we have seen, Reginald taut and formal, suggesting the strain of his mental imbalance. Yet they are alike in their staunch certainty of their godlike superiority to the savage lower orders. Reginald in his rages, however, speaks no less extravagantly than Ralph:

> Look, murdering villain, upon the destroyer of thy race--the avenger of his own! Die, thou human wolf, infuriate tiger, die! (Hurry [music]. Grapples with Wenonga, wrests hatchet from him, and kills him.) And with thy dying glance behold the fearful fiend, the Jibbenainosay, in Reginald Ashburn! Ha, ha, ha! Mother, sister, wife--at last ye are revenged![23]

The play ends with the most violent possible wish fulfillment: total, bloody destruction of the Indians, the stage ablaze in a tableau of their burning wigwams, watched by a ring of gloating whites.

Perhaps Ralph and Reginald are two aspects of the same personality (and both a projection of that of their creator, Robert Montgomery Bird). Singly and together, they demonstrate effective means of dealing with obstacles to westward progress along with appropriate emotional reactions to the circumstances encountered in that progress. In a perceptive analysis of the developing western attitude, Richard Drinnon compares Ralph to Mike Fink:

> Stackpole shared this chuckling contempt for the victims of white cruelty and like Fink believed it to be "as praiseworthy to bring in the scalp of a Shawnee, as the skin of a panther." As had the original

alligator-horse, Stackpole illustrated what Benjamin
Botkin once characterized as "the essential vicious-
ness of many of our folk heroes, stories, and expressions." To Stackpole's mind, Indians were
merely "red niggurs." Nick's skill as a super
slaughterer clearly won his wholehearted admiration. [25]

And, considering the less public impulses that may have been
at work, he adds:

> Bird went further than Simms and Paulding in re-
> vealing his own delight in the destruction of forest
> brutes. In scenes reeking with latent homosexuality
> he exultingly carved crosses in red corpses with
> his pen while Nick thrust his keen knife into their
> naked breasts. Penetration of red bodies presum-
> ably destroyed such temptations to instinctual grati-
> fication by butchering their embodiments: Bird was
> visibly upset that Indians, grown children at best,
> swung easily from laughter to anger and back, ex-
> pressing desires and venting tensions on the way.
> He did cynically grant, in his 1853 preface, that
> "the Indian is a gentleman, but he is a gentleman
> with a very dirty shirt." "Civilization" was what
> the Indian did not have, and "civilization" meant for
> Bird a real gentleman, himself, with sterilized or
> subdued urges and with proper order imposed on
> his life.... Doctor Bird's shirt was always spotless,
> and this starched self-control probably made his not
> "uncommon passion" of Indian-hating especially ran-
> corous. That rigidity, and some secret psychic
> wound of his own, may have given him a sense of
> the dammed-up aggressions underlying Nathan
> Slaughter's Quaker professions of philanthropy....
> What is clear is that in his violent pornography he
> verged on explicit acknowledgment that white Ameri-
> cans were the real devils in the woods, proud of it,
> and, to his mind, justifiably so. [26]

Louisa Medina was a superior melodramatist, and she
succeeded in capturing and projecting in her dramatization
Bird's fearsome Indian-hating. Presumably similar qualities
were retained in play versions we no longer have of William
Gilmore Simms' novel The Yemassee, performed in 1830 and

1842, and other works, no doubt, now lost to us even by title.

A later play continues the line of the bluff, Indian-hating Frontiersman, but with a slightly different emphasis of character that brings it closer to the friendly, familiar ones often seen in twentieth-century films performed by actors such as Gabby Hayes and Walter Brennan. This is the lovable and over-talkative comic type who nevertheless can always get the better of the red devils, and in the play in question, Nick Whiffles, he is the title character. The name gives a clue to the content of the piece: Nick, suggesting the uncontrollable Old Nick we saw in Ralph Stackpole and Reginald Ashburn, but beneficial to all white people who come to know him, and Whiffles, a proper surname for a sweet-tempered, aging and fatherly frontier leader who cannot stop rambling on. "If you want to kill me, tie up my tongue," he says. "I'll fight for ye--die for ye; but I must talk. I was borned talkin', and must talk on to the eend." His function in the play is to create suspense with his bumbling, slow movement and talk; his function in the life described by the play is to clear the way for proper white settlement of Indian lands.

Nick Whiffles is a three-act melodrama of 1858[27] typical of its time but also carrying forward a traditional view of Frontiersmen and brave pioneers. Two points in particular mark it as somewhat different from previous Indian plays. First, and for the first time on our stage, the setting is the rolling prairies considerably west of the Mississippi, and the characters are some of those countless pioneers who streamed westward during and after the Gold Rush years. Secondly, the Indians are no longer seen as quite the fearful horrors that had brought on the extreme defensiveness of a Nathan Slaughter. They are held in contempt not so much as terrible villains but merely as dirty, low creatures the whites naturally despise. When the villain, a squaw man called Lot Halliday, has trapped the heroine, Blanche, and tries to seduce her, she expresses her disgust at his machinations with, "Leave me, ruffian, and herd with that degraded race which you pride yourself in aping. Thou art at best but a painted brute." Halliday's wife, Molly Molasses, is a comic-relief "squaw" who echoes many a dusky maiden before her and since by giving aid and comfort to the whites, at one point helping Blanche to escape Halliday's clutches.

The Indians in this play have not been disposed of entirely, and their removal to those bleak western plains has only resulted in turning them into a minor, constantly present annoyance to the whites who are taking over still more of the country. They have only become, therefore, slightly less than human creatures for whom one need feel no respect, nor even much fear. Leopard, another Indian, is introduced as eager for revenge against a white who has struck him like a disobedient dog or child, but he gives little feeling of menace. The only other Indian in the story is Le Loup, a friend of the whites who also helps the heroine in her time of trouble.

Nick Whiffles has a complex plot concerning the recovery of a lost child (the heroine, Blanche), the actions of her several good protectors including Nick himself and a young hero who will marry her, and the wiles of a white villain, one of whose major flaws is his association with Indians. Being white, however, even he is allowed a sympathetic note, and the thought of a Christian hell in his final dying speech:

> My sight is failin'! A word more. I don't expect
> to be forgiven--I don't ask it. No! No! Fate
> must take its course, I must go as I am--as black
> as the blackest of the infernal host.

Whether the black infernal host includes any Indians is a moot point, but seems unlikely. Elaborate production effects added to this plot include Nick's first entrance on a real horse; a trained dog that howls on cue during a song Nick performs and later pulls the old scout out of a lake; a storm on this "working water," as the script describes it; a burning cabin; and, for the final tableau, a prairie fire. But the disastrous complications are brought on by whites; the bad Indians are peripheral presences and only mildly villainous, and the one or two good ones are defined only in terms of their aid to the white characters. Whatever the degree of his diabolism, the red devil, as Brian Dippie has pointed out, is no more than a fallen Noble Savage.28

By the mid-nineteenth century, as we have seen, the Native American as a stage character has gone through three phases. He shows a metamorphosis from his earliest theatrical form as a fantasy creature in farces and musical entertainments into an idealized Noble Savage whom playwrights eventually attempted to relate to real Indians, and finally as a representative of a dying race of undesirables who would inevitably be replaced by white settlers.

There was, of course, much overlapping and blending of the character stereotypes throughout their theatrical history. Some of the noblest savages came very early, as in Robert Rogers' Ponteach, a character largely based on Rousseau's popular concept of the Natural Man and just as largely in the unnatural supermen of seventeenth-century heroic tragedy. But that play, though read, was not performed in its own time. More familiar in the eighteenth century was the Indian as a fantasy figure of musical pieces such as Mrs. Hatton's Tammany, or in Panattatah and other pantomimes and ballets, and, spilling over into the next era, in Barker's The Indian Princess. Early in the nineteenth century the still much-used tradition of artificial nobility did not prevent forward-thinking playwrights from trying to show Indian characters as real people--or at least as realistically as any other characters in melodrama, the predominant form of the day.

With the era of Jacksonian democracy and the vast changes then coming about in the United States, the Noble Savage was more often thought of as a dying savage and shown as such on the stage. Expansion of the republic was the order of the day, requiring the taking over of Indian lands on a larger scale than ever before and either removal of tribes or their wholesale destruction. As both were questionable practices, the Indian came to be thought of as a greater problem than ever before--a problem much harder to solve in good conscience.

In stage representations, therefore, as in general public thinking, he grew to be more of a menacing obstacle to fulfillment of the white man's desires. Metamora influenced the stage view of Indians in a sympathetic manner for at least ten years from its first performance in 1829; Nick of the Woods expressed a significantly darker view from 1838 onwards. It was this darker view that reflected the then-current mood of the public. Most people saw the expansion of the country as more important than the rights of a disenfranchised minority people. The Noble Savage had been transformed into an objectionable Red Devil.

This last change of personality, less subtle, much more open and blunt in its anti-Indian feeling than the previous ones, is the form that has lasted longest. With few exceptions, plays featuring Native American characters in the past century and a half have shown them negatively, sometimes as joke characters of a low order, or as despicable drunken outcasts, or, most often, as fearsome villains to be overcome by supremely brave and capable white heroes as unrealistically depicted as their red opponents. Until after World War II, Americans rarely accepted that only a xenophobic naiveté caused them to find Indians funny because of their different customs, mores, and skin color; that it was white traders and settlers who turned displaced Indians into drunken tramps kept on the outskirts of society; and that supposed white bravery was no more than a compensatory measure of white men in their offenses against people whose property they were stealing. As the real Indian world was irretrievably destroyed, a distorted and negative one came to be the accepted norm on the stage.

NOTES

1. Brian W. Dippie, The Vanishing American: White Attitudes and Indian Policy (Middletown, Ct: Wesleyan University Press, 1982), pp. 58-59.
2. Hugh Henry Brackenridge, Indian Atrocities [1782], (Cincinnati, 1867), p. 62.
3. Roy Harvey Pearce, The Savages of America, A Study of the Indian and the Idea of Civilization (Baltimore: Johns Hopkins Press, 1953), pp. 73-74.
4. Ibid., p. 73.
5. John Augustus Stone, Metamora; or, The Last of the Wampanoags, in Barrett Clark, ed., America's Lost Plays, 20 vols. (Princeton, N.J.: Princeton University Press, 1940-41; reprint ed., Bloomington: Indiana University Press, 1969), vol. 14, p. 12.
6. Anonymous, Philip; or, The Aborigines, 1822; Robert Montgomery Bird, King Philip; or, The Sagamore, 1829; James Kennicott, Metacomet, 1829; John Augustus Stone, Metamora; or, The Last of the Wampanoags, 1829; G. Blanchard, Metamora; or, The Indian Hunters, 1830; John Brougham Metamora; or, The Last of the Pollywogs, 1847; Robert B. Caverly, King Philip, 1884; A. A. Furman, Philip of Pokanoket, 1894. Of the earlier version only the anonymous play

and Stone's are extant; the last two named are unperformable
closet dramas.

7. Stone, Metamora, p. 23.

8. Ibid., p. 25.

9. James E. Murdoch, The Stage, or Recollections of
Actors and Acting (Reprint edition, New York: Benjamin
Blom, 1969), pp. 298-99.

10. Pearce, The Savages of America, pp. 74-75.

11. Josephine Fishman, "The Dramatization of the
Novels of James Fenimore Cooper" (M.A. thesis, Stanford
University, 1951), p. 92.

12. [Anonymous], The Wept of Wish-Ton-Wish. A
Drama in Two Acts. From J. Fenimore Cooper's Celebrated
Novel of the Same Name. French's Standard Drama, no.
CLIV (New York: Samuel French, [n.d.]).

13. Fishman, "Dramatization of Cooper," pp. 92-97.

14. Stephen Glover (attrib.), "The Last of the Mohicans." In Four Acts. Unpublished manuscript promptbook.
New York Public Library, Manuscript Division.

15. According to William Dunlap in his Diary, who
stated that C. P. Clinch, the playwright who had dramatized
The Spy, had so informed him. Quoted in Fishman, "Dramatization of Cooper," p. 2.

16. Dale Van Every, Disinherited: The Lost Birthright of the American Indian (New York: William Morrow and
Company, 1966), p. 29.

17. Curiously, two of the most famous frontier leaders,
Davy Crockett and Sam Houston, who had lived with Indians
and actively campaigned against removal and other forms of
victimization of Native Americans, never appeared as dramatic
characters in this period. The much later Davy Crockett; or,
Be Sure You're Right, Then Go Ahead (1872) is a fanciful
melodrama in no way based on Crockett's actual career.

18. Herman Melville, The Confidence-Man: His Masquerade. Norton Critical Edition, Hershel Parker, editor
(New York: W. W. Norton, 1971).

19. All details on J. S. Jones' plays from playbills in
the Boston Athenaeum Library.

20. George C. D. Odell, Annals of the New York Stage,
15 vols. (New York: Columbia University Press, 1927-1949),
vol. IV, pp. 239-240.

21. Richard Drinnon, Facing West: The Metaphysics
of Indian-Hating and Empire-Building (Minneapolis: University of Minnesota Press, 1980), p. 204.

22. Known, in addition to Medina's, are a version by

George Washington Harby, Nick of the Woods; or, The Salt River Rover, performed in New Orleans in 1839, and Nick of the Woods; or, The Altar of Revenge by J. T. Haines, played the same year at the Royal Victoria Theatre in London.

23. Louisa Medina, Nick of the Woods; or, The Jib-benainosay, in James L. Smith, Victorian Melodramas: Seven English, French, and American Melodramas (London: Dent, 1976), pp. 72-73.

24. Ibid., p. 95

25. Drinnon, Facing West, p. 156.

26. Ibid., p. 158.

27. John Hovey Robinson, Nick Whiffles. A Drama, in Three Acts. (New York: Samuel French, 1858). There seem to have been two other versions of the story, one by John F. Poole written for the Bowery Theatre and first played there on August 23, 1858, according to Odell, Annals, vol. VII, p. 134, and another listed by Joseph N. Ireland, Records of the New York Stage from 1750 to 1860 (New York, 1888; reprint ed., New York: Benjamin Blom, 1966), vol. II, p. 683, as Nick Whiffles, the Trapper Guide.

28. Dippie, Vanishing American, p. 25.

Chapter V

THE VANISHING (STAGE) INDIAN

In March 1800 William Dunlap produced his adaptations of both
Pizarro and The Virgin of the Sun at the new Park Theatre
in New York. Sixty years later, in December 1859, Dion
Boucicault appeared as the Indian Wahnotee in his new melodrama The Octoroon at the new Winter Garden Theatre on
Broadway. During the years between these two events at
least one hundred and twenty plays featuring Native American
themes and characters were written in the United States.
The 1820s and 1830s were most fecund: no fewer than sixty-
four Indian plays came out in those two decades.

Most of these dramatic works were performed in American theatres and some in theatres abroad. A few were un-
performed closet dramas treasured, with reason, only by
their writers and a handful of loyal readers. Many were
hackwork pieces of the poorest kind which deservedly survived only a few performances. Some were the products of
skilled professional playwrights, and a few of these are landmark plays of the century.

Considering this remarkable number of playscripts about
Indians, it is only to be expected that the quality of most
was not very high. Yet pieces such as The Indian Princess,
She Would Be A Soldier, Metamora, Owen's Pocahontas, Medina's Nick of the Woods, and, as we shall see, The Octoroon
and Brougham's Po-Ca-Hon-Tas, extravagant as they are and
adhering to the sentimental and melodramatic conventions out
of which they grew, are works of strong dramatic values.
If their quality as literature is low, their honest theatricality
and the playwrights' intelligent handling of dramatic materials
was respectable, no less so than in comparable types of plays
in our late twentieth century theatre.

Reasons for the flood of Indian plays in the 1830s and

1840s are many. First, there was, as the new century and
the young nation developed, an increasing demand from audi-
ences--and consequently, writers learned, from theatre man-
agers--for plays on American subjects. In the earlier years
of the republic, American playwrights had found little encouragement for their work; managers could produce European plays without paying for them (since no copyright laws
protected them) and attract the public with European stars
as well. But no matter how strong the influence of European
(particularly British) plays and performers, nationalist feeling grew daily stronger in the early decades of the century.
By the time of Andrew Jackson's first administration, with
nationalist attitudes and desire for expansion reaching their
peak, American audiences found that American characters
could be quite as interesting as any from the old world, and
many excellent native-born actors were performing these
roles in theatres throughout the land.

The patriotic play, which touted the virtues of democratic American ways of life and of the down-to-earth, anti-
aristocratic American people, led the way, from the time of
Royall Tyler's The Contrast (1787) onward through the Fed-
eralist period.[1] Tyler's Jonathan was the first of a long line
of beloved Yankee characters. But several other peculiarly
American personalities soon peopled the stage, including the
Frontiersman (sometimes blended with the Yankee, as we have
seen in characters like Henry J. Finn's Sergeant Welcome
Sobersides) and, of course, the Indian. When not seen in
an earlier historical context, as in The Wept of Wish-Ton-
Wish, The Armourer's Escape, or Metamora, the stage Indian
usually shared the world of the adventurous pioneer of that
day, as in Oolaita, Catherine Brown, Nick Whiffles, or The
Mormons, giving theatregoers the added thrill of immediacy.

Because of the attractiveness of Indian themes and the
ease with which an Indian melodrama could be constructed
(along with the managers' constant concern about filling out
their multiple-play bills), another reason for the numbers of
such pieces presents itself. Any amateur or hack playwright
who could turn out a formula piece with Indian characters
and one or two ideas for spectacle scenes in it (not necessarily original ones) could get it considered for production
and find a buyer. We must eternally regret that most of
these plays, perhaps as many as two-thirds of the scripts
written,[2] are no longer extant, and we will never know how

poor or how excellent they may have been, or what attitudes
were displayed in their presentation of Native Americans.
These can only be conjectured from the implications of the
titles and from plays still available for study. Even playscripts by the more successful professional playwrights written for the larger theatres or more organized companies often
did not survive. Of Louisa Medina's half-dozen plays written
for the great Bowery Theatre, for example, only one, Nick
of the Woods, remains to us. Probably a pièce d' occasion
such as Black Hawk, played at the Bowery on January 27,
1834, was typical of many productions of the day. The Sauk
chieftain Black Hawk, in New York for some unnoted reason,
was taken to the theatre, presumably in an attempt to attract
a large and well-paying house that wanted a look at the exotic celebrity as well as a dramatic thrill on the stage. Odell
recorded the event:

> A recent visit to town of the great Indian Black
> Hawk was commemorated at the Bowery with the pro-
> duction on the 27th, of Black Hawk, with Rice as
> Marshal of the City, Collins as the Indian Chief,
> Marble as the Prophet, and Sowerby as Timbertoe.[3]

The play itself was never performed again; the playwright,
presumably paid for his quick work, remains anonymous.

Of known writers, some worked as "house" playwrights.
John F. Poole, Nathaniel H. Bannister, and Louisa Medina
(whose husband, Thomas Hamblin, then owned the theatre)
were employed over a long period of time to supply plays for
the Bowery Theatre, and Joseph Stevens Jones wrote con-
tinuously for two Boston theatres. Playwriting, rarely possible as a full-time profession, also attracted people from
other fields: James Kirke Paulding and George Morris were
editors and journalists; Thomas English and James Nelson
Barker were politicians; J. S. Jones was a physician, as was
Robert Montgomery Bird (although he was better known as
a novelist); and several actors, Henry Finn, John A. Stone,
and John Brougham among them, turned out polished and
playable scripts. But the skill and polish did not necessarily
make fine drama. For the most part, they all wrote so much
within the melodramatic conventions of the day, and their
work so strongly reflects then-current popular thought about
Indians, that it is difficult for later generations to see any
universality their plays may have had.

Thus, as theatre managers found there was a market for native plays and actors to play them, they began to look for American comedies, Yankee plays, Revolutionary plays, frontier plays, Indian plays. With the new pride in our brief history and with the nationalist urge to express it, the idea of showing aspects of real American life on the stage caught on, never again to be stilled.

There were also many Indian plays intended to be performed only in their readers' imaginations. In every era there has been a body of closet drama, and in the nineteenth century it made up a large bulk of published material, and presumably there were many more such works written but never published. A random choice shows the variety of material treated; the attitudes in all the pieces examined was positive and pro-Indian.

One of the few well-known writers of closet dramas in this period was Henry Rowe Schoolcraft. Famous as one of the first scholars to make and publish ethnological studies of Indians, Schoolcraft wrote Alhalla; or, The Lord of Talladega in 1826 (although he did not publish it until 1843). Subtitled "A Tale of the Creek War," Alhalla is a kind of miniature epic poem in dramatic dialogue form in six cantos, composed in very cliché rhymed verse. Having neither a poetic nor a dramatic gift, Schoolcraft fell back on stage Indian stereotypes, nobly spoken and painfully dignified, for his characters, and a thin plot burdened with harangue and discussion, whose minimal events have little to do with the Creek War.

A work carpentered out of the imagined adventures of Christopher Columbus' followers is The New World, published in Boston in 1848 in the Dramatic Poems of a lady called Harriette Fanning Read. A verse drama emulating the styles of any of the Romantic poets who might have written a play, it tells a standard story. Alana, a Carib Indian girl of "Hayti," is in love with Guevara, a virtuous and handsome young Spaniard, but is harrassed by the villainous adventurer Roldan. The latter kills Guevara, who, as he is dying and with her agreement, stabs Alana so that Roldan cannot possess her. Alana and her fellow tribesmen are, like most Indian characters in these nonprofessional "poetic" works, borrowed from commerical plays of the time and are no more than well-spoken, sympathetic white people disguised in red makeup.

One is left with the impression that Mrs. Read had been inspired by seeing a performance of Metamora.

A still more amateur work in verse so poor as to be
near-doggerel is W. B. Dailey's Saratoga, A Dramatic Romance of the Revolution, printed in Corning, New York, in
1848. Its characters include a cardboard figure of an Indian,
given the name Eagle, who is brought in to say a few lines
about the coming American nation.

Vastly more pretentious is a piece called Tan-Go-Ru-A,
"An Historical Drama in Prose," by Henry C. Moorehead.
Enormously long (280 pages of text), it is peopled not by a
"List of Characters" nor even a "Dramatis Personae," but by
"Interlocutors," and is divided not into acts and scenes but
into "Part First. Section I," and so on. There are four
"Parts," each with several "Sections." Buried in the mass
of words is a story of a Moravian missionary in eighteenth-
century Pennsylvania who wants his daughter Miriam to marry
a powerful young Indian chief named Tangorua (the hyphena-
ted spellings of character's names are abandoned in the text)
in order to keep the peace in their backwoods neighborhood.
This plot is crudely joined to another about the mismanagement of the colony by the British, which brings on war with
the Indians. Tangorua is killed and Miriam released from her
father's promise. The three Indian characters in the work,
Tangorua, Werahoochwee, an "Indian Powwow," and Kazuka,
Miriam's confidant, can only be described as talking props.

Typical of school dialogue pieces of the time is Kindness
Softens Even Savage Hearts, published in Chicago probably
in the 1860s by Delia A. Heywood, the pseudonym of a lady
named Polly Ann Pritchard, in a volume entitled Pritchard's
Choice Dialogues No. 1. It is a naively charming two-scene
playlet with much-idealized situations and characters. The
setting is the Maine frontier during the French and Indian
War. The writer gives a nutshell synopsis before the dialogue
begins: "The McLellans, more humane and less prejudiced
than their neighbors, are unmolested by the Indians, while
their neighbors are hunted down and murdered." In the
first scene the McLellans prepare to care for the wounded
from a battle, including Indians, and in the second scene
Indians come to thank and praise them for their generous
dealings with the natives. Despite its slightness, the piece
is unusually interesting for publishing so positive a point of

view in that place and time (the Midwest in the 1860s); Indian
troubles on the Plains and the implementation of the questionable new reservation system were already being publicized,
and public attitudes had begun to swing toward strong anti-
Indian views. In its naively idealized pro-Indian feeling it
bears a relationship to a similar earlier work, Catherine Brown,
the Converted Cherokee, and is a precursor of Helen Hunt
Jackson's writings of the 1880s and the later sentimentalizing
of Indians at the turn of the century.

Even though some playwrights tried to characterize
Native Americans truthfully and represent their speech with
some accuracy, we have seen that the plays were marked by
the artificial melodramatic plots accepted as high drama at
the time and filled with arch and rarely believable dialogue
of a kind once described by Arthur Hobson Quinn as "that
mixture of Indian and Ossian which became traditional upon
the stage."4 In a theatre already rich in comic performers
and playwrights, it is hardly surprising that as the conventions of Indian plays began to wear thin they should be guyed
and burlesqued in comic presentations.

By the end of the 1830s it was found that burlesque
productions so delighted audiences that they would sustain
the career of a theatre like William Mitchell's little Olympic
in New York. When an elaborate piece such as La Bayadère,
the Maid of Cashmere made a hit on the legitimate stage, it
was parodied as Buy It Dear, It's Made of Cashmere, and
Lucy Did Lam a Moor made fun of a stage version of Scott's
famous poem. It was only natural that Edwin Forrest's performance in his Indian play was burlesqued in a comic sketch
called Metaroarer (since Forrest's speaking of the role had
been compared to the sound of Niagara's roar). Of these
pointed satires and their creators, Constance Rourke wrote:

> They produced a lusty, gay and savage humor, full
> of barbs flung at the current scene, full of native
> extravagance. Through their incidental satire many
> of the cults of the day at last toppled into ridicule
> [of Indian plays].... Their great theme was the
> false romanticism of American sentiment for the In-
> dian.5

In 1847 John Brougham, our foremost burlesque satirist
of the mid-century, both as writer and performer, produced

Metamora; or, The Last of the Pollywogs. The hero Metamora keeps his name but is chief of the Pollywog tribe. Of
the original characters, Kaneshine the prophet, the traitor
Annawandah, Metamora's wife Nahmeokee, and Lord Fitzarnold
have become Whiskeetoddi, Anaconda, Tapiokee, and Fitz-
daddle. The latter is a dandy who carries a parasol on his
walks in the forest, and Metamora's titanic struggles with
wild beasts are parodied with his slow killing of a puzzled
bear to the tune of "Old Dan Tucker."

Because of the wide-ranging effects of various media
on our twentieth-century daily life, it may be difficult to
imagine the influence these popular burlesque plays had on
the production of serious works in the pre-Civil War theatre.
It is necessary to remember that the multi-talented Brougham
was one of the most successful and popular men of the theatre in the America of his time. Irish-born, he first appeared
on the American stage in 1842 and was particularly skilled,
and beloved, in Irish character roles. He wrote about seventy-
five plays, for which he was described as the Aristophanes
of the American drama, and was the manager at various times
of theatres such as Brougham's Broadway Lyceum (later re-
named Wallack's Lyceum), which had been built for him in
1850, and whose productions always had a broad popular appeal. There are probably no close modern parallels to Brougham's career, since most modern-day comedians are known
solely for their performing (and almost always in material
written for them by others). But artists such as Bob Hope
or Carol Burnett, or any whose sharply observed comments
and parodies burlesque popular culture and the public scene,
may be the nearest. The major difference is that Brougham
conceived, wrote, and produced all his own material in the
form of full-scale musical plays of which he was also principal
performer and director.

"In the area of farce-comedy and parody," a modern
commentary declares, "he is the one outstanding writer in
nineteenth century America." And, more to the point for us:
"Brougham is generally remembered because he almost single-
handedly brought an end to the tremendously popular plays
which celebrated the heroic American Indian" with his two
burlesques, _Metamora_, in 1847, and _Po-Ca-Hon-Tas; or, The
Gentle Savage_, in 1855.[6]

Po-Ca-Hon-Tas opened at Wallack's Lyceum Theatre on

Christmas Eve of that year to general praise. It continued
there as a main piece through the spring of 1856 and was
produced again in the fall at both the Bowery and National
Theatres. It continued to be popular as a standard burlesque afterpiece in many American theatres until 1884. It was
also popular with soldiers who performed it as a camp show
during the Civil War.[7]

Po-Ca-Hon-Tas; or, The Gentle Savage is a two-act
musical play in which the traditionally accepted version of
the Pocahontas story is turned topsy-turvy. In an elaborate
Dramatis Personae we find that the names of "ye salvages"
are mostly absurd puns, but no more absurdly concocted
than the names in most Indian plays. The play opens with a
lengthy prologue parodying Henry Wadsworth Longfellow's in
his recently published The Song of Hiawatha, its central section giving the gist of the plot along with a sly commentary
on the underlying self-righteous attitudes of most Indian
plays:

> Now, the natives knowing nothing
> Of the benefits intended
> By this foreign congregation,
> Who had come so far to show them
> All how much they'd been mistaken;
> In what darkness they were dwelling,
> And how much obliged they were to
> These disinterested people,
> Who had journeyed to enlighten
> Their unfortunate condition,
> Through these potent triunited
> Anglo-Saxon civilizers,
> Rum, gunpowder, and religion.
> Now, the natives, as I mentioned,
> Didn't see the joke precisely
> In the way it was expected,
> They believing, simple creatures,
> They could manage their own matters
> Without any interference--
> Thought the shortest way to settle
> Those gratuitous advisers,
> Would be quietly to knock them
> On the Head, like Bulls of Bashan.[8]

The satrical style utilized by Brougham demonstrates

reasons for Po-Ca-Hon-Tas' popularity with its audiences.
The music, the libretto, and the subjects guyed were all
pertinent to life in New York and the nation in the 1850s.

The musical score, organized and orchestrated ("Dis-
located and Re-set," as the title page has it) from popular
and folk songs of the day by the well-known theatrical musician James G. Maeder, is in the ballad opera tradition. The
opening number for King Powhatan and a chorus is set to a
pop tune called "King of the Cannibal Isles"; this is followed
by a pseudo-Irish number (to the music of "Widow Machree")
in which Powhatan rhapsodizes over his "dhudieen" (an Irish
clay pipe)--"To me by a wily Paddy whack sent," he sings,
"Who had an axe to grind, hence the broad accent." Later,
"Rosin the Bow," "Pop Goes the Weasel," and other songs
are used. Interspersed with these are recitative passages in
which Maeder parodied the fashionable styles of Italian romantic opera (which was then gaining a foothold among upper-
class theatregoers in New York). "Grand scena complicato,"
"Hibernoso affettuosamente," and "Inter-aria nigroquae" (introducing a minstrel-show number) are some of the descriptions given.

Virtually every line of the text set to this music is
filled with puns and topical allusions. "What iron fortune
led you to our shores?" the King asks John Smith, who re-
plies, "Ironic monarch, 'twas a pair of oars." (The italics
throughout are Brougham's.) Describing Powhatan in a later
passage, he pictures the king as "A portly savage, plump,
and pigeon-toed, / Like Metamora both in feet and feature,
/ I never met-a-more-a-musing creature!"

In Brougham's simplified version of the story, the
Englishmen arrive and argue with Powahatan about taking
over his country; John Smith meets Pocahontas at the finish-
ing school where she and her friends Lum-Pa-Shuga, Dah-
Lin-Duk, Luv-Li-Kreeta, and others are pupils, and Pocahontas falls in love with him; she saves him from her father's
executioners, and the play ends with their marriage. Her
father has wished that she marry John Rolfe (who is turned
into a vaudeville Dutch comic; his role includes a Tyrolese
yodeling song). But Smith tells Rolfe, in effect, that history took care of the real Rolfe and his Indian bride, and
writers of Indian plays are free to play hob with facts--and
legends, however sacred--as they please.

Often points in the slender plot give rise to commentary on current matters. For example, when Smith and his henchmen take over Powhatan's government, they describe how they will divide the spoils in a "Grab Game" song, telling us that practices like the more scandalous ones of the Boss Tweed years to come were already known in New York:

> Grab away
> While you may;
> In this game, luck is all,
> And the prize
> Tempting lies
> In the rich City Hall.
>
> . . . .
>
> Grab away
> While you may;
> Every day there's a "job,"
> It's a fact
> By contract
> All intact you may rob.[9]

Relaxing from their labors of unsurpation, the men join Smith in a divertissement describing the recent New York season of the famous tragedienne Rachel, who had performed, of course, in French. Her manager had touted her appearance as the social event of the year; he expected a wealthy upper-class audience for whom he pushed his ticket prices very high, thus excluding lower middle-class audiences like Brougham's. Smith sings the final chorus of the number:

> Now all you nice folks as are fond of a play,
> And like to be amused in a sensible way,
> Don't you be deluded by fashion's sheep-bell,
> But come here where our language you understand
> well.[10]

Women's rights were a new topic of some interest at this time also. When told by her father she must marry John Rolfe, Pocahontas responds with, "The king who would enslave his daughter so, / Deserves a hint from Mrs. Beecher Stowe!" When her girl friends think she is being forced to marry against her will, they march on Powhatan's palace:

[Enter Poo-Tee-Pet and all the Indian women. They execute sundry manoeuvres and finally form a hollow square around Smith, very pointedly pointing their arrows at the King and company.]

King: Hollo! Stop that! My goodness! I
       declare!

       Those arrows make me quiver!--as you
       were!

       What are you, that thus outrage propriety?

Poo-Tee-Pet: The Anti-marry-folks-against-their-will
       Society.

King: Why come you here?--as sorrowful spec-
       tators?

Poo-Tee-Pet: No! on the contrary, we're very gladia-
       tors!

       For Freedom every heart with ardor glows,

       On Women's Rights we're bent, and bent
       our bows!

       Your daughter dear must marry whom
       she may,

       Daughters, you know, should always
       have their way![11]

The actor who played John Smith in Brougham's burlesque play, Charles M. Walcot, was also a playwright with satirical talents. During the year following the successful opening of Po-Ca-Hon-Tas, he wrote a similar play again parodying Longfellow's Indian epic poem, The Song of Hiawatha, which had been published in 1855. Walcot called his play Hiawatha; or, Ardent Spirits and Laughing Water, and it was first performed, like its predecessor, at Wallack's Lyceum Theatre, on December 25, 1856. Although not quite the hit that Brougham's piece had become, Walcot's Hiawatha aided in changing the theatre-going public's mind about the old-fashioned Indian melodramas they had been seeing for so many years. Also, by the time Walcot's satire opened, platform readings of Longfellow's work had become very popular. Wherever Walcot's play was done, the effectiveness of the poetic readings was somewhat diminished.

Throughout that disturbed decade before the Civil War, a theatre public that had so long accepted the sophomoric inanities of most Indian plays came to reject them. Hardly a dozen serious plays with Indian characters appeared from 1850 to 1860, and Walcot's Hiawatha joined Po-Ca-Hon-Tas to laugh them off the stage. The enjoyment of pieces like Brougham's and Walcot's provided a way of laughing not only at the outdated and pretentious falsities of Indian melodrama but also a way of laughing away the festering problem of Indian-White relations instead of thinking about it seriously. Stage Indians had become passé, and the tiresome problem of how to cope with real Native Americans, a problem now minimized east of the Mississippi though growing more serious on the Western Plains, was put in the shade by swiftly developing frictions between North and South, frictions that disturbed both the political and private lives of Americans everywhere.

"A sense of popular relief, similar to that after Munich in 1938," writes a historian, "first greeted the Compromise of 1850"[12] (a group of related Federal statutes which settled some disagreements about whether states newly entering the Union were to be slave or free, though it included approval of the notorious Fugitive Slave Act of 1850). But the effects of compromise were vitiated by measures such as the Kansas-Nebraska Bill of 1854 which allowed the possibility of further new slaveholding states in the West and "looked like another victory for appeasement,"[13] and by the Dred Scott Decision of 1857, yet another victory for the South and the institution of slavery. And, further exacerbating aroused feelings, Harriet Beecher Stowe's novel Uncle Tom's Cabin had been published in 1852. Considered to be the most influential work of fiction in the history of literature, it was turned into a play within a few months of its publication, and the stage version in its turn exerted enormous influence as the most widely seen theatrical production of all time.

Not surprisingly, the stage Indian did not stand up well against the competition of such conflicting interests. New views of the Indian were coming into focus, and they were not positive or flattering. We have reviewed Noble Savages and the newly discovered villainous Red Devils who opposed the brave Frontiersmen and pioneer settlers. Now we come upon a rarer breed for the stage, the landless and displaced unfortunates left behind after the forced migration of the 1830s.

This type is exemplified by a secondary but focal character in Dion Boucicault's The Octoroon; or, Life in Louisiana, first played at the Winter Garden Theatre on December 5,

1859. The greater historical importance of Boucicault's play (aside from its qualities as a well-planned sensation melodrama) is rooted in his sympathetic, balanced presentation of both Southern and Northern points of view on slavery. But his clearcut characterization of Wahnotee, the Indian hanger-on at Terrebonne Plantation, shows for the first time some effects of the removal and dispersal of tribes and families. Not for another sixty years would writers describe culturally disrupted Indians so realistically.

Wahnotee's first appearance in the play elicits sharply contradictory comments. When the villain, McCloskey, comments, "He's too fond of thieving and whiskey," the heroine, Zoe, defends him with:

> No; Wahnotee is a gentle, honest creature, and re-
> mains here because he loves that boy with the
> tenderness of a woman. When Paul was taken down
> with the swamp fever the Indian sat outside the hut,
> and neither ate, slept, nor spoke for five days, till
> the child could recognize and call him to his bed-
> side. He who can love so well is honest--don't
> speak ill of poor Wahnotee.[14]

But poor Wahnotee's fatal weakness is commented on almost immediately by the slave child, Paul, of whom the Indian is so protective. When Paul is told to go to the boat-landing shed where the plantation's mail is delivered, this dialogue ensues:

Paul: I'm 'most afraid to take Wahnotee to the shed, there's rum there.

Wahnotee: Rum!

Paul: Come, then, but if I catch you drinkin' O, laws a mussey you'll get snakes! I'll gib it to you! now, mind.[15]

But it is Wahnotee, proving his final worth and faith after McCloskey has murdered Paul, who hounds the villain through the swamp and kills him. Yet, however good his higher nature and his honorable love for the slave child (who may be seen as a replacement for the tribal family he has lost), Boucicault lets us know in a realistic manner that an Indian like this was perceived in civilized communities as no more than a town drunk, an accepted parasite but the more contemptible for being red-skinned. The variable dimensions of character with which Boucicault was able to invest his stage people are one of his notable achievements in melodrama.

Wahnotee is remarkable--despite the wild melodramatic action that involves him--for the believability with which he is presented by Boucicault. Thus he is a stark contrast with most Native Americans shown on the stage before him and most that were to follow for many years. An example of shallower dramatic thinking is displayed in an interesting amateur work, In Quod; or, Courting the Wrong Lass, by an unidentified playwright. Its Indian characters are somewhat thin background figures, but they bring on stage for the first time the reservation Indians of the Plains. Described as "A Comedy in Two Acts. Only One Stage Setting," the scene being "A Military Fort among the Indians of the western frontier of the United States," its cast includes, apparently, the only Indians in a play written during the war decade. It seems safe to conjecture that, like Alexander Macomb's Pontiac of a generation before, this play was written by an army man who well knew the setting of a military post, the social life of the soldiers, the officers, and their resident families, and the visiting Indians whose affairs were administered from the fort. It was probably written to be performed at a social event by the men stationed at just such a fort.

In Quod is a farce featuring a conflict between a Dutch comic old man, a similar Irish one, and a pair of young lovers. The plot, such as it is, is one of the oldest known: the young heroine is desired by one of the older men, but she loves the young hero, eventually gets him, and all ends well. The Indians appear in occasional scenes, adding some local color and a bit of depth to the story, but they are nameless, rather shadowy figures, a group presence taken for granted. There is no antagonistic feeling expressed toward them. Sometimes they are seen selling trinkets at the fort; in one passage they have come in from their reservation to get their periodic supply of government rations and to engage in a peacemaking council. The distributing of supplies is treated as a joke, the Indians being shown as amusing cadges getting what they can for free. The peacemaking business is taken no more seriously--the superiority of the soldiers stationed at the fort leaves no doubt about their ability to control the Indians of the area.

It is tempting to try to establish a date for this play. The generally peaceful atmosphere suggests that it was written before the Plains Wars began, perhaps in the later 1860s. If it was written by an officer at a frontier army post, he was a man who, though he looked down on Indians, was not yet bitterly unsympathetic toward them. Also, he was a man who had a genuine interest in and knowledge of theatre. He remembered pieces and performances like those of John Brougham, featuring the simplest of plots highlighted by the antics of Dutch and Irish comics. The Indians, in a foolish song they perform, refer to "Father Abraham" (a fond nickname for Lincoln in his later years), and this may indicate that it was written earlier, during the Civil War, when he was still alive.

In any case, In Quod; or, Courting the Wrong Lass shows Indians in an unantagonistic manner, at a time of peaceful intercourse with whites, and in comparatively everyday situations for them, rather than in the highly theatricalized style of melodramas of the 1830s, 1840s, and 1850s. Neither Dion Boucicault nor the anonymous author of In Quod made their Indians impossibly Noble Savages or unbelievably bloody villains, but showed them as accepted presences in American life, looked down upon but well known in those places and times. In the great heyday of Indian plays well before the Civil War, and again in the next spurt of Indian-play writing in the 1870s and 1880s, the classic fantasy or villain clichés were maintained. But Boucicault's Wahnotee and the reservation parasites of In Quod stand out in the period between as more nearly realistic representations of Indians on the stage than any others written before the middle of the twentieth century.

In view of the widely held theory that the Native Americans were a vanishing race, theatrical writing seems to be contradictory. The "Last Indians" of so many earlier plays like Metamora were superseded by strong Indian presences in plays like Nick of the Woods in which they are villainized to show the pioneers' struggles against them in a favorable light. Such plays upheld, it is true, the popular belief that Indians were hopelessly savage and therefore incapable of adjusting to white civilization and for that reason would eventually die out. But, on the other hand, the more the theory of the vanishing Indian was propounded, the more white Americans became aware of Indians in their midst. The removal policy got many Indians out of sight and out of mind for a time, but its failure was shortly seen by westward-bound settlers as they encountered not only the removed tribes but still more resident Indians on the Plains.

Confusion as to whether the native population was actually dying out was compounded by inaccurate population estimates. Since the first exaggerated guesses were made in the Renaissance, there were extraordinary differences in estimates of how many Indians lived in what became the United States. In a single decade of the nineteenth century, wildly varying estimates were published: in 1820, 471,036; in 1825, 129, 366; in 1829, 312,930.[16] Despite such variations, however, the estimates seemed (or were used by convinced publicists of the theory) to indicate a decline from seventeenth and eighteenth century guesses. The public wished to believe the theory, and did so. Brian Dipple has described the situation in colorful and precise terms:

> Extermination as policy was unthinkable, but a fully rounded version of the vanishing American won public acceptance after 1814. By its logic, Indians were doomed to "utter extinction" because they belonged to "an inferior race of men ... neither qualified to rise higher in the scale of being, nor to enjoy the benefits of the civilized and Christian state." A popular convention, premised on a moralistic judgment, had become natural law. Romantic poets, novelists, orators, and artists found the theme of a dying native race congenial, and added those sentimental touches to the concept that gave it wide appeal. Serious students of the Indian problem provided corroboration for the artistic construct as they analyzed the major causes hurrying the Indians to their graves. Opinion was virtually unanimous: "That they should become extinct is inevitable."[17]

But the vanishing race theory was constantly contradicted by everyday reality. Despite removal from the South and nearly forgotten wars of extirpation in the North, there were still Indians living in the Eastern states. West of the Mississippi, as the Santa Fe Trail and the Oregon Trail were developed, travelers' tales were filled with news of Indian encounters. Practitioners of the new science of anthropology such as Lewis Henry Morgan and Henry Rowe Schoolcraft were studying Indians in the field and publishing their findings. Our best historians, William Hickling Prescott and Francis Parkman, were writing extensively of the Indian past.

All of these sources supplied pertinent material for popular writers, including playwrights. Traditional character stereotypes of Noble Savages and Pathetic Dusky Maidens came to be accepted less wholeheartedly, as we have seen, and were eventually put out of commission--at least for a time--by the burlesques of John Brougham and Charles M. Walcot.

Perhaps the real value of the burlesque plays was not in doing away altogether with Indian plays (which, of course, they never did), but in showing new possibilities for the treatment of stage Indians, interesting new departures from the absurdly false ones the public had been seeing for so long. Incipient realists such as Dion Boucicault (who brought out The Octoroon less than two years after the production of Po-Ca-Hon-Tas and Walcot's Hiawatha) could more easily take on the challenge of portraying an Indian whom the audience could accept as an actual human being. In the years to come, more playwrights would try to do the same.

By mid-century, then, the age of innocence for the stage Indian was well in the past. After the Trail of Tears, after Nick of the Woods, after the Gold Rush of 1849 and the flood of white migration across the great trails of the West, the stage picture of the Native American moved away from fantasies of injured nobility and pathos to a view far more negative and bleak. The insistent presence of Indians in American life proved false the theory that they were a vanishing race and caused them to be seen, on the stage as on the western mountains and plains, as a burden and an obstacle.

NOTES

1. Bruce Marchiafava, "The Influence of Patriotism in the American Drama and Theatre, 1773-1830" (Ph.D. dissertation, Northwestern University, 1969), pp. 9 and 14-15.
2. A. H. Quinn's estimate in his History of the American Drama from the Beginnings to the Civil War (New York: Appleton-Century-Crofts, 1953), vol. II, p. 269.

3.   George C. D. Odell, Annals of the New York Stage, 15 vols. (New York: Columbia University Press, 1927-1949), vol. III, p. 680.

4.   Quinn, Beginnings to Civil War, vol. II, p. 272.

5.   Constance Rourke, American Humor, A Study of the National Character (New York: Doubleday Anchor Books, 1953), p. 104.

6.   Walter J. Meserve and William R. Reardon, "Introduction" to John Brougham, Po-Ca-Hon-Tas; or, The Gentle Savage, in Barrett Clark, ed., America's Lost Plays, 21 vols. (Princeton, N.J.: Princeton University Press, 1940; reprint ed., Bloomington: Indiana University Press, 1969), vol. 21, p. xiv.

7.   Richard Moody, ed., Dramas From the American Theatre 1762-1909 (Boston: Houghton Mifflin, 1969), p. 401.

8.   John Brougham, Po-Ca-Hon-Tas; or, The Gentle Savage, in Clark, America's Lost Plays, vol. 21, p. 121.

9.   Ibid., p. 132.

10.   Ibid., p. 134.

11.   Ibid., p. 152.

12.   Robert E. Spiller et al., editors, Literary History of the United States, third edition, revised (New York: Macmillan, 1963), p. 505.

13.   Ibid.

14.   Dion Boucicault, The Octoroon; or, Life in Louisiana, in Arthur Hobson Quinn, Representative American Plays, 7th ed. (New York: Appleton-Century-Crofts, 1966), p. 378.

15.   Ibid., p. 379.

16.   Brian W. Dippie, The Vanishing American: White Attitudes and U. S. Indian Policy (Middletown, Conn.: Wesleyan University Press, 1982), p. 125.

17.   Ibid., pp. 10-11. Dippie's quotations are from "Indians Removing Westward," (Jan 7, 1828) House Rep. No. 56, 20th Congress, First session, p. 2, and from Nathan Hale. "Heckewelder's Indian History," NAR IX (June, 1819), p. 170.

Chapter VI

REDSKIN VILLAINS: THE DOWNWARD PATH
TO RACISM IN THE AMERICAN THEATRE

Native Americans are characterized in varying ways in the
mixed lot of plays that illustrate the great Westward Movement of emigrants from the Mississippi to the Pacific. From
the later 1850s through the 1880s--in contrast to the bumper
crop in a similar period in the first half of the century--no
more than a couple of dozen plays dealing with Indians were
brought out. These, however, include burlesques, satires,
and vaudeville sketches, melodramas of the newly developed
ten-twent'-thirt' variety, and more serious and expensively
produced pieces, not to speak of closet dramas and even a
pantomime. An examination of their contents shows marked
contrasts in attitude. Some are highly favorable and supportive of Indians, while others are highly antagonistic and
racist in tone.

An intriguing and unfairly neglected play published in
1857 is Fashions and Follies of Washington Life. It is the
work of a Washington, D. C., writer called Henry Clay
Preuss, who was a keen-eyed observer of the social scene
there. Fashions and Follies is a bright and attractive satire
of political and public life in Washington in the form of a
melodrama, complete with a villain who traduces the character
of the sweet, smart heroine and almost brings on a tragic
duel, happily aborted when he is caught and exposed. Most
of the scenes, however, are little satirical vignettes, each
attacking one of the subjects Preuss had chosen to expose
and ridicule. They are all interlaced in a racy, funny style
with which he even satirizes the melodramatic story line with
its silly plot and characters.

An outstanding passage occurs in Act IV, scene 2,
when Tonawha, "a live Indian Chief," in the capital to call
on the President, is presented by the principal character

man, Captain Smith. Having fought beside Tonawha's father, "Old Thunder," in the swamps of Florida, Smith thinks highly of such Indians. "There he stands, Colonel," Smith says to a companion:

> a living monument of the wrongs of his people--son of a great chief--owner of thousands of acres--gagged by your government--cheated by its agents and now shivering at the doors of our great halls of legislation--pleading for a poor pittance until his hair is wet with the dews of the night! There he stands-- look at him, and blush for your color!

The answer is a pat one that must have been heard countless times in such arguments:

Colonel Cecille: Well, Captain, this is an unfortunate state of things, but I don't see how it can be otherwise. Progress is the eternal law of nature--and the Anglo-Saxon race must go onward. If the Indian race will not or cannot assimilate, they must go back. Those who cannot go with the tide must sink under. The Government, I conceive, is as just as the case will admit. It allows them a fair price--ratified by mutual treaties.

Captain Smith: Fair price? Brass rings and rotten whiskey! Treaties? Put a pistol to a man's breast, and ask him politely to hand you his purse! No, sir! Jack Smith knows what he's talking about--wasn't in the Everglades of Florida three years for nothing. I haven't time or occasion to argue the question now, but I will say this: when the secret archives are opened at some future day--when the bloody chapter of Indian wrongs is given to the world--my word for it--it will make a proud nation blush![1]

Tonawha comes into the conversation with some equally strong points, not weakened even by the pidgin English he is made to speak:

Tonawha: Ugh! Tonawha want to talk. Pale-faces say big words--me not no [sic] big words --me no little words--me no what you talk. Pale-faces vair bad to red man. Great Spirit give us plenty land--big hunting grounds: Pale-faces come, take our land, drive us way! Pale-faces give us hot red water, which make our heart feel bad and burn us up! ugh! Den Dey bring a good book, to tell bout Great Spirit, and make us good. Ah! I see other books white man write--ugh! bad pictures! vaire bad pictures! I see one pale-face--he toma-hawk, he burn, he kill other pale-face, 'cause he no believe in his Great Spirit, ugh! Indian no do dat.

Captain Smith: That's a clincher!

Tonawha: Long time go, Great Spirit send pale-faces one good chief--he tell you no cheat --no steal--he tell you many good tings-- what you do? you nail him to big crooked wood, (crossing his arms) and he die! Ugh! Indian no do dat!

Captain Smith: If that ain't a "ten-strike," I'll swallow my head! [2]

Tonawha's exceptional qualities are stressed as the scene progresses and he meets Smith's daughter, the sweet heroine. He is gracious and courteous with her, and she charms him with equally gracious behavior. But, having served Preuss' sly satirical purpose, Tonawha unfortunately does not appear in the play again.

Written in a day when most audiences would not have taken this kind of guying comfortably, it is not surprising that Fashions and Follies of Washington Life has no record of performance. Nevertheless, Preuss' optimism about the potential value of his play was expressed in an introduction:

It must be gratifying to every humanitarian to know that the evils here adverted to, are gradually yield-ing to a progressive and enlarged moral sense in the

> public; and should this humble effort aid, in any
> degree, in advancing the good work of reform, the
> author will deem himself amply repaid for the labor
> of the task.[3]

Preuss was unduly modest. The play is considerably more
than a closet drama with good intentions. Its excellent dialogue, interesting characterizations, and sharp satire give it
the potential for a delightful modern production.

In contrast to Preuss' satire is a news-of-the-day play
performed in San Francisco in the same year Fashions and
Follies was published in Washington. This was a "beautiful
and thrilling" three-act drama called The Oatman Family,
written by a San Francisco actor, C. E. Bingham, and first
performed at the American Theatre there on September 9,
1857.[4]

The Oatmans were an emigrant family traveling the Gila
Trail toward Fort Yuma and California in the spring of 1851.
Royse Oatman, the father, impatient with the slow progress
of the wagon train with which they had crossed the Plains,
struck out ahead of it in western Arizona. Shortly thereafter his single wagon was attacked by a band of seventeen
Indians, possibly Apaches but more likely Yavapais, who
killed the parents and four of their seven children. They
left the badly injured teen-aged son, Lorenzo, for dead and
carried off Olive, thirteen years old, and her ten-year-old
sister Mary Ann. Lorenzo recovered and got himself to California, determined to locate his two surviving sisters. It
was learned in time that the girls had been sold by the Yavapais to the more peaceful Mohave Indians who lived in settled
farming villages on the Colorado River. Mary Ann, always
a frail child, died, probably of tuberculosis, and Olive was
adopted by the Mohave family of a man named Aspenosay. In
their concern for her spiritual welfare, Aspenosay and his
family arranged to have an elaborate tattoo engraved on her
chin, as was done for all Mohave girls. Tattooing was a
ritual observed by Mohaves of both sexes so that, upon death,
the divine judge would recognize them and allow them to
enter the desired hereafter place which they called Sil'aid,
the land of dead people. Olive was "rescued" with little ado
in January 1856, rejoined her brother Lorenzo, and eventually
married a citizen of Sherman, Texas, where she lived until
her death in 1903. There is a fine photograph taken shortly

after her recovery that shows her neatly coiffed and wearing a modest crinoline gown, and with the chin tattoo which she of course wore throughout her life.[5]

Bingham's play apparently treated mainly the massacre and rescue portions of the adventure. It seems to have been based on a best-selling book, largely fictional, by a local preacher called Stratton, published in San Francisco in the summer of 1857. MacMinn informs us that in a preface to the third edition, Stratton

> pointed out that the chief value of his book lay in its revelation of the "wise intent of Providence," as shown in the fact that "these dark Indian tribes are fast wasting before the rising sun of our civilization." One can see that Bingham had plenty of inspiration for his drama.[6]

That the subject would be of special interest to San Francisco audiences goes without saying. Most of them had come there under difficult circumstances, either by ship or across the continent, and sometimes under threat of similar dire happenings. The story was familiar in the city and, sparked by Olive's reappearance only eighteen months before, was still comparatively current. The special interest of its use in a play lies in the fact that it was the only dramatization of a real occurrence of Western adventure that we know of.

Other plays focusing on the westward movement are not based on known factual incidents, but on generalized knowledge of the kinds of adventures western settlers experienced. For stage purposes, however, the experiences were exaggerated and sensationalized beyond any realistic description. Unfortunately we cannot know in detail how The Oatman Family compared to the ones we have preserved, as it was performed only once and Bingham's script has been lost.[7] But it is hardly likely that Bingham's descriptions or characterizations of Indians, if he gave them any, were as sympathetic as those of Henry Clay Preuss or even as neutral as those of John Hovey Robinson in Nick Whiffles.

A more positive view of Indians is found in The Mormons: or, Life at Salt Lake City by Thomas Dunn English, first performed at Burton's Theatre in New York on March

16, 1858. English was a writer and politician who settled in Logan County, West Virginia, became the first mayor of the town of Logan, and wrote a history of the county as well as some verse, a temperance play, and The Mormons. (In his history he recorded the story of the Shawnee girl Aracoma on which the outdoor spectacle drama The Aracoma Story, performed at Logan every summer, is based.)

The sole Indian in The Mormons is "a Kioway chief," Dahcomah, friend and aide of the hero, Walter Markham. Dahcomah is characterized as a man of parts who does not neglect his own interests while looking out for his friend's:

Markham: Ah, Dahcomah! you here, old friend of the prairies?

Dahcomah: Hugh! Bes' speak low. Mormon chief come back bime-by--dat Elder dam rascal.

Markham: Oh, no--he has rather led me to believe he is friendly.

Dahcomah: Ugh! Red Joe frien' too?

Markham: Not particularly, as you know. Why do you ask that?

Dahcomah: You brave man--my frien'--we hunt togedder --trabbil same war-path--save my life from Arapahoe tief. Mine Pratt an Hoe--dey goin' kill you.

Markahm: I know you to be a true man, Dahcomah; but think you mistaken. They can have no motive.

Dahcomah: Ugh! you lub white squaw--so do he.

Markahm: He! why the old fellow has a half dozen wives already.

Dahcomah: Dat so. Want more. Fond ob squaw. Dey talk--I lissen. Tink Ingin no understan'. Dey kill you. 'Pose dey try. I hab Joe scalp. Pooty scalp too. Red ha'r.[8]

Walter Markham's presence in the Mormon wagon train is accounted for in part by his skills as a brave frontier guide, but more importantly because he is trying to save Mary, the girl he loves, from being forced into marriage with Elder Pratt, one of the three Mormon villains of the piece. Markham is also out for revenge on a dastardly character called Neville, also with the train, who has seduced Markham's sister and left her dying in New York and has now become a Mormon. Markham's only aides in the nest of Mormon vipers are an old frontiersman, Whiskey Jake, the Indian Dahcomah, and, at the last minute, the U.S. Cavalry. Of course he overcomes Neville, Pratt, and the other Mormons and carries Mary off to a happy marriage with him.

The so-called Latter Day Saints, driven out of Illinois in 1846, had made their famous trek to the West in the winter and spring of 1846-47. In the decade since then, they had surmounted severe obstacles in setting up their enviably well-organized community in Utah, and, for that reason and particularly because they clung to the peculiar institution of polygamy, they continued to attract sensational national attention, most of it antagonistic. Not unnaturally, they were defensive about their faith, and that defensiveness--as in more recent years their proselytizing and the racist tenets of the Mormon faith--made many enemies for them.

The Mormons; or, Life at Salt Lake City is a standard kind of propaganda piece of the 1850s that went some distance toward satisfying public feeling about the would-be saints. It shows Mormonism in the worst possible light, as a shield for criminals like Neville, and as a trap for helpless young girls like Markham's Mary--not unlike the use of white slavery as a stage cliché that became popular fifty years later in melodramas that are distant relatives of this one. Dahcomah's presence in the play serves two purposes: first, there is the old familiar one of the example-setting Indian who is acceptably good because he helps good white men in pursuits such as taking his land away from him; but second, in this play he also serves by his goodness to show up the badness of the chosen villains, the Mormons. General Sherman's famous rejoinder to the Indian who claimed to be a good man could be altered to read: "The only good Mormons I ever saw were dead." That might well be taken as the purpose and point of Thomas Dunn English's play.

After the hiatus of the Civil War decade, Native American characters again began to appear in new plays during the 1870s. Most of these were transient melodramas of the poorest kind, such as the Buffalo Bill plays. There were a few dramatizations from books including three new pieces from J. F. Cooper's novels, The Last of the Mohicans by J. C. Stewart in 1870, The Life and Death of Natty Bumpo [sic] by Thomas B. DeWalden (utilizing all five parts of the Leatherstocking series) in 1873, and Leatherstocking; or, The Last of the Mohicans by George F. Rowe in 1874. Also, one of Augustin Daly's little-known failures, Roughing It, produced in 1873, was adapted from Mark Twain's book and presumably included his famous scathing descriptions of what he called the Goshoot Indians. None of these scripts is extant.

The 1870s began, however, with one of the most famous sensation melodramas of its day, Across the Continent; or, Scenes From New York Life and The Pacific Railroad by James J. McCloskey. Beginning like a temperance drama, the play's first act is a prologue; the other three take place twenty years later. John Adderly, saloon owner and underworld figure up to no good in the first act, continues his evil machinations in the later period, progressing to the attempted ruination of a gentleman called Goodwin, his adopted daughter Louise, and Joe Ferris, Louise's suitor, who has had some mysterious previous involvement with Adderly for which he had been sent "up the Hudson" for a three-year stretch. In the fourth act, Ferris, now gone straight, has become a station manager on the Union Pacific Railroad at Station 47, somewhere out West. Louise arrives and they declare their love, but their future is threatened when John Adderly also turns up in cahoots with an evil Indian, Black Cloud. The latter, along with his tribe, is seen solely as the villain's tool, a cliché bad element with no redeeming qualities. Adderly identifies himself with the Indians and bluntly categorizes them in his big speech just before the climax and his ultimate downfall:

> Now, Joe Ferris, your hours are almost numbered....
> And now to come here and find everything as if I
> had planned it. The daughter who so despised me,
> the father who hated me ... at last in my power!
> Oh, I could shout with very joy until the rocks re-
> echo with laughter! Rejoice, you red-skinned devils!
> For this I have sold myself to you, and become one

of your tribe. My measure of crime is almost complete, for with the wealth which I now possess and the gold, I am told, is hidden here, I will return to civilization. [9]

When Adderly convinces the Indians to cut down the telegraph lines which are the station's only connection with outside help, one of his Indian henchmen reports to him (in the only line in the play given to a red-skinned devil), ("Indian do what white man tell him--climb pole--cut wire--so." The Indians, at Adderly's behest, then attack the station. But Joe Ferris cleverly improvises a telegraph connection with another station, wires for help, and a train soon arrives on stage filled with soldiers who shoot Adderly and Black Cloud and put an end to the raging battle.

Across the Continent was one of the greatest dramatic successes of the nineteenth century. After a false start in a Brooklyn theatre in the fall of 1870, it opened on March 13, 1871, at Wood's Museum in New York City for a continuous run of six weeks, then reopened at Niblo's on July 17 for another six-week run. It was revived repeatedly into the last decade of the nineteenth century as a vehicle for the original star, Oliver Doud Byron (in the role of Joe Ferris), always featuring the realistic New York tenement, saloon, and street scenes, and in the last act the suspenseful telegraph scene, the Indian battle, and the spectacular arrival of the train. In the 1870s, these elements were new and exciting to audiences: the first transcontinental telegraph message had been sent from San Francisco to President Lincoln in Washington in 1861, the Plains Indian wars had reached their peak at the end of the sixties, and the Union Pacific railroad was opened in May 1869. The play must have seemed a kind of living newsreel to theatregoers of the time.

The somewhat cynical attitude toward Indian characters on the stage exemplified by J. J. McCloskey became standard in many theatre pieces of the 1870s. One group of plays in particular, the melodramas written to be played by William F. Cody (Buffalo Bill), spread negative views on Indians to enormous numbers of receptive people across the country, since most of Cody's performances were given not in large urban centers but in provincial theatres.

William Cody's colorful career as a young army scout

and Indian fighter, and of course his highly publicized ex-
ploits as a buffalo hunter, had made him a nationally known
celebrity. He was the subject of much public print, including popular dime novels and magazine serials, one of which,
Buffalo Bill, The King of Border Men, serialized in The New
York Weekly in 1869, was turned into a play in 1871. The
author of the story was "Ned Buntline," the pseudonymous
byline of Edward Zane Carroll Judson, an opportunist, self-
appointed patriot and defender of things American, temperance lecturer (between drinking bouts), and promoter of certain public figures and causes. Typical of his adventures
had been his work as a rabble rouser (attaching himself to
Edwin Forrest's coattails) who helped bring on the Astor
Place Riot in 1849. Now, twenty years later and twenty
years better known through his self-publicizing, he decided
to make a stage star of Buffalo Bill Cody.[10]

Judson had met Cody briefly on one of his temperance
lecture tours out West. Cody then looked him up on an invitation to visit New York in the spring of 1872, and Judson arranged for a performance of the play adapted from his
story at the Bowery Theatre. He also publicized the fact
that Cody would be present in a box from which the glamorous young celebrity would be well seen and could see himself played on the Bowery stage by an actor called J. B.
Studley.[11] Judson's campaign to con young Cody into appearing on the stage under his aegis was flattering. The
bait took, and Cody agreed to play himself in a production
of the play. Late in 1872, Judson set up a meeting in Chicago, where he planned to engage a theatre and actors and
prepare Cody for his theatrical debut.

Confusion exists as to the titles and identities of the
plays Cody appeared in, probably because of the careless or
devious record-keeping and advertising indulged in by Judson as well as Cody and his later managers.[12] The largely
fictional biographies and "autobiographies" about Buffalo Bill
are little help. Cody perpetuated a story that at their meeting in a Chicago hotel Judson sat down and wrote, in four
hours, the play they were to perform a few days later. Obviously, Judson merely altered the existing play, shrewdly
throwing in a part for Texas Jack Omohundro, a friend Cody
had brought along to be a fellow actor (and whom Judson had
featured in a Ned Buntline serial) and adding a role for himself (as a temperance lecturer) so that he could be on stage

to feed the new actors the cues and lines they were never able to memorize. He advertised the play in the Chicago Times as The Scouts of the Prairie; or, Red Deviltry As It Is with an alluring announcement:

> A sensational drama of the red-hot type, written by Ned Buntline, the prince of sensation-mongers, will be produced on to-morrow evening.... The lovers of realistic romance will have a chance to gorge themselves in this highly flavored food. Mlle. Morlacchi, the danseuse and pantomimist, will appear as Dove-Eye, the Indian Maiden.[13]

The play opened at Nixon's Amphitheatre in Chicago on December 16, 1872. A notice in the Chicago Times concludes its bemused commentary on the proceedings with:

> On the whole, it is not probable that Chicago will ever look upon the like again. Such a combination of incongruous drama, execrable acting, renowned performers, mixed audience, intolerable stench, scalping, blood and thunder, is not likely to be vouchsafed to a city a second time, even Chicago.[14]

Accurate as the Chicago critic may have been esthetically, he was wrong about the uniqueness of The Scouts of the Prairie. An extraordinary financial and popular success, it was only the first of a series of sure-fire money-makers featuring Cody during the next ten years.

Like McCloskey's Across the Continent, Judson's Scouts of the Prairie attracted audiences by the currency of its content: Indian fighting and the wild western life of newspaper and dime novel stories were brought to the audience's local theatre and made even more attractive by the presence of actual heroes of that romantic life. The play itself seems to have epitomized the narrow range of pieces starring Cody. It is simplistic in the extreme, and every character is cardboard and cliché, the Indians most of all. It is also viciously anti-Indian and antagonistic in tone: the Indians are always tied in with any bad-guy characters the sentimentalized good characters don't like, and all the bad ones are bushwhackers and Northerners. A strong element, which may have been added by Judson in his Chicago rewrite, is a notably jingoistic pro-Southern, anti-Union sentiment. The addition seems

the more likely to be his, as the first version of the script
was put together by a New York hack called Fred Meader
and was originally performed in New York only four years
after the end of the Civil War.

In the first act of <u>Scouts of the Prairie</u>, two white
villains are thought to be inciting local Indians to attack the
Cody homestead. One of their hirelings is an Indian drunk-
ard called Fire-Water Tom, who is caught, hazed, put through
a phony trial, and publicly whipped. The observing crowd
takes all this as a great joke, as the audience is expected to
do. We are to understand that all Indians are drunken louts
at heart, natural-born villains who will do any dirty work
for a renegade white man, particularly a Northerner, if the
Indian gets a little liquor for pay. The "trial" is conducted
by old Major Williams, who is also permanently drunk, but,
being a white man, is comically and acceptably so. A veteran
of the War of 1812, Williams goes on endlessly about having
"fit inter the Mexican War," and about being an expert Indian killer, as he claims the soldiers in that war learned to
be. His son, Snakeroot Sam, also present, is another noisy
Indian-hater.

<u>Scouts of the Prairie</u> is a remarkably hate-filled and
violent play. The frequent stabbings and shootings throughout are varied by scenes such as one in which a stockade
wall is blown open and another in which Buffalo Bill, hiding
in a hollow log, tosses his powder flask into the Indians'
campfire and blows them up. All these episodes result in the
bloody maiming or death of Indians. In the last act, several
white women are captives in an Indian camp and are insulted
and mistreated by Wa-no-tee Ma-no-tee, "the Turtle Dove"
(the "Dove-Eye" of the newspaper story), a violent-tempered
"Princess of the Ogallala" (and the only female Indian villain
found in an American play). The show ends with a great
fight scene in which Buffalo Bill, with a little help from some
minor characters, overcomes the white bushwhackers, killing
a couple of them and most of their Indian allies.

Playing dates for the <u>Scouts</u> tour included not only
smaller towns but also St. Louis, Cincinnati, Boston, and New
York. The tour closed in June 1873 at Port Jervis, New
York, having shown some ugly Indians to audiences East,
West, North, and South. Its great success made Cody de-
cide to take it out again for another season. The script was

slightly rewritten and the title changed to The Scouts of the Plains, and under that title it was toured again for a third and even a fourth season, into the spring of 1876.

During the summer break between tours, Cody always returned to his home in Nebraska and took jobs as a scout or guide for the U.S. Army or for well-to-do hunters. Some of these adventures supplied material for new plays. On an army expedition in the summer of 1876, after Custer's fiasco at the Little Big Horn, Cody was involved in a skirmish with hostile Indians during which he killed a Cheyenne warrior named Yellow Hand. Almost immediately the New York Weekly carried a story called "The Crimson Trail; or, Custer's Last Warpath, A Romance Founded Upon the Present Border Warfare, as Witnessed by Hon. W. F. Cody." In the fall of 1876, the Buffalo Bill Combination Company opened in Rochester in a new piece called The Red Right Hand; or, Buffalo Bill's First Scalp for Custer. Its climactic scene was a recreation of his hand-to-hand fight with Yellow Hand in which Cody ripped off the Indian's scalp, held it up for the audience to see, and shouted, "The first scalp for Custer!" This show was toured with success as far west as California.

In 1877 Cody experimented with hiring real Indians to appear in his show. These were a group of Sioux from the Red Cloud Agency, and the play they appeared in seems to have been Mountain Meadow Massacre, dramatizing a recent sensational crime in Utah, a multiple killing allegedly perpetrated by Mormon fanatics; how the Sioux were integrated into the plot remains a mystery, as no copy of the script is extant. For the 1878-1879 season, Cody opened in Baltimore with an unusually large company including a troupe of Pawnee Indians. During that season he had a play written for him called The Knight of the Plains; or, Buffalo Bill's Best Trail; its success caused the tour to be extended to California again. His combination companies continued their lucrative tours into the 1880s, with titles such as May Cody; or, Lost and Won, Buffalo Bill at Bay; or, The Pearl of the Prairie, Twenty Days; or, Buffalo Bills' Pledge, and The Prairie Waif. Odell comments that in the New York run of the Waif, "a band of Cheyenne Indian chiefs added verisimilitude in scalp and war dances, doubtless horrific indeed."[15] There seems to have been a change from Cheyenne to Pawnee in the native portion of the cast in the plays' national tour, if the publicist and a typical newspaper advertisement are to be believed:

The Only and Original
BUFFALO BILL
Hon. W. F. Cody
Late Chief of the Scouts of the U. S. Army
and his Mammoth Combination
in his great Sensational Drama, entitled
"The Prairie Waif"
Introducing the Western Scout and Daring Rider
Buck Taylor, King of the Cowboys.
A Genuine Band of Pawnee Indians,
Under Pawnee Billy, Boy Chief and Interpreter
24 First Class Artists   New and Beautiful Scenery
Mr. Cody, "Buffalo Bill," will give an exhibition of fancy
rifle shooting holding his rifle in twenty different
positions, in which he is acknowledged preeminent.[16]

A Fourth of July celebration in 1882, organized by
Cody at North Platte, Nebraska, was the origin of the Wild
West circus that was to be his chief occupation for the re-
mainder of his life. The show's origin was in a patriotic
gesture Cody made that summer, when he helped arrange a
display of wild steer and buffalo riding, horse races, rop-
ing, and other cowboy skills, preceded by a grand parade
and concluding with fireworks. The idea of combining an
outdoor entertainment such as this with some of the content
of his "house" shows, as he called them, was conceived.
Gestating through the time of Cody's winter tour, it was
brought to fruition at Omaha, Nebraska, when the Wild West,
Rocky Mountain and Prairie Exhibition opened on May 17,
1883. From his own ideas, and with the aid of several Western friends including his first partner, the sharpshooter Dr.
W. F. Carver, William Cody had created an original American
form of entertainment.[17]

The Wild West show was a success from the beginning,
and the easier performing requirements for Cody drew him
away from the more exacting labor of stage work. But to
help pay the salaries and traveling costs for a huge company
of cowboys, Indians, roustabouts, managers, and animals, he
continued his winter tours for three more seasons, into the
spring of 1886. The first tour of the outdoor show, though
it was well-received wherever it played, was ill-planned and
disorganized due to the inexperience of Cody and Carver at
managing and transporting so large and disparate a company
of nonprofessional performers. Carver left the company at

the end of the summer and Cody persuaded Nate Salsbury, an experienced professional show manager, to become his partner. It turned out to be the perfect collaboration, and thereafter--for the next thirty years--the Wild West show never failed to draw crowds and make fortunes for Cody and his managers.[18]

Apart from displays of trick riding and sharpshooting, Buffalo Bill's Wild West always included elaborate recreations of western adventure scenes, almost all of them featuring actual Indians as performers. In a program of the 1890s, five of these scenes are distributed among the twenty-four numbers listed, separating groups of virtuoso horsemanship and sharpshooting acts. Number 6 showed "a Prairie Emigrant Train Crossing the Plains. It is attacked by marauding Indians, who are in turn repulsed by 'Buffalo Bill' and a number of Scouts and Cowboys." Number 18 was the "Attack on the Deadwood Mail-Coach by Indians, repulse of the Indians, and rescue of the stage, passengers and mail, by 'Buffalo Bill' and his attendant Cowboys." Number 23 was an "Attack on Settlers' Cabin and rescue by 'Buffalo Bill' and a band of Cowboys, Scouts and Frontiersmen." The Indians in the company had only one number to themselves, and even that was an aggressive one, Number 15, in which members of the Sioux, Arapahoe, Brulé, and Cheyenne tribes showed "the Indian mode of fighting, war dances and games." Even a classic buffalo hunt, Number 22, was not theirs alone, but was conducted by Buffalo Bill, accompanied by Indians.[19]

The season of 1885-1886 was highlighted by the appearance of the aged Sioux medicine man, Sitting Bull. To break away from the tedium of life at the Standing Rock Reservation, he agreed to travel with Cody's company for four months. A souvenir photograph of him with Cody, both in full regalia, bearing the caption "Enemies in '76, Friends in '85" was hawked to the public. When Sitting Bull rode into the arena, silent and dignified, he was booed and jeered at as Custer's purported killer. When he left the company Cody gave him a fine show horse. Four years later, when Sitting Bull was murdered by Indian members of the U.S. Cavalry at Standing Rock, the horse took their gunshots as a cue, sat down on his haunches, and offered a hoof to "shake hands" with any comer.[20]

Buffalo Bill Cody's two innovations in show business,

creating the Wild West show and hiring real Indians to appear
as performers, were emulated by many other entrepreneurs
with varying degrees of success in later years. The last
attempt as a large-scale Wild West entertainment on Cody's
pattern was one organized by the film star Tim McCoy, a
failure in the late 1930s.

As for the kind of melodramas Cody performed, the
popular theatre of his time was well supplied with similar
hackwork pieces. Three plays in this vein show us three
sharply defined Indian character types familiar from earlier
plays. One is a joke drunk, one a heroic figure who helps
white people, and the last an isolated instance in this period
of the Pathetic Dusky Heroine.

The first of these works is a comedy-melodrama called
Luck by Joseph I.C. Clarke, published in 1877, which utilizes
some of the most pertinent interests of the time, silver mining
out West (in this case Utah), the making of quick fortunes
and the "luck" involved in the experience, and, though a
bit passé by 1877, the Mormons. The story has to do with
a dubious mining claim and two comic villains' attempts to
wrest it from the rightful owner, the young hero. In the
happy outcome, it makes him a very rich man. The single
Indian character is called Injun Joe, a tribeless drifter who
is treated in a condescending joke manner. He is set up as
nothing more than a drunken parasite who makes himself useful in catching the villains in exchange for a supply of whiskey. But he is the catalyst who turns the plot for the hero's
benefit by obtaining some documents, "heep paper," which
turn out to be a group of confessional notes and letters
dropped by the villainous lawyer Blynders ("Sto'pipe," as
Joe calls him) and the crooked Mormon Apostle Bloxham
("Bloxy"). Joe describes his adventure, in the primitive
speech form concocted by the playwright, thus:

> Me see Bloxy an' man weet sto'pipe.... Much talkee
> Bloxy's house--me plenty look all time; sto'pipe want
> go, Bloxy want no go--moh--more much plenty talkee.
> Bloxy give sto'pipe heep paper. Sto'pipe put heep
> paper hole in coat (in pocket). Sto'pipe get on hoss
> --no good on hoss--Me run down trail, get behind
> big tree, me trow little tree at hoss; den sto'pipe
> in sage brush; me run put sto'pipe on hoss; me see
> heep paper in sage brush; me no talkee; sto'pipe go

> 'way, so bad; me take heep paper; me run; me no
> laugh; me heep dam glad![21]

Clearly, no advance in characterization of Indians or
the writing of dialect was attempted by this playwright. As
for the name Injun Joe, while it may have been borrowed
from Mark Twain, since The Adventures of Tom Sawyer had
been published the previous year, the impression given is
that it is merely a descriptive substitute for purportedly un-
pronounceable Indian names and a common usage like Sambo
or Jemima as a sort of racist catch-all to indicate the white
man's contempt for the subject to whom he applies it.

The second play is a more derivative melodrama, The
Emigrant's Daughter by Len Ellsworth Tilden, rather in the
vein of Ned Buntline but distinctly a grandchild of Monk
Lewis and Pixerécourt. A wagon train crossing the Plains
falls into the ambush of a bandit gang called the Coyotes.
But the Coyotes are foiled by the appearance of the ghostly
"Black Spirit," a black-draped apparition which always turns
up just before a spot of trouble. An Indian attack heralded
by an appearance of the masked warrior throws the Coyotes'
evil plans for the wagon train out of kilter. The bandits,
however, kill all the Indians except their chief, Black Eagle,
who expresses a dramatic lament for his tribesmen:

> Ugh! Great Father no smile on Black Eagle. War-
> riors die fever. Big thief Coyotes kill rest. Black
> Eagle alone. Braves all gone to Happy Hunting
> Grounds. All left Black Eagle graves of father.
> Him die by 'um fighting for 'um. All he got--all
> poor Black Eagle got. Me death to all Coyotes.
> (draws tomahawk and dances wildly about) Um,
> death to Coyotes! Death! Death! Kill 'em.[22]

This nutshell history is further explained to Minnie, the
emigrant's daughter of the title, by Austin Fynes, the train's
guide and her honest suitor. (She is also pursued by the
villain.):

Fynes:　　... an old prairie friend of mine, Black Eagle,
　　　　　whom I met in the forest today.

Minnie:　Black Eagle is an Indian name.

Fynes: Yes, and its [sic] the name of as honest an Indian as ever lived. The government assigned
him a reservation just south of here. A band
of desperadoes, known as the Coyotes, established headquarters on it, and Black Eagle, Indian like, waged war against them. He was out-
numbered in men, but he made things exceedingly
warm for them, and Indian as he is, he has saved
many an emigrant train from destruction. Fever,
yellow fever, attacked the tribes, and many of
them died. Soon after he unwisely sought another fight with the Coyotes, and suffered defeat, all the tribe being killed except himself.
Not content with this, the Coyotes attacked Black
Eagle's village, killed all within it, old men, women, and children. Black Eagle now roams the
woods, dealing destruction to the outlaw band.23

Tilden may have been an aspiring playwright who created this play for a local stock company in Ohio. It is neatly
fashioned on a pattern already very old-fashioned in his time,
with hero, heroine, villain, standard comic relief (in this
case a henpecked soldier, Irish of course, and his harridan
wife), and the ghostly savior of the good people.

In contrast with its old-fashioned tone, the most striking element in The Emigrant's Daughter is Tilden's sympathy
toward the Indians. It is as if the attitude reflected a shift
in public thought, as if the news of the Army's persistent
destruction of the Plains tribes and the horrors of prison-
camp reservation life had caused a groundswell of reaction
against government policies. (The year this play appeared,
1884, was also the year Helen Hunt Jackson published her
explosive best-seller, A Century of Dishonor, as well as her
novel Ramona.)

Four years later another melodrama appeared that displayed both old and new interests. This was a piece called
Border Land, by Charles Townsend. The new element is
represented by its setting, the Arizona mining country. The
old is shown in the standardized plot and the use of a Pathetic Dusky Heroine, the first to appear on the stage for many
years but a continuation of a type that has come down into
our own time. This character is Winona, an Indian girl who
secretly loves the hero, Jack Ralston. When the villain,

Dempsey, kidnaps Mary Lester, Jack's beloved, Winona helps him save her. In a confrontation between Dempsey and Ralston, Winona is conveniently killed when she throws herself in front of the endangered Ralston. Later, in a big spectacular knife fight, Jack gets the better of Dempsey and the final tableau shows him in an embrace with Mary.

The characterizations are shallow, and the dialogue for Winona is even less-advanced baby talk than that of the Indians in <u>Luck</u> and <u>The Emigrant's Daughter</u>. When she overhears Dempsey plotting with one of his henchmen to abduct Mary, Winona soliloquizes:

> What say--carry off Mary? What for--money? Old Lester heap rich--give big ransom. Winona stop that!

Later on, when she is explaining it all to Jack Ralston, this exchange occurs:

Winona: Bad mens here--talk--say carry her off to mountains--git ransom--kill you. They here soon.

Ralston: You heard this?

Winona: Yes--Winona heard.[24]

And in her last scene:

Ralston: (<u>bends over Winona ...</u>) Winona! Look up! Speak to me, child. It's Jack; don't you know me?

Winona: Dear Jack--lift me up--me love you--me save you (<u>throws her arms around his neck</u>) Winona happy--Great Spirit calls her home--love--love --ah! (<u>arms fall and head sinks down.</u>)

Ralston: Winona! Winona! Dead, dead, dead! (<u>Lays her down.</u>)[25]

During the last quarter of the nineteenth century, the Indian participation in the performing arts continued to increase. Native Americans in Buffalo Bill Cody's plays and Wild West show were not the only ones to be seen by a theatre-

going public. In vaudeville, a form that crystallized in this
period, Indians continued to appear occasionally as they had
done in variety shows since the eighteenth century--or for
that matter since Columbus had presented his Carib troupe
at the court of Aragon. Some appeared in circus-like sur-
roundings, and their acts partook more of sports events
than of theatre. A group of Iroquois and Onondaga Indians,
for example, played their native lacrosse game for the public's
delectation in March 1878 at a New York arena called the
London Circus, and the next year, as Odell informs us, "Indian riders, Comanche and Iriquois [sic] made thrilling the
week of April 14" at the Aquarium.[26] On the west coast in
1887 a Seattle vaudeville house advertised Alaska Sam and
his Eskimo singers and dancers. The Eskimos were of course
free to roam as they wished in their homeland, since whites
had not yet discovered its hidden wealth, but for reservation
Indians, getting into show business must have been a welcome change from the monotony of their usual constricted
lives.

Despite their long history in vaudeville and circus,
however, Indians, like other ethnic performers, did not appear as intelligent speaking performers in stage productions
before the mid-twentieth century. The Indians in the Buffalo
Bill plays do not really count as actors since they were only
there to do an occasional specialty dance number and then to
fight and die on cue. In higher-class productions Indian
characters who had to speak lines, like Negro characters,
were always played by white actors in greasepaint of the appropriate tint.

Two serious plays, given excellent productions about
twenty years apart, show the consistency of the anti-Indian
attitudes of the time. They were written and produced by
two of the major figures of the American theatre, Augustin
Daly and David Belasco. The first is Daly's Horizon, first
performed at the Olympic Theatre in New York on March 12,
1871. One of Daly's few original pieces, Horizon is often considered his best play.[27] As in most of his plays, its polished
dialogue carries a note of satire, as in this first-act exchange
about Indians by a group of naive Easterners:

Mrs. Van Dorp: But the Indians--

Mr. Smith: Ah yes--the noble savage. I'll speak to

	him as his paleface brother. I've read the Leatherstocking stories, and I think I can manage 'em.
Alleyn:	No quarter to the savages, who murder women and children. But to the weak and oppressed I may be a friend. Duty commands no more.
Rowse:	Well, I'm going to take a case of dollar store jewelry out with me, and trade it for furs with the simple-minded red man. There's nothing like carrying civilization into the Far West. [28]

Mrs. Van Dorp's burden in life is that her husband and daughter vanished from Eastern society into the safe anonymity of a westbound emigrant train, and it is the destiny of heroic young Alleyn to go out West, locate them, and marry the daughter, Med. Sundowne Rowse, a lobbyist, turns out to be one of those enterprising movers who will hornswoggle Congress and the railroad interests out of land on which to build a pioneer town.

But in the elaborately worked-out plot of Horizon, a more focal character is an Indian, Wannemucka. Apparently a drunken young lout, Wannemucka is thrown out of the town of Rogue's Rest by the local vigilance committee along with other "undesirables," including an old sot named Wolf and his lovely daughter, Med. When Wannemucka offers to take care of Med, however, he finds that being companions in misfortune does not necessarily eliminate racial bigotry:

Wannemucka:	(Coming forward): Wannemucka friend! No leave old Wolf to die by the dogs. In-jun honest! Take care of young white girl.
Wolf:	You! Trust my child to you!
Wannemucka:	Indian honest! ... Wannemucka chief of tribe. Take white maiden there. Be a princess.
Med:	(Terrified): Oh, father! (Clinging to Wolf)

Wolf: You copper-colored scoundrel. You dare to
               think of my daughter--a lady-- (Strikes him)[29]

From this point, in Act II, Wannemucka becomes the
play's villain. First he kills Wolf, then, with the aid of
other Indians, he attacks a river boat from which he abducts
Med and takes her to his village to be his second wife. His
Indian bride, Onata, becomes concerned:

> The maidens rejoice that their warriors have re-
> turned, but not that they bring white women to the
> tribe.... Onata needs no slave whose face is like
> the white moon, and shines through all the lodge.[30]

But her objection is overruled. Alleyn discovers that Med
is Mrs. Van Dorp's long-lost daughter and rescues her from
the Indians. So Wannemucka is foiled in his villainy and
then killed, and the play ends with the white people safe,
the Indians put down, and "progress" promised for the
prairie.

More than twenty years separate Daly's Horizon from
David Belasco's two plays of western adventure, The Girl I
Left Behind Me (1893, in collaboration with Franklyn Fyles,
a New York Sun play reviewer) and The Girl of the Golden
West (1905), yet in them no advance is noticeable in characterization of Indians on the stage, nor any development of
understanding of the Indian problem that brought on the
Plains Wars. Charles Frohman had apparently asked Belasco
to write a play for the opening of his beautiful new Empire
Theatre at 39th Street and Broadway in New York, and
Belasco complied with The Girl I Left Behind Me, which
opened there (after a tryout week in Washington), on January
25, 1893.

> I had made up my mind [Belasco wrote] to try to
> bring on the American stage a phase of American
> life, on our Western frontiers, involving the Ameri-
> can Indian, in a new way.... At that time, early
> in 1892, the Indian troubles in the West were much
> in the public mind. The fierce insurrections of 1876,
> under the leadership of Sitting Bull, Crazy Horse,
> Spotted Tail, and others, and the lamentable slaugh-
> ter of the gallant Custer and his intrepid followers
> in the terrible battle at the Little Bighorn (June 25,
> that year), had not been forgotten.[31]

In other words, he intended to utilize saleable, currently popular subject matter and perpetuate attitudes, rigidified sixteen years before, for a public he shrewdly expected to think as he did. As for the "new way" in which he had decided to bring the American Indian on the American stage (in phraseology worthy of Ned Buntline), a few lines in the first act suffice to make an Indian character sound a bit more outspoken than other such characters in similar plays of the time. In these lines, John Ladru, or Scar Brow, a Blackfoot chieftain, describes his tribesmen's grievances, but the effectiveness of the speech is quickly dispelled by his taking action against a frontier outpost when its commanding officer bluntly refuses to do anything about the injustices Ladru has complained of. Audience sympathy is then twisted toward the white dramatis personae, and the Indians become the blackest of villains.

The Girl I Left Behind Me is a military melodrama rife with sentimental concern about soldiers' honor in a Plains outpost and laden with manufactured suspense over Indian menace and the fate of the post's occupants. Kate Kennion, visiting her father, a general at this Plains redoubt, is unhappily betrothed to Lieutenant Parlow but in love with Lieutenant Hawkesworth (both serving in the post's garrison). Parlow, a dastard who has seduced and abandoned another officer's wife, causes the loss of several men during a skirmish with Indians through his cowardly behavior, for which he blames Hawkesworth. But, after a thrilling Indian attack on the fortress, Parlow is exposed, the Cavalry arrives to save the "lost" outpost, and Kate marries Hawkesworth.

A highlight of the first act is the council scene in which the Blackfoot leaders Ladru, Fell-an-Ox, and Silent Tongue come to the post to confer with General Kennion and Major Burleigh:

Ladru: General Kennion, your soldiers are scattering our braves at the sun dance.

Kennion: Your education, Ladru, should free you from these old superstitions.

Ladru: The good priest taught me much, but he did not make me forget the wrongs of my people....

Burleigh: Our government provides liberally for you.

Ladru: (Addressing Kennion) Since Last winter's cold
and hunger, the rations have grown smaller
and poorer, and last month there was no food
at all.

Burleigh: (Brusquely) Silent Tongue's men seemed ready
enough yesterday to help themselves.

Kennion: Let us listen, major.

Ladru: (Ignoring Burleigh) When Silent Tongue's men
take the cattle to feed their hungry women and
children (Turns to Burleigh) you call them
thieves and drive them back to their tepees,
where the next snow may fall upon their graves.
General, I did not come to speak of these
things, but to ask you to keep your soldiers
from interfering with our worship.

Kennion: The military has no option.

Ladru: You are Christians, because you choose to be,
but you deny to us the sacred rites handed
down from our fathers. (Pointing to Fell-an-
Ox and Silent Tongue) These are human
beings. Raise your voice for them.

Kennion: I am powerless.

          . . .

Ladru: Then if we begin our great annual sun dance
tomorrow, you will stop it?

Kennion: (Firmly) The order is imperative.

Ladru: (Rising and speaking with vehement protest)
This is monstrous. (With intense feeling) You
have taken from us every earthly right, and
now are we to have no God?

Kennion: I must enforce the policy directed from Washington. [32]

Unlike the military, playwrights of Belasco's old-fashioned melodramatic persuasion believe in obeying orders to the letter, stressing the "policy dictated from Washington" to a "powerless" commanding officer who "has no option" before an "imperative" order. Some of the worst disasters of Plains warfare (Custer's, for one) were the result of a cavalier flouting of orders sometimes as arbitrary as Kennion's, but sometimes more humane and reasonable than the officers in question liked. Intentional misconstruction of orders resulted in the My-Lais of the nineteenth century, such as the massacre of undefended villages by Chivington at Sand Creek, Colorado, in 1864 and by Custer at the Washita River in 1868, among numerous others. Kennion's cold negativism is of a piece with the thinking that brought on those atrocities: Belasco's vaunted "realism" is present much less in his exact reproductions of place and his dictatorial stage directions than in his dramatizing of anti-Indian attitudes to which he clearly subscribed without reservation.

The improbable plot of Belasco's later western thriller, The Girl of the Golden West, includes two supposed Indians. The white heroine, Minnie, though absolutely pure and virtuous, runs a saloon in a California mining settlement of Gold Rush days. The plot turns on Minnie's falling in love with a notorious bandit who, we are asked to believe, turns out to be her equal in virtue and purity of character. Minnie has a maidservant called Wowkle, an Indian girl, apparently the only other female (if barely a human one) in the camp. Wowkle also has a boyfriend, a thieving redskin drunk named Billy Jackrabbit. Billy appears in the first act cadging drinks at Minnie's saloon, the Polka, and then has a brief scene at the opening of Act Two with Wowkle, intended as comic relief from the seriousness of Minnie's romantic story. Though they are unmarried, Wowkle has born Billy a child which she carries about in its cradleboard. They discuss, in the crudest pidgin English, their white superiors' promises that if they will get married there will be some attractive gifts of beads and whiskey for them. They agree that they may not want to stay married to each other for more than a few months, and the scene ends with Billy's insistence that she come and sleep with him as soon as she can leave her mistress for the evening. Belasco has sketched in these comic grotesques--and they might be of the same tribe--in the manner of Mark Twain's Indians in Roughing It, for whom Twain showed such contempt.

The plays examined in this chapter show that the Native American seemed to have no stage future except as a despised comic figure or an outright villain, in neither case drawn as anything more than a caricature of a human being. The most typical and successful plays of the entire period showed Indians in the worst possible light. Although intended for different classes of audiences, the plays of Augustin Daly, J. J. McCloskey, and David Belasco served the same purpose as those of the lesser hacks who provided Buffalo Bill Cody with pieces to perform. All these plays perpetuated racist attitudes which the creators and purveyors of such material accepted and thought (with some reason) most acceptable to a general audience and quite in line with government thinking of the time. And they all reached far wider audiences than any in which Indians are shown in a more positive way--and more nearly human--such as Thomas Dunn English's The Mormons, The Emigrant's Daughter, and probably the latter-day reworkings of the Leatherstocking tales. The considered attitudes of Henry Clay Preuss in his unfortunately little-known Fashions and Follies of Washington Life and later interesting attempts at characterizing Indians, as in The Mormons, were far from common. It is also unfortunate that even the most sympathetic creators of Indian characters were unable to make them speak anything other than a cliché pigdin English which does credit neither to author nor character.

As for believable Native American presences on the stage in the latter half of the nineteenth century, the score is not high. Indians in vaudeville and circus appearances were rare exotics whom audiences looked at as they looked at animals in a zoo. It was easier to accept the old patterns of Noble Savage and Pathetic Dusky Maiden, and the newer one of bloody Redskin Villain. Of the three, however, it was the Redskin Villain, increasingly present, who won out in visibility and numbers. The Indian characters are caricatures, and most often the white characters are no more subtly developed. The purpose, and the effect, in the drawing of both white characters and red is to display a condemnation and sternly negative view of Indians. It now remains to be seen what more positive appearance Native Americans made on the stage in the years between the Civil War and World War I.

NOTES

1. Henry Clay Preuss, Fashions and Follies of Washington Life. A Play in Five Acts. (Washington, D.C.: The Author, 1857), pp. 58-59.

2. Ibid., p. 59

3. Ibid., p. 3.

4. George R. MacMinn, Theatre of the Golden Era in California (Caldwell, Ida.: Caxton Printers, 1941), pp. 185 and 245.

5. Gene Jones, Where the Wind Blew Free (New York: W. W. Norton, 1967), pp. 82 ff. (Chapter 5, "Search for the Tattooed Girl").

6. MacMinn, Golden Era Theatre, p. 245.

7. Frank L. Fenton, "The San Francisco Theatre, 1849-1859" (Ph.D. dissertation, Stanford University, 1942), p. 406.

8. Thomas Dunn English, The Mormons; or, Life at Salt Lake City. A Drama in Three Acts (New York: Samuel French, 1858), p. 7.

9. James J. McCloskey, Across the Continent, in Richard Moody, Dramas From the American Theatre 1762-1909 (Boston: Houghton Mifflin, 1966), p. 531.

10. Jay Monaghan, The Great Rascal: The Life and Adventures of Ned Buntline (Boston: Little, Brown, 1952), pp. 19-21.

11. Nellie Snyder Yost, Buffalo Bill, His Family, Friends, Fame, Failures, and Fortunes (Chicago: Sage Books, The Swallow Press, 1979), pp. 60-61.

12. The extant copy of this play in the Harvard Theatre Collection is a typed promptscript with a title page which reads "Buffalo Bill The King of the Border Men. Dramatized from Ned Buntline's Story by Fred G. Meader Esq." It may be assumed that, despite retention of the original title (which was not kept after the various New York runs), this was a copy used during the 1873-1874 season, since it is altered to include a role for Wild Bill Hickok, who joined the company in the fall of 1873.

13. Yost, Buffalo Bill, pp. 69-70.

14. Quoted in Yost, Buffalo Bill, p. 70.

15. George C. D. Odell, Annals of the New York Stage, 15 volumes (New York: Columbia University Press, 1927-1949), vol. XI, p. 278.

16. Yost, Buffalo Bill, p. 166.

17. Thomas C. Cochran and Wayne Andrews, eds., Concise Dictionary of American History (New York: Charles Scribner's Sons, 1962), p. 1017.

18. Henry Blackman Sell and Victor Weybright, Buffalo Bill and the Wild West (New York: Oxford University Press, 1955), pp. 135-136.

19. Ibid., pp. 223-224.

20. Brian W. Dippie, The Vanishing American: White Attitudes and U. S. Indian Policy (Middletown, Conn.: Wesleyan University Press, 1982), p. 201.

21. Joseph I. C. Clarke, Luck. A Comedy in Three Acts. Printed But Not Published (New York: DeLacy and Willson, 1877), p. 39.

22. Len Ellsworth Tilden, The Emigrant's Daughter. a Border Drama, in Three Acts (Clyde, Ohio: The Ames Company, 1884), p. 5.

23. Ibid., p. 8.

24. Charles Townsend, Border Land. A Drama in Three Acts (Chicago: Dramatic Publishing Co., c. 1889), pp. 18-19.

25. Ibid., p. 25.

26. Odell, Annals, vol. X, pp. 487 and 694.

27. Arthur Hobson Quinn, A History of the American Drama From the Civil War to the Present Day, 2 vols. (New York: F. C. Crofts, 1939), vol. I, pp. 14, 38.

28. Augustin Daly, Horizon. An Original Drama of Contemporary Society and of American Frontier Perils. In Five Acts and Seven Tableaux. (New York: Printed, As Manuscript Only, For the Author, 1885), p. 16.

29. Ibid., p. 29.

30. Ibid., p. 60.

31. Quoted by Glenn Hughes and George Savage in their introductory note to The Girl I Left Behind Me in Barrett Clark, ed., America's Lost Plays, 21 vols. (Princeton, N.J.: Princeton University Press, 1940; reprint, Bloomington: Indiana University Press, 1965), vol. XVIII, p. 104.

32. David Belasco, The Girl I Left Behind Me, in Clark, ed., America's Lost Plays, vol. XVIII, pp. 120-121.

Chapter VII

GOOD INDIANS, NOT DEAD

Despite the low point the Native American had reached on
the stage (as in reality) in the last quarter of the nineteenth
century, there was an undercurrent of sympathetic consideration for him in this period that eventually emerged in strong
statements made by several playwrights.

The most scurrilous libels of his character and way of
life were seen at the lower end of the dramatic scale, in the
Buffalo Bill plays and their close relations in popular melodrama. But at the higher end, in successful "class" plays
such as Daly's and Belasco's, there was little difference in
attitudes of hate and denigration. To these writers the Indian was a drunken bum, a murderous villain, a white villain's
willing tool, or a white hero's comic sidekick. He was never
simply a respectable everyday man whose cultural background
differed from that of Americans of European ancestry.

The countercurrent that led away from these views of
the Indian may be seen in the closet drama of the time and,
more particularly, in the revival of theatrical interest in Pocahontas and other Indian heroines. This latter development
may have been the result of a feminine stimulus that had
never before been so strong. From the time of the first convention on women's rights at Seneca Falls, New York, in
1848, women's movements constantly increased in power,
changing and strengthening the position of women in American society in countless ways. By extension, women's influence in literature and the arts also increased. The far-
reaching effect of one woman's articulate interest was more
than conspicuous in Harriet Beecher Stowe's Uncle Tom's
Cabin and would be repeated, albeit on a far smaller scale,
with Helen Hunt Jackson's two books on the 1880s, A Century
of Dishonor and Ramona. In the future, when the twentieth
century began, the current would flow on in the growing

pageant movement (supported largely by women's groups) and in a few important commercially produced plays.

In the closet drama of the 1870s, however, markedly different views are sometimes propounded, and most examples of these non-theatrical plays show the Indian in a positive light. In a short, pageant-like school piece called <u>Home</u>, four girls are given sentimental verse speeches about the virtues of America as "Home."[1] Two are immigrants, one Scotch and the other Swiss, the third is an "American" girl, and the last is an Indian (of no specific tribe). The first three girls spout platitudes that must have been much in the air in those years just before the great Centennial celebrations of 1876. The "Indian maid," however, delivers a tearful soliloquy about how the white men hounded her people off their homeland. The speech is of particular interest for its sympathetic, if sentimentalized, view of Indians at this time. It was published in 1873, at the height of the Plains Wars and well before champions of the Indian such as Helen Hunt Jackson published anything reflecting the real state of Indian life at the time.

A differing view is expounded in a piece called <u>Centennial Movement, 1876</u>, apparently a failed attempt at a commercial play and intended (with little success) as a satire.[2] It contains a scene in a hotel lobby in which a Wild West character, a kind of Buffalo Bill parody, appears and patronizingly introduces three Indian chiefs he has brought with him. They are clearly intended to be part of some profit-making venture for him, but this is not elaborated on. The Indians do not speak for themselves. A Negro congressman arrives and is insulted by the frontiersman, who pushes him out of the way to present his Indians, commenting that he supposes nowadays everyone will have to get used to letting Blacks get into front positions at the expense of the Indians. The writing is clumsy and uncertain, but the playwright's attitude toward Indians (and Blacks) is as sour and unpleasant as that of his one-dimensional characters.

A much more ambitious project is a vast five-part dramatic epic of the New England Indians, <u>Battle of the Bush</u> by an amateur historical dramatist, Robert Boodey Caverly; after his name on the title page of each play appears the identification "Poet and Historian." "Drama No. 1," as he categorizes it, is <u>Last Night of a Nation</u>, and it is concerned

with Sassacus, "King of the Pequots," and the end of his
tribe in the Puritans' war of 1637. "Drama No. 2," Miantonimoh, brings us a character familiar from the play versions
of Cooper's Wish-Ton-Wish, ending with his murder in 1643.
Typical of the dialogue in all these pieces is the entrance
speech of Canonicus, a follower of Miantonimoh in this play:

> Ah! me fear ye. White-man me no trust more!
> Government no trust me! English accuse Miantonimo
> of wrongs! He my friend! English wolves in sheep-
> skins! Ye be guilty of many wrongs.[3]

All the Indians throughout the five plays exclaim their lines
in this same cryptic pidgin language.

"Drama No. 3" is a version of the Wampanoags' story
called King Philip. "Drama No. 4," The Regicides, is about
the killers of King Charles I in America, who occasionally
communicate with Indians for ulterior purposes. "Drama No.
5," Chocorua in the Mountain, is the story of a legendary
"Last Indian." Each piece is preceded by a long introduction, a retelling of the "Legend," as Caverly heads it, on
which the play is based. He begins each introduction in a
vein sympathetic to his Indian heroes but allows his comments
to fall into the standard clichés of his time. In the introduction to the first drama, he comments, "From the lamentable
destruction of the 'heathen tribes' by the combined agencies
of war and the plague prior to their coming here, the Pilgrims took courage,"--the accepted implication that the Indians were a doomed and vanishing race before the Puritans
began their genocidal relations with them--and then repeatedly
quotes, with apparent approval, from Cotton Mather's anti-
Indian diatribes and refers to the "necessity" of exterminat-
ing the Pequots.[4] All the plays are heavily footnoted, partly
with references to reliable historical sources, but equally
with references to Caverly's own verse "epics," as he calls
them, apparently as voluminous as these pretentious "plays."

A livelier piece, Canonicus, by a playwright with a
famous namesake, Alexander Hamilton, is the most interesting
and dramatically valid of all closet dramas about Indians.[5]
But, like most closet dramas, it is derivative and old-fashioned
in style and form. Canonicus was a real historical figure
(like his compatriot Miantonimoh), as were his son Samosacus
and, of course, Roger Williams, with whom Canonicus has some

dealings in this play. Samosacus has been kidnapped as a boy and taken away on an English ship. Now an adult, he returns, rejects his affianced bride Moina, and marries Nyana, a girl who turns out to be treacherous and unfaithful. Moina throws herself from a high rock into a lake, Canonicus laments at length, and Samosacus, seeing Moina dead and finding that Nyana has betrayed and deserted him, stabs himself. Canonicus also dies, apparently of grief.

Canonicus is written in rather inflated, "antiqued" prose. When the hero encounters his friend Roger Williams after Williams' rejection by his fellow Puritans, Canonicus comes out with: "Pale-face brother, thou hast my heart; here art welcome. Last moon thou wert in favor; what thy fault with thy pale-faced friends?"[6] In later passages, Canonicus, addressing his white and Indian enemies, has speeches reminiscent of some in Metamora:

(Thunder heard)

Canonicus: Hear'st thou that voice? Aye, thou tremblest at the sound. Canonicus knows its portent. In the voice of truth, which he has ever worshipped, ever followed, Canonicus has no fear! Canonicus bows to no man![7]

In his long dying speech, which closes the play (reminding us of Ponteach's final harangue in Rogers' play), he curses the green and well-watered spot of ground where he has fallen:

Canonicus: A thousand deer have fattened here and fallen. Not a blade shall it ever bear, for the pale-faces' use. My curse is on it.
Canonicus, the last of the Naragansetts, is avenged!
(He swoons and dies, and the curtain falls to slow music)[8]

In a cast of fifteen, only five are whites, and Hamilton has taken the opportunity to make his Indian characters, for all their dated rhetoric, distinct and interestingly varied, although Canonicus, Samosacus, and Moina are portrayed only as familiar Noble Savages of the most admirable noble-Roman type. The general tone of the piece is entirely sympathetic toward these latter-day fantasy Indians, at least implying that the writer's attitude toward actual Native Americans would not be unsimilar.

The New England Indians continued to hold interest for study-bound dramatists, as in Alfred A. Furman's <u>Philip of Pokanoket</u>, in which the principals are "Pometacom, called Philip, Chief of the Wampanoags," and his son Metacomet. [9] Furman's approach to the material, though not unlike Hamilton's, is somewhat more stilted. We are asked to believe that Philip and his cohorts always speak in neo-Jacobean lines such as these:

> Wake, dogs of war! and with your ulcered tongues
> Lick up the drops that so untimely flowed,
> Till your swart veins shall swell to mountain-size
> And burst in pitiless havoc on the land.
> With solemn hand married to your redress,
> I now unbelt my hatred of the whites;
> And bid it roam sleepless the bounds of earth
> In quest of blood to sate its appetite. [10]

Philip is an eminently Noble Savage, but the playwright gives us to understand that he had quite the wrong idea about holding on to his tribe's ancestral lands. The Puritans, he implies, were justified in their assaults on those Red Devils the Wampanoags. To keep the peace, it was necessary to slaughter them all.

<u>Philip of Pokanoket</u> has a subplot of some interest. A female "sachem" called Wenonah has been having a love affair with Church, a white officer captured by Philip during the course of the play. In trying to save Church when the vengeful Philip orders his death, Wenonah is killed. Church escapes back to the Puritans' ranks, mourning his dusky love, and then overcomes the Wampanoags for his poeple. The best one can say for this overblown piece is that it gives equal weight, unlike most other pieces utilizing both, to the themes of the Noble Savage and the Pathetic Dusky Maiden.

A notable put-down of a Dusky Maiden occurs in a weak closet melodrama, <u>Blennerhassett's Island</u>, in which one of the most interesting stories of intrigue in the entire realm of American history is wasted. [11] Aaron Burr, in the later part of his career, conspired to get control of western lands to create a new country of which, it was said, he dreamed of becoming the first emperor. In this wild conspiracy, he involved the army explorer General James Wilkinson and a man called Blennerhasset, who owned an island in the lower Ohio River from which some of the actions of the conspiracy were conducted. Little of this story is used in the script. The only Indian character in it is a girl called Mahala. She appears only in comic-relief scenes with two pointedly lower-class men, "Mike Fink," with whom she is eventually induced to make a sexual arrangement, and another older man whom she rejects. Mahala displays no native characteristics whatever; she is written more in the tradition of the Romp character. By any standard the character is false and shallow, and apparently present only because the writer felt that a sluttish female who commended no respect would be amusing paired with the rugged Frontiersmen-comics. In the 1890s the label "Indian" served the purpose.

Quite opposite thinking is propounded in an interesting piece that features a Mexican Indian heroine. The playwright, Daniel Brinton, was a practicing physician and also a scholar on the subject of the early post-Conquest history of Mexico and its Indians. His play, Maria Candelaria, is based on historical fact.[12] It is about a revolt in the state of Chiapas in 1712, led mainly by a twenty-year-old girl, the heroine of the title. Maria carries on an ancient Mayan tradition of a priestess being a dominant leader of her community in war and in peace. To the Spaniards' dismay, the Indians have blended their own pagan religious practice with Catholicism in services conducted by Maria. The Indians fight to be free of Spanish oppression, but their rebellion fails. Maria's fiancé is killed in battle, and she leaps from a cliff-edge into an abyss.

Brinton's play is partly in verse and partly prose, with unexceptional uses of both. Although overlong and not well organized, it treats an appealing subject and is filled with ideas that were coming to the fore at that time about women's rights and equality of the sexes and of races. It even contains some rather erotic passages that would not have been spoken on the stage in the Nineties. Also it is one of the most pro-Indian of all these closet pieces.

Several Canadian writers of this period also found Indians a stimulus for non-theatrical drama. In Laura Secord,

The Heroine of 1812,[13] a verse play about a woman who foils a Yankee attempt to take a British fortification, the Americans are made to look bad, but "Mishe-Mo-Qua (The Great Bear), a Mohawk Chief" and his small band of noble native followers are rewarded with kind words from a British officer when they save Laura Secord from the wicked Yankees.

A more flamboyant piece is De Roberval, a story of the time of Cartier's explorations in Canada told in arch and imposing blank verse. The Sieur De Roberval, an early governor of Canada, is characterized as a swashbuckler skilled at coping with bad situations such as argumentative conflicts with Indian chiefs. Not unexpectedly, there is a girl, Ohnawa, an Iroquois, who attaches herself to him. But colonial politics take precedence in this plot, and little time is wasted on the Indian characters.[14]

Both Tecumseh and Thayandenegea (also in verse of sorts) treat Indian problems of the Canadians' southern neighbors. The former,[15] strongly pro-Indian, makes heroes of its historical Indians so shallowly that they emerge as characterless, "noble" cyphers. Thayandenegea (the Indian more familiarly known as Joseph Brant, who supported the British forces in the Revolutionary War) shows its hero as an admirable warrior, but makes other Indians dubious allies of the whites who should be extirpated for the sake of the white man's progress. Unfortunately, the verse in Thayandenegea is so obfuscated that its complexities sometimes need a kind of translation before the action or point of a scene can be made out.

The Columbus quadricentennial and its attendant public celebrations in the early 1890s inspired several pieces about the discoverer, which included appearances of Caribbean natives. In Columbus; or, A Hero of the New World,[17] two Carib women, the enforced wives of Spanish settlers, are seen briefly. This piece was intended for amateur production. A later Columbus, in stilted verse, has the familiar scene of the hero presenting his Carib charges at the Spanish court. He describes them as "these brave people, sons of God like us, / With generous natures and compliant wills."[18] The writer liked the period enough to include with publication of this work a pseudo-historical Indian drama called The Aztec God. Still another work, Christopher Columbus,[19] described on its title page as "The Catholic Play of the Year.

The World's Fair Drama ... Written for the Quadricentenniel
Celebration of the Discovery of America." In the landing
scene in San Salvador, Columbus punishes a sailor for trying to tear gold rings from the nose and ears of an Indian,
and of course a native group is shown later in the usual
court scene. But they are uncharacterized, nameless props
rather than people.

Yet, despite the minimizing of Indian characters in some
of these works and the reiteration of character stereotypes
in many others, the aggregate effect of this group of non-
theatrical dramas is a pro-Indian point of view. "Pro-Indian,"
however, does not necessarily mean that Native Americans
were dramatized as real human beings. When such attempts
were made by these amateur authors, the effort at characterization was put into white characters. In pieces such as
Centennial Movement, 1876 and Blennerhassett's Island, Indians were made the butt of racist jokes, while in R. B.
Caverly's five-part work and Furman's Philip of Pokanoket
they are heroized, but their extirpation is accepted as necessary for "Progress." Nevertheless, a general sense of acceptance of Indians and Indian life is present, and it is
stressed in plays such as Canonicus and the Canadian pieces.
As we shall see, this feeling continued and grew, so that in
general a more sympathetic concept of Indians was to become
common in the theatre as in the library by the turn of the
century. Soon after it, "Bad Injuns" were to become the
property of the movies.

A popular rediscovery of this period was the national
Indian heroine, Pocahontas. Considering the plays that were
turned out, it is one that would have profited from a re-
viewing by more professional theatre writers. The first of
these works is a curiosity very like an early nineteenth-
century pantomime, colorful, melodramatic, and fantastic, but
using Indians only as a taking-off point. It is called Pocahontas and is described by its author as "A Melo-Drama in
Five Acts."[20] Interest in the Indian characters is incidental;
the plot focuses on the English colonists' internal conflicts,
set in a fanciful Jamestown that never was. Powhatan and
his priests are noble but shifty, and Pocahontas is a sweetly
cute, wholly unbelievable singing lady. Typical of the writing, with obvious borrowings from Longfellow, is the description of her entrance:

Citizen: Aye, sure she is enchanted!!

Rolfe: What I told you, she's a fairy,
And a princess of the forest,
And this troop who wait upon her,
Are her courtiers--maids of honor,
And, though like some gipsy's daughter,
She is often here among us--
Singing songs the winds have taught her,
Singing songs the birds have sung us,
She's not less a chieftain's daughter--
Chieftain of the woods, the prairies,
King of all the tribes of warriors.[21]

Indian "royalty" is given this kind of verbal treatment, but when the commoner braves come to attack the colony a descriptive line reads, "Look how they crouch and skulk among the trees"--unhuman and animal-like. But the plain-living white pioneers' way of life is hardly a match for the Indians' style. "Act 3rd, Scene 1st" opens in Powhatan's "court" in the woods. "He is surrounded by his most beautiful women and greatest warriors. The king reclining on beautiful skins. The scene is eastern. An Indian girl dances before the court...."[22] Another production number closes the act, a "ballet and Indian corn-dance," during which "the harvest goddess, clothed as Ceres, enters and is welcomed by the chorus."[23]

Ten years after this fantasy piece was published, there appeared in Chicago a fantasy of a different kind, a "burlesque operetta in two acts," also called Pocahontas by Welland Hendricks.[24] The "airs" for its songs were not original but, in the tradition of ballad opera, included familiar tunes such as "Polly-Wolly-Doodle" and "Jingle Bells."

Although lacking the wit and pungency of its ancestor, John Brougham's Po-Ca-Hon-Tas; or, The Gentle Savage, the libretto is competent, professional, and pertinent. It comments on current events, and it draws in the "Darky" and the "Injun" as standard joke stage figures of the time. Mahogany, a comic black servant, introduces himself with, "I'm a dusky dude from Darkeyville," and there is much joking about his potential sexual connections with Pocahontas and other Indian girls. The attitudes toward land-grabbing and money-centered Americans resembled those that had been

popular in the 1850s, as Brougham showed us. When John
Smith meets Powhatan in Act I, he sings:

> Now, Mister Powhatan,
> Just listen unto me;
> We've come from Mother England
> That's across the sea.
> Our island's getting crowded,
> We'd like to buy some land;
> We'll pay your higher price, sir,
> For we boys have got the sand.

Chorus: O Mister Injun, please listen to our song;
               We're tender hearted fellows who never do a
               wrong.

> We don't want very much, sir,
> Say, from the Gulf up to the Lakes;
> And at the broad Pacific
> We'll set the western stakes.
> We'll pay a silver dollar
> (Aside) That's worth only eighty cents,
> And draw our note to balance
> (Aside) Payable fourteen centuries hence.

Chorus: O Mister Injun, please listen to our song;
               We're tender hearted fellows who never do a
               wrong.

> We shall start a little nation
> On the mutual benefit plan,
> Where birth and brains are nothing,
> And where money makes the man.
> We'll make gov'nors of your sachems,
> Put a state house in the thicket,
> And run you for our pres'dent
> On the Demipublican ticket.

Chorus: O Mister Injun, please listen to our song;
               We're tender hearted fellows who never do a
               wrong.[25]

Powhatan, who is a rather bland, sad character, mildly accepts this folderol without objection. At the beginning of
the second act he sings a little song to his daughter with
words that expressed an old yearning of the palefaces:

And now, my darling dear, I must soon go away;
Away to the woods I must go, dear,
And this gift I leave,
The best to receive,--
The blessing of your father on you, dear.

. . .

The pale-face has come; the red man must go,--
Go from the grounds that he loves, dear,
And you who remain
Shall sing this refrain,--
The blessing of your father on you, dear.[26]

Burlesque operettas such as Hendrick's Pocahontas
were competing in these years with the rising form of entertainment called vaudeville, which not infrequently included
the Indian presence in its variety format. Real Indians sometimes appeared in vaudeville, but more often their presence
was shown in one-act farcical scenes in which Indian characters were part of an elaborate joke. Two pieces by a performer called Charles White ("the celebrated Ethiopian come-
dian") and offered to the audiences of the Theatre Comique
in New York in the 1870s indicate to us what was laughable
about Indians to variety-show audiences then.

In The Rehearsal; or, Barney's Old Man, a young actor, stymied by a visit of his naive and over-curious parents
to the big city, takes them to rehearsal, with disastrous results. The harassed stage manager, to get them out of his
hair, dresses up actors as Indians and has the old couple
chased out of the theatre.[27] In The Bogus Indian, the title
is misleading since the Indian is real. A failing lawyer cons
a rich young lady out of five hundred dollars for his "char-
ity" for the "Oregon Indian tribes." He also promises to
bring her a real Indian chief, an object she thinks would be
decorative in her parlor; she gets an actress friend to dress
as a squaw so the chief will feel at home there. The lawyer
finds a medicine show quack who sells him an Indian for
fifteen dollars, one of a troupe the quack has hired but who
got drunk on their advance pay. At the lady's home, the
Indian cavorts in a wild dance which terrifies the lady, her
friend, and her comic black servant, and wrecks her parlor.[28]

The targets of ridicule in these pieces are less the

meddlesome white parents than the supposedly frightening wild Indians, less the ostentatious rich lady than her comic black servant and her pet Indian. The attitude is patronizing, assuming that Indians are drunk whenever possible and can only behave in a wild and uncontrollable manner in any white society.

A similar piece called Society Acting satirizes a social fad of the 1890s, private dramatic performances in the elegant drawing rooms of the well-to-do, and shows little change of attitude toward Indians.[29] While the master and mistress are away, Jenny, the chambermaid, gets the other servants to participate in her boyfriend's play. One of the servants is dressed up as Metamora and spounts parodies of lines from Stone's still-famous play. When Mr. Somerset, a friend of the master, turns up, the servant-Metamora scares him with much comic whooping and war-dancing and beats him with a comic war-club like a Greek comic actor's bladder. In a Keystone Kop-like chase scene, the other servants join Metamora to send Mr. Somerset on his way.

Slight and absurd as these sketches are, their Aristophanic social attitudes and dramatic elements give them a value equal to many more pretentious plays of the time. The championing of lower-class working people such as actors and house servants and the satirizing of nouveau-riche "society" people and shady lawyers give them strong dramatic thrust. The only unfortunate element is the racial bigotry that weighs as heavily as their positive virtues.

In the midst of this milieu of shallow, limited thinking and widespread rejection of Native Americans, in the theatre as in everyday life, there appeared in the 1880s first a novel and then its dramatic adaptation that were intended to be the Uncle Tom's Cabin of the Indians. Helen Hunt Jackson wrote Ramona to publicize the unhappy plight of the California Indians, and if it did not have quite the effect that Mrs. Stowe's bombshell had thirty years before, it nevertheless was quickly seen to be--and remains--a strong and clearsighted objection against injustices to Native Americans, as well as the most popular Indian story (except for those of Cooper) ever written.[30] Ina Dillaye's dramatization of the novel helped spread its fame. It was particularly popular as a road show and was eventually seen by millions more in its various film versions, as well as in an outdoor pageant production in Southern California from 1948 on.

Mrs. Jackson already had a long career as a writer of romantic hack fiction when she became interested in the history of the American Indians. In 1881 she published A Century of Dishonor, a stern indictment, carefully documented, of the United States' ruinously dishonest mismanagement of the Indians. It still reads, a hundred years after its publication, with considerable power. The book caused such controversy that the government appointed Mrs. Jackson to examine the problems of the Mission Indians of California, where she then lived. She completed a report in 1883, but the project became an exercise in futility. The character of the frustrated Indian agent in Ramona must have been based on her experience. Ramona was published in 1884. Mrs. Jackson died in 1885 at the early age of fifty-five.

Ina Dillaye's play Ramona is a romantic melodrama superior in its dialogue writing and dramatic effect to most such works of the period.[31] Several remarkably advanced points are made, mainly that Indians can be worthy, intelligent, and honorable people who have recognizable human instincts, including strong parental concerns, like the best of white people. Half-breeds are not necessarily devious and dishonest. Miscegenation, far from being a necessary taboo with ugly results when violated, is the accepted final action of the play. Considering the welter of incident and the several years' span of time it covers, Ramona is perhaps a little too economical, even arbitrary, in its adaptation of the novel, yet it strikes the reader as a cogent and well-made play.

Ramona lives on the California ranch of Señora Moreno, who is antagonistic to her because the Señora's wayward brother was Ramona's father and the girl's mother was an Indian. The Señora's son Philip loves Ramona, but she falls in love with Alessandro, a full-blood Indian and a brilliantly clever young hand on the ranch. Ramona elopes with him. Señora Moreno refuses to let them return to the ranch, and they are victimized and knocked from pillar to post by the new American owners of the country. Two years later, when their child lies dying, Alessandro, in a distracted state, takes a horse that does not belong to him to get to a white doctor. The doctor refuses to come out to help Indians, and Alessandro is killed by white vigilantes who find him with the missing horse. Ramona is taken in by Aunt Ri, a character representing the better kind of American pioneer settler than the rednecks who have harassed Ramona and Alessandro. Some time later, Ramona and Aunt Ri are resettled at the

Moreno ranch at Philip's invitation. Señora Moreno has died.
Philip persuades Ramona to marry him, so her future is
finally secured.

Dillaye's characters are clearly delineated, and the dialogue is polished. The three Indian characters in the play,
Ramona, Alessandro, and Carmena (a small role in Act IV),
speak everyday unstilted English, which is a nice enhancement of their portrayal as human beings rather than ethnic
grotesques. The white characters are mostly differentiated
by their dialects. Aunt Ri is a wise and open-minded Tennessee country woman who sees the good in Indians as she
does in whites. The Agent to whom Ramona appeals is an
educated, upper-class man helpless in the face of government
stupidity in its arbitrary dealings with the Indians. The
vigilantes are sharply limned as quite believable redneck
hoodlums--far more real than one-dimensional melodrama villains.

Ramona is a straightforward drama of decent people
victimized by bigotry. In contrast, the more simplistic action melodramas of the popular theatre persisted in maintaining their categories of good white men and villainous Indians
throughout this period, ultimately delivering the stereotypes,
neatly pigeonholed, to the movies. A group of melodrama
scripts from the end of the century stresses these harsh contrasts. The first is a five-act play, standard in form and
content and not unlike--and no less shallow than--the pieces
in which Buffalo Bill Cody chose to tour. Written by James
A. Herne (much admired for his later naturalistic drama,
Margaret Fleming), it is called The Minute Men of 1774-1775.
It purports to have to do with the Revolutionary War.[32]

The Minute Men is a contrived, sentimental, and violent
melodrama, part of whose plot turns on the discovery that
Roanoke, apparently a subservient but handsome and noble
young Indian, is really the long-lost son of an upper-class white
man. This allows Roanoke to marry one of the play's two
ingenues and shows up the villain as worse than we had at
first thought, since we learn that he had abducted poor Roanoke and sold him to a "Mohawk chief" when he was only a
toddler. There is also a crew of ogre-like redskins, the villain's henchmen, who are disposed of in a spectacle scene in
which a house where they are hiding is blown up, killing all
of them. Herne's attitude toward Indians was the standard

commercial one of the time--the only good ones were dead or, like Roanoke, could be proved to be white and the victim of some kind of villainy that put them in Indian hands.

A Southwestern curiosity, apparently never produced, is a very amateur "verse" play, Geronimo's Summer Campaign of 1885.[33] Clearly the work of an Indian-hater propagandizing against the Apaches, the work is not only nearly formless but so remarkably naive in writing and presentation, filled with wrong words, misspellings, and misconstructions of words, that it reads like a medieval folk play. Geronimo is described as an evil lecher and his "campaign" takes the from of abducting and trying to seduce a white rancher's wife. Throughout, there are references to the Apaches as bug eaters (one of them is called Wormsucker), and they all talk much like the naughty characters (such as Mak the sheep-thief) in Medieval cycle plays, continually boasting of their thievery. There are repeated sneering references to the Apaches as wearing little or nothing, and the writer seems obsessed with childish sex-talk. One is reminded of the expressions of latent homosexuality pointed out by Richard Drinnon in Nick of the Woods. This patch, in a scene with a white captive, is typical:

Geronimo: Well, well
These ball-headed [sic] agents from the East all lie
And steal. Tarantulahawk, you cut a strip
Of buck-skin from your long gee-string, and make
A slit thro' both his ears, and fasten them
Unto the bended branch with that good thong.

Tarantulahawk: I hate to shorten up my gee-string, chief,
You know I had to rustle hard to get
The buckdeer's hide to make it from. I scalped
The Mexican while he was tanning it.

Geronimo: You don't need much gee-string upon your front,
As pale-face says "three-inch" is long enough

For you.   Now there is our old neighbor
  chief
Eskiminzen, he's had so many wives,
It makes him need a gee-string to his
  knees.
       (They tie Dubran's ears to a limb
       with the thong)[34]

Remarkably, however, the naughty-little-boy, would-
be smutty talk gives these Indians a kind of reality that
never came about with the pretentious diction or pidgin English of most native characters in earlier plays.   The real conflict with the Apaches in 1885 is disregarded, and the piece,
hardly a play, ends inconclusively with a report that the Indians have retreated and been beaten.   It may be conjectured
that the playwright, G. D. Cummings, was a local writer,
perhaps a newspaper reporter caught up in the area's fear
of and savage retaliation against the Apaches.   Probably he
was occasionally exposed to performances of Shakespeare's
plays of those of nineteenth-cnetury playwrights and merely
emulated what he remembered of their style and technique.
The piece was apparently set up in type (and not edited or
proofread, if the writer was even aware of such practices) and
distributed by a printer in Phoenix or Albuquerque.

Writers who aspired to greater professionalism in melodrama tended to use Indians more as accent or comic relief
characters.   The Golden Gulch, a "Drama in Three Acts" of
1893, is typical.[35]   The writing is crude and glib, and hoary
with clichés.   Its sole native character is "Old Magnus, a
Degenerate Indian"--a blunt description of an unwanted parasite reminiscent of Boucicault's Wahnotee in The Octoroon.
The only attempt at characterizing him comes in the playwright's "Remarks" preceding the text: "Magnus is an Indian
of uncertain age.   He is straight and dignified in spite of
his rags.   Use the regular shade of 'Indian' greasepaint and
wear an Indian wig."[36]   Magnus appears in two brief scenes
in the second act, written like vaudeville skits.   In the first
his drunken mutterings frighten a Negro comic and a stage
Irishman; in the second he startles an amorous old maid who
at first mistakes him for a man she is after.

In The Girl From Klondike; or, Wide Awake Nell, "A
Comedy-Drama in Three Acts," this pattern is repeated.[37]
(The writer is Frank Dumont, who supplied the variety stage

with Society Acting, previously examined herein.) The Indian's name here is "Temperance Tom." He has no lines at all and is identified only by his bedraggled feathers and his flask. His purpose is to accent again a comic scene--he is posted as a guard over a recalcitrant black comic character who is being temporarily restrained. Temperance Tom takes several pulls on his flask, falls asleep, and then is dragged off stage and forgotten for the rest of the play.

A somewhat different tone is notable in Tatters, the Pet of Squatters' Gulch, "A Border Drama in Three Acts."38 The heroine is Titinia Timberlake, or Tatters, the respectable daughter of the local hotel owner. Tatters is in love with Robert Ferris, the young hero, who, however, is half-Indian and scorned by the rest of the community for that reason. But Robert also turns out to be the land-rich heir of a long-lost (white) father, who conveniently appears and explains all. The play ends with Tatters and Robert in a happy embrace, looking forward to a bright future.

The playwright is much in sympathy with Indians, as shown through his heroine and his hero--Robert and his recently deceased mother, although Indians, are hopelessly, sentimentally good people--and through his villainous characters who have only bad things to say about Indians. These villains also antagonize and mistreat Mose, a black servant, toward whom both Tatters and Robert are so friendly that Robert, through Mose's efforts, is saved from a lynch mob. Yet, contradictorily, the playwright seems to go out of his way to make all his characters antagonistic toward Jews. When Robert is disguised as a "Jew peddler" (so described in stage direction), Tatters calls him a "dirty old sheeny" and sends him on his way as a tramp. Tatters appeared in 1912, a time when, perhaps, the minorities Americans were most conscious of were Blacks, Indians, and Jews, and a playwright may well have had an almost compulsive urge to include his opinions on all three in his work. The most interesting dimension in this rather shallow play is the writer's sentimental, positive acceptance of the long-familiar American native and the Black man, coupled with rejection of the newest American, the immigrant Jew.

The American drama at the end of the nineteenth century, then, was marked by an ambivalence in treatment of Native Americans and other minority characters. Yet the

under-current of sympathy for Indians that had been growing for a quarter of a century was bound to have its day.
Stereotyped Indians continued to appear, but in some plays
the stereotypes gave way to near-naturalistic characterizations, and this in turn seems to have influenced a newly
broadminded view of Indians as real people. For the most
part the stereotypes would pass on to the movies, and sin-
cere attempts would now be made by playwrights to show Indians as natural and believable characters like the palefaces
whose world they were beginning more and more to share.

NOTES

1. Mary L. Cobb, Home, in Poetical Dramas for Home
and School (Boston: Lee and Shepard, 1873).
2. Nathan Appleton, Centennial Movement, 1876 (Boston: Lockwood, Brooks and Co., 1877).
3. Robert Boodey Caverly, Miantonimoh (Boston:
The Author, 1884), p. 78.
4. Idem, Last Night of a Nation, p. 5.
5. Alexander Hamilton, Canonicus. A Tragedy in
Five Acts. In Dramas and Poems (New York: Dick and Fitzgerald, [1877]).
6. Ibid., p. 38.
7. Ibid., p. 52.
8. Ibid., p. 54.
9. Alfred Antoine Furman, Philip of Pokanoket. An
Indian Drama (New York: Stettiner, Lambert & Co., 1894).
10. Ibid., p. 12.
11. Donn Piatt, Blennerhassett's Island, in Poems and
Plays (Cincinnati: Robert Clarke and Co., 1893).
12. Daniel Brinton, Maria Candelaria. An Historic
Drama from American Aboriginal Life (Philadelphia: David
McKay, 1897).
13. Sarah Anne Curzon, Laura Secord, The Heroine
of 1812. A Drama (Toronto: C. Blackett Robinson, 1887).
14. John Hunter Duvar, De Roberval (St. John, N.B.:
J. & A. McMillan, 1888).
15. Charles Mair, Tecumseh [1887], in Tecumseh ...
and Other Canadian Poems (Toronto: William Briggs, 1901).
16. James Bovell Mackenzie, Thayandenegea. An
Historico-Military Drama (Toronto: n.p., 1898).
17. Daniel S. Preston, Columbus; or, A Hero of the
New World. An Historical Play (New York: G. P. Putnam's
Sons, 1887).

18. George Lansing Raymond, Columbus [1893], in Collected Works (New York: G. P. Putnam's Sons, 1900).

19. Very Reverend M. M. A. Hartnedy, Dean, Christopher Columbus (Steubenville, Ohio: The Columbus Club, 1892).

20. Samuel H. M. Byers, Pocahontas (N.p.: n.p., [1875]).

21. Ibid., p. 16.

22. Ibid., p. 37

23. Ibid., p. 47.

24. Welland Hendricks, Pocahontas (Chicago: T. S. Denison and Company, 1886).

25. Ibid., pp. 6-7.

26. Ibid., pp. 10-11.

27. Charles White, The Rehearsal; or, Barney's Old Man (Chicago: Dramatic Publishing Co., 1876).

28. Charles White, The Bogus Indian (New York: Robert M. De Witt, 1875).

29. Frank Dumont, Society Acting (Chicago: Dramatic Publishing Co., 1898).

30. Robert E. Spiller et al., eds., Literary History of the United States (New York: Macmillan, 1963), p. 869.

31. Ina Dillaye, Ramona. A Play in Five Acts, Adapted from Helen Hunt Jackson's Indian Novel (Syracuse, N.Y.: Printed by F. LeC. Dillaye, 1887).

32. James A. Herne, The Minute Men of 1774-1775 in Barrett Clark, ed., America's Lost Plays, 21 vols. (Princeton, N.J.: Princeton University Press, 1940; reprint, Bloomington: Indiana University Press, 1959), vol. VII.

33. G. D. Cummings, Geronimo's Summer Campaign of 1885. A Drama (N.p.: n.p., 1890).

34. Ibid., p. 50

35. Charles Townsend, The Golden Gulch (New York: Fitzgerald Publishing, 1893).

36. Ibid., p. 6.

37. Frank Dumont, The Girl From Klondike; or, Wide Awake Nell (Chicago: Dramatic Publishing Co., 1898).

38. Levin C. Tees, Tatters, the Pet of Squatters' Gulch (Philadelphia: n.p., 1912).

Chapter VIII

FIRST AMERICANS ON THE AMERICAN
STAGE IN THE NEW CENTURY

As American theatre moved into the twentieth century, increasingly milder views of Indians continued to gain ground, slowly but steadily, with the theatre-going public. Of course the popular melodrama circuit persisted in showing Indians as the blackest villains, and that version of Indian character was swiftly being transmuted into the film medium, which would continue for almost another half century to see dead Indians as the only good ones. In vaudeville, the Indian was good for a laugh; in pageants and on the opera stage, his way of life could be elaborated on for spectacular effect. And in several major plays the old clichés of Noble Savage and Pathetic Dusky Maiden were reworked in attractive ways to gain the greatest audience sympathy and interest.

William C. DeMille's Strongheart was a notably successful example of the new thinking about Native Americans on the legitimate stage. Strongheart opened at the Hudson Theatre in New York on January 30, 1905, with a much-admired star, Robert Edeson, in the title role.[1] Presented as a smooth "society drama" in the vein of Pinero (and it is a skillful American example of that vein), Strongheart is built on an old familiar pattern of hero and heroine, clever villain, comic relief characters, and a plot about important papers in the wrong hands. The melodramatic plot manipulations, however, are rather less than convincing. The real interest of the play is in DeMille's dramatizing of the problem of miscegenation. Could interracial marriage, as seen by middle-class Eastern society in 1905, be made acceptable? The playwright would have it accepted, and he indicts a bigoted society for refusing his Indian hero and white heroine the emotional fulfillment they richly deserve.

Soangataha is a gifted and handsome young Indian, called Strongheart by his admiring fellow students at Columbia

149

University, where he is a much-heroized star athlete. A
cynical and worldly-wise older student, Ralph Thorne, has
involved Strongheart's closest friend, Frank Nelson, in a
football gambling scandal. When Strongheart tries to cover
for Frank, he--more because he is an Indian than for apparent mishandling of a list of secret signals for a big game
--immediately loses status and is thrown off the football team.
This crisis comes at the worst possible time, when Strongheart has proposed marriage to Frank's sister Dorothy, whom
he has loved for three years. When Frank and his non-
Indian friends hear of the proposal (from Ralph Thorne, of
course), they turn on Strongheart and reject him out of
hand in a strong third-act scene, the climax of the play:

Dick: You have made love to her!

Strongheart: (proudly) Why should I not?

Dick: Because you are an Indian.

Strongheart: I am proud of it.

Frank: Strongheart[,] you are one of the finest
               men I know, but you are not one of us.

Thorne: You see!

Strongheart: Neither is any European, yet you would
               give your sister to one of them.

Frank: It's not the same thing.

Strongheart: No--I have a greater claim. I am the Ameri-
               can. You are foreigners.

Dick: At any rate, we're different.

Strongheart: In what way-- I speak your tongue. I
               obey your laws. I have lived with you,
               slept with you, eaten from the same dish:
               yet I am not one of you.

Dick: You have done all this, yet it has not
               changed the color of your skin!

Strongheart: The color of my skin does not prevent your calling me "friend."

Dick: But I'm your friend no longer--when you spoke of love to her, you betrayed our confidence.

Thorne: (quietly) You see--

Frank: Not so fast, Dick-- He did not realize--

Strongheart: No--let him speak-- It is true we understood one another. I have seen men of your race as dark as I am, with exposure to the sun. Am I different from them?

Dick: Yes--

Frank: It may be unjust and against reason, but it cannot be denied.

Strongheart: I have the same education as you, the same customs, the same feelings.

Dick: Still you are an Indian.

Strongheart: You do well to remind me of that. You have taken the land of my fathers, yet when I live by your laws you will not call me brother-- I am the son of a chief. In what way am I not your equal?

Frank: It's not a question of logic.

Dick: It's physical repulsion against the intermingling of races.

Strongheart: If she has not that feeling what can it matter to you-- If it were natural I too should feel it-- Why do I not?

Frank: It cannot be explained but it makes what you ask quite impossible.[2]

Dorothy, in an effective emotional scene in Act IV,

agrees to marry Strongheart and return with him to his western home. However, an Indian messenger, appropriately called Black Eagle, arrives to inform Strongheart that his father has died and he must return to become his people's leader. Here, unfortunately, DeMille succumbs to old clichés that have marred Indian plays from their beginnings. Strongheart is now understood to be an important "Prince" or "Chief" of his tribe (but what tribe has never been mentioned). He is suddenly--for dramatic effect only--subject to a kind of royal succession very uncommon among American Indians and required to return to his Graustarkian western kingdom and take up the reins of government over his adoring people, eschewing his worthy but inappropriate mistress for, presumably, a suitable Indian "queen." In his last scene with Dorothy, he tells her:

> Strongheart: Your people will not take me-- My people will not take you--
>
> Dorothy: <u>Your</u> people--
>
> Strongheart: Out of their poverty, their need, their suffering--they educated me to be their chief-- my life belongs to them--and they demand it--
>
> Dorothy: And they demand our happiness--[3]

Strongheart then concludes the scene with a blunt statement, "It is the law of races--," accepting the taboo of miscegenation as absolute and sending Dorothy away. The curtain then falls on a "tragic" solo moment for the hero, who prays: "Oh great spirit of my fathers. I call to you for help, for I am in the midst of a great desert--Alone."[4]

Yet however doubtful the credibility of William DeMille's final plot solution, his unsentimental dramatization of the arrogant hypocrisy of educated, supposedly liberal white men is nearly unique in Indian plays.

Similar arrogant attitudes are somewhat glossed over in Edwin Milton Royle's The Squaw Man, which opened in New York a few months after Strongheart with an even more glamorous leading man, the English matinee idol William Faversham.[5] But there was a difference in the ultimate success of

these two plays. Strongheart had a successful run and was
made into a film in 1914, but it was not revived and is now
a forgotten play. The Squaw Man, re-using the familiar sentimental tale of the pathetic Indian girl who dies for her
white lover, was so popular that the story was reworked as
a novel (by William Faversham's wife) and then successfully
turned into a film three times, in 1913, 1918, and 1931 (all
three directed by William DeMille's nephew, Cecil B. DeMille);
in addition, a sequel, The Squaw Man's Son, appeared on
the screen in 1917.

A squaw man is a white man who cohabits with an Indian woman for a protracted length of time, usually in an exclusively Indian milieu. The earliest dramatic relatives of
E. M. Royle's hero are Bacon in Mrs. Behn's The Widow Ranter; or, The History of Bacon in Virginia (1689) and Inkle
in Colman's Inkle and Yarico (1787), though neither is truly
a squaw man because they do not live out Indian lives.
Neither are Hampden, the officer who loves Pocahonte in A
New World Planted (1802), nor the Rolfe character in any of
the Pocahontas plays. The first fully developed squaw men
in drama are a dissimilar pair, the noble Alonzo in the two
Kotzebue plays (1791 and 1795), who settles permanently with
Cora in their Inca world, and a villainous renegade character
called Abel Doe in Nick of the Woods (1838). Doe is not only
the first full-fledged squaw man in our drama but is also the
father of a Dusky Maiden who dies aiding the white man she
loves.

As for the reverse situation, the white woman who marries an Indian was always a rarity, at least in the theatre.
The earliest was Polly Peachum in John Gay's Polly (1728/
1777), who settles happily with her Caribbean chief. The
only nineteenth-century example is Ruth (or Narramattah) in
The Wept of Wish-Ton-Wish (1830 et seq.). In a more realistic setting--not distanced by history as Cooper's heroine
was--Dorothy Nelson in Strongheart is not allowed the kind
of satisfactory liaison Polly or Narramattah enjoyed. An interesting comment on attitudes toward both male and female
connections with Native Americans was made in a study of the
Indian in the media:

> One index of the Indian's entrapment in pseudo-
> history was the peculiar tolerance whites gave to
> Indian miscegenation. When it came to interbreeding,

Indians clearly outranked Negroes. The best of Wasps, horrified at having one drop of Negro blood, somehow imagined that all went well in the family tree after an illustrious male ancestor stepped off the Mayflower and mated with the first available Indian princess. Such pride in having a select type of Indian blood was only extended to female royalty of an otherwise inferior race. To claim a male Indian, even a chief, as an ancestor was a faux pas. It might suggest that the family bloodline was susceptible to the warrior ways of the savage. But a well-groomed kind of Pocahontas as a great-great-grandmother--that was real Puritan get-up-and-go. Such a family would have greater social clout, since history has cushioned the first shock of white touching red.[6]

But if, as in Royle's The Squaw Man, the noble hero has mated with an Indian woman less brilliantly desirable than Pocahontas, it was easy enough to dispose of her with considerable dramatic effect.

The hero of Royle's play is Jim Wynnegate, an honorable young Britisher who, to avoid an unhappy love affair with his cousin Henry's wife, Diana, takes the blame for an embezzling scandal Henry is involved in and leaves England. He becomes a Wyoming rancher, using the name Jim Cranston. In Act Two his life is threatened by a vicious bully, Cash Hawkins, whom he has rightly accused of rustling his cattle. Hawkins attempts to gull an Indian, Tabwana, in a crooked cattle-buying deal, but he is frustrated by Tabwana's daughter, Nat-u-ritch. When Hawkins tries to kill Jim, Nat-u-ritch shoots him dead. In the third act, five years later, Jim and Nat-u-ritch are married and the parents of a son, Hal. The Wynnegate family solicitor, Mr. Petrie, searches Jim out to tell him that his cousin Henry is dead and Jim is heir to the earldom. But Jim feels bound by his allegiance to the way of life he has chosen with Nat-u-ritch and Hal. Petrie convinces him that Hal should be sent to England and educated for his eventual inheritance. Nat-u-ritch is heartbroken, but the squaw man's will is law to her. Meanwhile, a sheriff who had been a friend of Hawkins discovers that Nat-u-ritch was his killer. Nat-u-ritch realizes the insoluble difficulties of her situation when Diana arrives to take Hal away. So she avoids arrest and solves the dilemma by shooting herself, thus leaving Jim free to return to England with Hal and Diana.

Nat-u-ritch, though a role short in lines, is a strong and decisive character. Yet Jim is always concerned about her conflicting emotional strengths and weaknesses. In his long scene with Petrie, he describes the success of his marriage with her but sets up the final action of the play with this exchange:

Petrie: Believe me, I would advise nothing unbecoming to a man. But aren't you idealizing Nat-u-ritch a little?

Jim: On the contrary; we never do these primitive races justice. I know the grief of the ordinary woman. It doesn't prevent her from looking into the mirror to see if her bonnet is on straight, but Nat-u-ritch would then throw herself into the river out there, and I would be a murderer as much as if I pushed her in.

Petrie: Why not take her with you to England?

Jim: Impossible. We'd both be much happier here. Even here I am a "Squaw-Man"--that means socially ostracized. You see we have social distinctions even out here.

Petrie: How absurd!

Jim: Social distinctions usually are.[7]

Though the central focus of the play is on the title character, the memorable climactic action is that of the pathetic Indian girl ending her life so her white husband and child can continue to enjoy theirs. With this well-tried, tear-jerking situation as the core of the play, it is not surprising that Royle's use of it is maudlin in the extreme. Jim's farewell scene with his son is so crudely sentimental as to seem a joke to the modern reader, and his self-sacrificing goodwill toward his English relatives and later toward Nat-u-ritch nullify his credibility. The lack of originality in plot and character are also remarkable, seeming to be no more than a rehash of stories popular at that time. Hal is set up to be merely another Little Ford Fauntleroy, and the entire third and fourth acts are little more than a rewriting of the second half of Madame Butterfly.

The Squaw Man, like DeMille's Strongheart, demonstrates audience attitudes of 1905--a new awareness of Indians as people, yet a cautious holding back from wholehearted acceptance of their integration into modern life. The titillation of the exotic drew audiences whose tears could flow and tongues could cluck satisfyingly at the sad state of affairs involving Indians--some of whom seemed to be decent and likable human beings after all. It was comforting to find in Soangataha and Nat-u-ritch the old familiar stereotypes--a really Noble Savage, a man one could respect for not taking advantage of a white woman, and a Pathetic Dusky Maiden whose suicide served white humanity--but displayed as morally responsible characters in polished modern entertainments.

The next step in making Native Americans more acceptable to white audiences was to show their ways of life as not only attractively colorful but also culturally well-organized (the anthropologists' day had come) and something less than the war-dance-and-torture orgies of nineteenth-century fiction. The glamour and spectacle of Indian life was made use of in pageants such as The Masque of Montezuma by Thomas Wood Stevens and Kenneth S. Goodman, produced in 1912.

Similarly, repeated attempts were made to introduce such exotic glamour to the operatic stage, in works mostly forgotten after one or two performances. Poia, a singing heroine of 1906 by Arthur Nevin and Randolph Hartley, seems to have been the first. Some of the better known composers of the day soon followed suit. Natoma (1911) was Victor Herbert's contribution (and his only serious operatic work), on a libretto by Joseph Redding: Azora (1917) was Henry Hadley's (libretto by David Stevens); and Shanewis (1918) was the work of Charles Wakefield Cadman and Nelle R. Eberhart. Cadman, a sound musical researcher, had visited the Omaha Indians to study their dances and ceremonial music, and he successfully utilized such materials in several compositions. Also he worked with the Indian musician Francis La Flesche on Bureau of Ethnology publications on Indian music.[8] Nevertheless, although Natoma (sung by the great Mary Garden and John McCormack) and Shanewis survived a season or two, operatic Indians were soon abandoned. It would be many years before American composers and characters, Native or otherwise, would succeed on the serious musical stage.

In the legitimate theatre, a work of somewhat stronger

substance was offered at the New Theatre in New York in
the Spring of 1911. This was Mary Austin's play, The Arrow-
Maker, which dramatized the life and customs of a specific
kind of Southwestern Indian community.[9] The playwright,
a westerner who had lived with the Indians of the California
desert, was also a prominent feminist and one of that rich
trove of American women writers who came to the fore at the
turn of the twentieth century, including Willa Cather, Kate
Chopin, Sarah Orne Jewett, and others. Mary Austin's finest
book, The Land of Little Rain (1903), is infused with the
harsh realities of the desert country she loved; she felt
strongly the influence of realism in the arts, and accurate
observation of her subjects was a keynote of all her work.
Her incisive comment on the writing of plays about Indians
puts forth the reasons for the failure of most such works:

> The greatest difficulty to be met in the writing
> of an Indian play is the extensive misinformation
> about Indians. Any real aboriginal of my acquain-
> tance resembles his prototype in the public mind
> about as much as he does the high-nosed, wooden
> sign of a tobacco store, the fact being that, among
> the fifty-eight linguistic groups of American abori-
> ginals, customs, traits, and beliefs differ as greatly
> as among Slavs and Sicilians. Their very speech
> appears not to be derived from any common stock.
> All that they really have of likeness is an average
> condition of primitiveness: they have traveled just
> so far toward an understanding of the world they
> live in, and no farther. It is this general limitation
> of knowledge which makes, in spite of the multiplica-
> tion of tribal customs, a common attitude of mind
> which alone affords a basis of interpretation.[10]

Apart from Mary Austin's fascination with Indian life,
her other dominating interest was the position of women in
society. The principal character of The Arrow-Maker is not
the artisan of the title but a woman of unusual gifts, and
the play may be construed as a parable of the value of women
in the social milieu they inhabit.

The Chisera (she has no other name) is a young woman
born with a gift for contact with the powers that control the
earth and man's life. The tribe makes use of her as counse-
lor for their welfare, but as a priestess she must live apart

and is not allowed to partake of the everyday lives of other women of the tribe as woman, wife, or mother. The meaning of the play grows out of the conflict of these interests and how the tribe has developed its relationship with her:

> How they did this, with what damage and suc-
> cess, is to be read, but if to be read profitably,
> with its application in mind to the present social
> awakening to the waste, the enormous and stupid
> waste, of the gifts of women. To one fresh from
> the consideration of the roots of life as they lie
> close to the surface of primitive society, the obses-
> sion of the recent centuries, that the community can
> only be served by a gift for architecture, for ad-
> ministration, for healing, when it occurs in the per-
> son of a male, is only a trifle less ridiculous than
> that other social stupidity, namely, that a gift of
> mothering must not be exercised except in the event
> of a particular man being able, under certain re-
> strictions, to afford the opportunity. There is per-
> haps no social movement going on at present so
> deep-rooted and dramatic as this struggle of Femi-
> ninity to recapture its right to serve, and still to
> serve with whatever powers and possessions it finds
> itself endowed.[11]

The plot of The Arrow-Maker is comparatively simple. Simwa, the arrow-maker, is an ambitious young man who wants to be a tribal leader. He has been having an illicit affair with the Chisera, but he jilts her to marry a younger girl, Bright Water, daughter of an important man of the tribe. Enraged by the rejection, the Chisera withdraws her blessings and good counsel from the people, and their fortunes decline sharply. Skirmishes with neighboring Indians bring about loss of their homeland and general misery. The Chisera, having for nearly a year avoided communication with the gods and counselling of the tribe, finds she has lost her divine gift. The people, driven to the wall by their enemies, beg her to aid them, but she cannot. When she exposes Simwa as the ultimate cause of her trauma and loss, he shoots and kills her with a magic arrow she had given him to protect himself. The greed and lust of man, and disrespect for the gifts of God, have brought about the downfall of the entire community.

Another Westerner who wrote plays, none of them remotely of the quality of Mary Austin's single dramatic product, was the California poet Joaquin Miller. As a playwright
he is best known for The Danites in the Sierras. He had
had a mild stage success with that piece and another western
thriller, Forty-nine, in the 1870s and '80s. A later piece,
An Oregon Idyl [sic] (never produced), is a thin melodrama
having to do with Indian land rights in California.12 John
Logan is a noble-hearted and soft-spoken half-breed whose
father, a French doctor and land speculator, has long since
deserted John and his dying mother. When the father re-
appears, he and John have an argument during which the
doctor falls into a river. The villain of the piece, an Indian-
hater who hopes to take over both John's land and the heroine, accuses the young man of murder and tries to collect a
reward for capturing him. But the father turns up unhurt
for another reunion, this time a happier one, with his long-
lost son, and sees him joined to the heroine, Carrie, daughter
of a Southern gentleman settler.

Even if An Oregon Idyl were more original in style and
structure, the archness, sugary sentimentality, and sophomoric humor in Miller's writing probably would have precluded
much success for it. Every character and situation seems to
have been borrowed from some other play, and Miller only
points up the falseness of the borrowed elements by turning
them into a crude and tasteless pastiche. The point of view,
however, is entirely pro-Indian and against anti-Indian whites,
and the writer firmly champions the "mixed" marriage of the
half-Indian hero and the Anglo-Saxon ingenue.

From the time of the Civil War, and particularly since
Ina Dillaye's play version of Mrs. Jackson's Ramona, we have
seen that a strain of positive, sympathetic thinking toward
Native Americans had been growing in American playwriting.
Running parallel, of course, were negative, racist attitudes
in many plays. Both in plays showing positive and those
showing negative views of Indians, the old character stereotypes continued to be used. Plays like Strongheart and The
Arrow-Maker, and even The Squaw Man, were giant steps
forward in persuading the public to see something more than
cliché stereotypes. But--not unexpectedly--playwrights,
their audiences, and play reviewers often found the old ways
of seeing Indians comfortably acceptable, requiring no effort
of searching thought on the subject.

This reactionary, cynical approach to the use of Indian characters for commercial purposes is vividly illustrated by one of David Belasco's later productions, The Heart of Wetona, and by the critical response ot it. Wetona was a romantic melodrama developed by Belasco and the nominal playwright, George Scarborough, through several tryout playing dates and with much rewriting before it opened at Belasco's theatre in New York on March 4, 1916.

Originally titled Oklahoma, the plot showed the working out of a moral dilemma among a group of white religious figures. The heroine was a deacon's daughter who had gone astray with a less than honorable young clergyman but eventually made a more appropriate connection with a young man who had loved her all along. These roles were strong ones, apparently, but the piece did not seem to jell until Belasco decided to keep the setting but change the race and background of the characters. Indians were drawing crowds to the moving pictures--in the five years before Wetona was produced, Belasco's own play, The Girl I Left Behind Me, as well as Strongheart and The Squaw Man, had been filmed in company with dozens of "original" Indian filmscripts--but there had been little Indian competition on the legitimate stage. In any case, Belasco had always opted for an exotic touch in his productions, and that touch always seemed to make them audience winners--and, of course, financial hits. With Belasco's supervision, Scarborough changed the father and daughter characters into Oklahoma reservation Indians-- the deacon was now Quanah, a Comanche chief, his daughter was called Wetona, and the heroine's seducer became an attractive but dissolute young army officer. The patient true lover who finally wins Wetona was John Hardin, Indian agent for the reservation.

Details of the script, now lost, can be reconstructed from newspaper reports. On January 21, 1916, reporting on a tryout performance in Stamford, Connecticut, the New York Telegraph commented, perhaps unkindly, that it was like "going back to the days of the old time melodrama." The play was

> the story of an Indian reservation near a United States army post. It concerns the love affair of an army officer and an Indian maiden, but the former turns out to be considerable of a blackguard. He

meets his Waterloo at the hands of an agent, who, it develops, has been in love with the Indian girl from the start.

The situations are tense and the story has many gripping moments.[13]

When the play opened in New York, the reviewer for the New York Sun wrote:

> It is the appeal of young love that adds its force to the Indian play. Here there is continuing peril to the young man whom the Indian maiden loves, [to] the man she subsequently grew to love in reality, and then to her so long as her chieftain father threatened punishment for her step aside. There is not a minute [in] "The Heart of Wetona" in which there is no peril impending closely and the audience responds sympathetically to every suggestion of growing danger or nearing safety.[14]

Wetona was played by an appealing young actress called Lenore Ulric (then spelled Ulrich), one of the long series of women performers whom David Belasco turned into stars. In the second act, Belasco's direction emulated a currently sensational scene in Hartley Manners' play Peg O' My Heart in which another rising young star, Laurette Taylor, charmed her audience by playing with a live dog. Miss Ulric was given a kitten to play with. "Her fondling of the animal," the Sun reviewer noted, "occupies a considerable part of the second act. It is a most ingratiating episode, [a] human, gentle and amusing performance.... Mr. Belasco has devised a scene which shows her in a most attractive light."[15]

The most interesting passage in the Sun review is a revealing comment on Belasco's stage Indians, representing, presumably, the way in which both audiences and reviewers of the time still most often viewed Native Americans in the drama:

> Mr. Belasco has proven his skill in treating the Indian as a stage type before this. In "The Girl I Left Behind Me" and in "The Girl of the Golden West" he treated red men with the same picturesqueness and imagination. Usually the Indian is an unspeakable and grunting bore on the stage. He is

as unconvincing as he is ludicrous. But the Belasco
Indian is not of the tobacco shop type. He is real.
Then there is never too much of him, which is, after
all, the possible reason of his greater plausibility.
In "The Heart of Wetona" he is, excepting in the
case of the chief, so admirably played by William
Courtleigh, but a decorative detail.[16]

Since Belasco's Indians--seen from a 1980s vantage
point as only slightly less fantasy-bound than any in an
1830s melodrama--were the long-accepted norm, it is hardly
surprising that attempts at more believable Indians like those
created by Mary Austin or William DeMille might be received
with some skepticism by the reviewer quoted above. Belasco's false realism was the wonder of the day, enhanced by
the fact that the Indian stage presence was, for the most
part, minimal--"but a decorative detail," like the other "realistic" props with which Belasco littered his stage.

As Strongheart and The Arrow-Maker were steps forward in the long progress of Native Americans on the stage,
The Heart of Wetona seems a step backward, particularly in
a time of swift and profound changes in theatre all over the
western world. After its production, few plays on the subject appeared until very recent years. The impetus that had
brought stage Indians into the twentieth-century American
theatre seemed to have run out by the time of the First
World War. Then, after a brief hiatus (similar to that of the
Civil War years), dramatic interest in Indians rose again, and
from 1918 to 1982 about forty Indian theatre pieces were
brought out.[17] There are one or two operas, two ballets,
a few comedies, musicals, and dramas, and a large number
of pageant-like outdoor shows in the "symphonic drama" genre
established by Paul Green in 1937. The characters in most
of these works are far removed from the fanciful exotics of
the eighteenth century, yet vestiges of outworn stereotypes
still remain. But however believable some characterizations
may be, and however idealized others are, stage Indians are
actively with us still.

NOTES

1. William C. DeMille, "Strongheart." Unpublished

manuscript promptbook. Lincoln Center Library for the Performing Arts, New York Public Library.

2. Ibid., pp. III-29-32.

3. Ibid., p. IV-20.

4. Ibid., p. IV-22.

5. Edwin Milton Royle, "The Squaw Man." Unpublished manuscript promptbook. Lincoln Center Library for
the Performing arts. New York Public Library.

6. Donald L. Kaufmann, "The Indian A Media Hand-
Me-Down" in Gretchen M. Bataille and Charles L. P. Silet,
eds., The Pretend Indians: Images of Native Americans in
the Movies (Ames: Iowa State University Press, 1980), pp.
27-28.

7. Royle, "Squaw Man," p. III-16.

8. Edward E. Hipsher, American Opera and Its Composers (Philadelphia: Theodore Presser, 1927; reprint ed.,
New York: Da Capo Press, 1978), p. 101.

9. Mary Austin, The Arrow-Maker. A Drama in Three
Acts (Boston: Houghton Mifflin, 1915). Rev. ed.

10. Ibid., p. vii.

11. Ibid., p. xi.

12. Joaquin Miller, An Oregon Idyl in Joaquin Miller's
Poems, 6 vols. (San Francisco: The Whitaker and Ray Com-
pany, 1910), vol. 6, "Poetic Plays." None of the "Poetic
Plays" are written in verse.

13. All newspaper quotations are from clippings in the
Robinson Locke Collection of Scrapbooks, Series 5, volume
53. Unpaged. Lincoln Center Library for the Performing
Arts. New York Public Library.

14. Ibid.

15. Ibid.

16. Ibid.

17. See Appendix.

Chapter IX

SUMMARY AND CONCLUSION

In almost all of the nearly three hundred theatre works featuring Native Americans that were created between 1753 and
1916, the subjects were characterized in a few stereotypical
ways rather than as individuals with distinct personalities.
Many white characters were also stereotypes, but, as the
skills of modern playwrights have grown--particularly under
the influence of Naturalism and the local color movement in
the past hundred years--white characters escaped the pigeon-
holing that Indians never got out of except in a few latter-
day plays.

The most common Indian types were the Noble Savage
and the Pathetic Dusky Maiden, both adaptable for the plots
of tragic, comic, fantastic, or musical pieces, or any combination thereof. In time there was the fearsome Indian villain,
and later still, the parasitical drunken Indian, both of these
usually--though not always--appearing in viciously anti-Indian
plays. It was only very late in the period considered in this
study that the Indian's human qualities would be explored to
some extent and he would be shown sympathetically as a victim of fate.

Indian characters illustrated these stereotypes in varied
ways. In some plays their presence is important though they
have few lines or none at all, as in In Quod; or, Courting
the Wrong Lass (ca. 1865) and Centennial Movement 1876
(1876), although the political and social views of those years
on Indians could hardly be more explicit. In other plays,
Indians have small but crucial roles, such as the Indian Chief
in Mordecai Noah's delightful comedy She Would Be a Soldier
(1819), who has two of the most interesting scenes in the
play; or Wenonga, "the Black Vulture of the Shawnees," in
Nick of the Woods (1838), the villain of the first major anti-
Indian melodrama; or a girl called Nat-u-ritch in The Squaw

164

Man (1905), whose devotion to the white man she loves is so great that she does not hesitate at killing herself to benefit him.

Many plays, of course, focused solely on featured native characters. One of the earliest, Ponteach; or, The Savages of America (1766), glamorizes the career of a great warrior, and it had important successors in Metamora; or, The Last of the Wampanoags (1829) and Strongheart (1905). Heroic male figures have been balanced by the beloved character of Pocahontas in at least fifteen theatre pieces about her legendary life, and there were equally strong heroines in Ramona (1877), who struggles to cope with the white world, and the Chisera, the dominating figure in The Arrow-Maker (1911), the only play dealing entirely with conflicts within an Indian community.

The size of the role, however, was less important than the focus on it and the way playwrights and audiences reacted to these characters. Most of the plays, though interesting as relics of other eras in the theatre, are not, by any standard, good plays. But they are extraordinarily interesting for the entirely different reason that they mirror the way in which white audiences viewed Native Americans-- and accepted or rejected them as people--at any given period.

In the eighteenth century, Indians were transmuted into stilted cardboard figures or shadowy clichés. Three works based on actual historical incidents are typical. Ponteach, the only play that treated the natives' real grievances against whites and therefore was never produced, makes of the great warrior a one-dimensional Drydenesque hero. In The Paxton Boys (1764), no Indians appear at all; the whole piece is a discussion of colonial civil rights, with a passing lament that the Indians had none. In Nootka Sound (1792), Indians were farcical figures, apparently so that a terrifying experience of white men could be laughed off, leaving the whites with their dignity--and assumed superiority--intact. Indians were also popular in pantomimes, ballets, and in musical fantasies such as the operatic pastiche Tammany; or, The Indian Chief (1794). But in all these works, the Indian characters were no more than white concepts performed by whites disguised with red makeup and exotic feathered costumes unlike any real Indian clothing.

As the new melodrama form developed in the nineteenth century, the Indian seemed a perfect stock figure to be involved in colorful adventures in American scenes that would match the melodramatic thrills of European theatres. Elements of the outdated heroic tragedy and the drame were revivified in melodrama, blending well with the new interest in forceful women characters fostered by the Romantic Movement. A new awareness of Native Americans came about as the country began to expand after the Louisiana Purchase in 1803, particularly in the 1830s when large-scale immigration from Europe began. Correspondingly, there was a remarkable vogue for Indian plays lasting from the 1820s to the 1850s, when the great migration to the West began.

Most of these popular Indian plays, reinforcing the stereotypes, showed Native Americans in sympathetic, heroic roles. This was probably, to some extent at least, a reaction against the government's policies culminating in the brutal Indian Removal Bill of 1830. But as westering pioneers found Indians to be increasingly greater obstacles to their desires, positive attitudes toward them began to decline, and by the later 1830s audiences wanted to see frightening Indian villains overcome by brave white pioneers, as they did in Nick of the Woods in 1838 and for years afterward. Pro or con, however, in a few more years the Indian play had outworn its vogue. The falseness of Indian melodramatics was laughed off the stage by John Brougham's great burlesque, Po-Ca-Hon-Tas; or, The Gentle Savage in 1856.

The results of uprooting the tribes from their ancestral homes was shown even before the Civil War in Dion Boucicault's The Octoroon (1859), in which a pathetic displaced Indian aids his white benefactors by killing the villain. Stage Indians were few in the war years but began to reappear in the 1870s as the Plains Wars spread across the mid-continent. Soon, Indians became the bloodiest of villains in cheap melodramas such as those written for Buffalo Bill Cody.

But again a reaction arose against the traducing and mishandling of the native population by a misguided government and land-greedy settlers. Ramona spoke for many in the 1880s and long after as the first play since Ponteach to admit that Indians had legitimate grievances, and also that they might be considered and portrayed as real human beings just as white characters were, and therefore might be given

realistic dialogue, thoughts, and actions. Disasters culminating in the massacre at Wounded Knee in 1890 also probably
affected much public thinking and the widening view of Indians on the stage. After the turn of the twentieth century,
though stereotypes still prevailed in most plays, a concept
of Indians as living people came to be accepted. The cliché
Indians had passed on to the movies. White people's need to
mask their fears of Indians by refusing to see them on the
stage as anything other than stereotypical cardboard figures
had finally begun to fade away.

The masking operation carried out by white playwrights
for white audiences passed through several phases: in the
eighteenth and nineteenth centuries, it was based in a general ignorance of Indian life and character; throughout much
of the nineteenth century came a great fear of Indians as
enemies, followed by expressions of race hatred; by the beginning of the twentieth century, there developed an awareness of guilt as the cause of the deplorable fate of the Indians and a limited acceptance of them as real human beings
for the first time in history.

Throughout the history of Indian-play writing, from
the eighteenth-century emulators of Dryden to David Belasco,
stereotypical Indian characters were rarely more than disguised white people acting as whites wanted the Indians to
do. But the changing playwriting conventions of this period
brought them from farfetched fantasy Indians through a stage
of hardly more realistic melodrama redskins, both heroic and
villainous, and then on to characterizations as believable
modern stage figures. It seems logical to conclude that this
latter state is an improvement over the racist stereotypes of
earlier years and is advantageous to the understanding of
Native Americans as human beings and fellow citizens.

The principal forces that helped to bring about the
desirable change to a realistic presentation of Indians on the
stage were five in number. First, there was the influence of
the women's movement toward emancipation, in the arts as
well as in social and political life; second, a growing sense of
pride in all things American, including Indians, accented by
the Centennial celebrations of 1876; third, the end of any
presumed Indian menace on the vanishing Western frontier in
the 1890s; and fourth, the American transliteration of Naturalism and Realism in our local color movement in which so

many writers, including playwrights, dramatized the everyday life of plain people. Fifth and last was the naturally
shifting point of view of American audiences brought on by
urban growth and technological changes and their effect on
American social life, including the entertainment industry.

The ultimate aim of the women's movement that had
begun early in the nineteenth century was, of course, suf-
frage, but positive side effects were felt in many other areas
of American life besides politics. The arts in particular were
felt to be a feminine province; a new respect for women novelists
and playwrights grew, and their thinking on subjects other
than domestic welfare was considered pertinent. Mrs. Stowe's
work had demonstrated the effects on public life that a woman's creative effort could have. Mrs. Jackson followed suit,
and the play version of Ramona is a theatrical landmark that
showed Indians for the first time as believable everyday human beings rather than die-cut clichés. Its long-lasting popularity suggests that audiences had changed their views about
Indians or, at least that they found the characters sympathetic. Thus it opened the way for still more realistic por-
trayals to come, such as the complex personalities drawn by
Mary Austin in The Arrow-Maker.

The Centennial Exposition in Philadelphia in 1876 celebrated the hundredth anniversary of the nation; the climate
of the time of which it was a landmark celebrated a growing
pride, even an arrogance, in things American. The Exposition in Philadelphia was specifically set up to celebrate the
one-hundredth birthday of the Declaration of Independence
by showing off the technological progress of the country in
the century since that document was written. But it also
supported a strong euphoria about positive values in every
reach of American life (the Woman's Building was a great attraction, for example) and did not exclude consideration of
the cultural contributions of Native Americans. With the set-
tling of the West and the fast-increasing network of railroads,
more people were traveling for pleasure in America (rather
than to Europe) and discovering not only the scenery but
also western people, Indian and white, on their own ground.
There was a new interest in bringing home souvenirs of the
cultures such as Indian pottery and other craft work. The
local color movement in writing was paralleled by the arts
and crafts of the day, which often found inspiration in Indian
design. The United States Bureau of Ethnology began pub-

lishing its great multivolume <u>Handbook of American Indians</u> <u>North of Mexico</u> in 1907. The so-called Indianist Movement in the arts, a branch of the local color interest, particularly in music, was much publicized in its heyday, the 1880s and 1890s, resulting in popular concert works such as Cadman's song "In the Land of Sky-Blue Water" and Arthur Farwell's adaptations of Navajo songs for choral performance.[1]

This new peaceable interest in Indians as colorfully attractive American possessions may be construed as a kind of national sigh of relief that the seemingly perpetual Indian "wars" of the Plains had come to an end. There were minor campaigns by federal troops against the Bannocks in 1895 and the Chippewas in 1898, but the last major conflict was the army's massacre of Sioux families at Wounded Knee, South Dakota, in 1890. Farms and ranches were felt to be safe from any fear of Indian attack, real or imagined, and travel was secure throughout the West. Fear of Indians was kept alive for youngsters by the wild delights of Buffalo Bill Cody's huge outdoor show--perhaps the most famous theatrical entertainment in the world at the turn of the century--in which real Indians pretended to be bested by white actors. But Buffalo Bill's circus gave a narrow, biased picture of a few bygone incidents, and everyone knew that any real danger was a thing of the past.

The Wild West show offered perhaps the freshest view of old-time Indian villains, played slightly tongue-in-cheek, for the fun of it, and distanced by the great arenas where it played. On the stage, while vaudeville and burlesque Indians became funny creatures of contempt, the popular melodrama most often continued to show the same stale cliché "bad Injuns" who had threatened brave palefaces for a hundred years. The most typical might be ogres such as those of <u>The Minute Men of 1774-1775</u> (1886), but also included merely "degenerate Indian" drunks as in <u>The Golden Gulch</u> in 1893. By 1912 there was hope for the melodrama Indian's rehabilitation, as seen in <u>Tatters, the Pet of Squatters' Gulch</u>, whose respectable young Indian hero is allowed to marry the white heroine, following the lead of more dignified dramas such as <u>Strongheart</u>. Only the less discerning audiences at the movies still saw many Indians as horrid, leering villains, since the old stage Indian, replete with his accretion of personality clichés, had been turned over to the sensational

cinema, which would not begin to scrape them away for another half century.

With these forces at work, an alteration in audiences'
views of Indians was inevitable. And there were many supporting causes that turned them away from the old clichés.
For one, the influence of Naturalism in drama was present,
first in our continual borrowing of Ideas from European theatre, and second in the discovery of the charm of local color
in American scenes. Believable motivation in plays, believable characters and acting--a real American slice of life--
were in demand. Other forceful impressions had also been
striking theatre-conscious Americans thick and fast since the
Civil War. The enormous growth of towns and cities gave
them a less insular, more sophisticated awareness of their
country and the world, as did the Americanization of un-
countable thousands of European and Oriental immigrants,
the new fashion for travel in Europe, and the expansion of
the performing arts. All of these were promoted by the as-
tonishingly swift advances in technology in United States industry, resulting in the newly affluent economy of the "Gilded
Age" and the recessions and recoveries that followed it to
the end of the century. The broadened world-view of Americans made them less patient with stereotypical entertainments.

The characters they saw on the stage in the two or
three decades before the Great War were more realistically
believable and had some understandable motivation for their
actions. The Squaw Man--and his playwright--may have been
patronizing toward his Indian wife, but they try to offer some
explication of her extreme behavior. Strongheart throughout
his drama performs consistent actions which we find to be
credible and logical developments from his character and the
situation--even his return to his playwright's fanciful Indian
world.

The Indian character types in The Squaw Man and
Strongheart are not new, but they are treated in a new way.
The Noble Savage had been the favored Indian male character
in our drama from the time of Le Père Indien, and in English
and French plays long before that. The Pathetic Dusky
Maiden, first appearing in Ponteach, became a staple early in
the nineteenth century and grew increasingly in prominence
thereafter. These were the admirable, idealized Indian characters originating in fantastic, heroic, or sentimental plays.

But as the nation expanded its territory and dealings with Indians grew more problematic, new racist caricatures intended to demean them were created. The great westward movement was illustrated in lurid chromo tints by the flood of popular Indian plays of the 1830s and 1840s. In 1838, Nick of the Woods set a precedent by featuring this new concept of Indian villains. Twenty years later, a closer approach to realism came with Dion Boucicault's drunken parasite, Wahnotee, in The Octoroon. Both these new types were eventually incorporated into vaudeville and burlesque as the fear of Indians diminished and it was possible to joke about them more. With this development, a new sympathy prompted by injustices toward the Indian produced another variant, the Indian as a helpless victim of fate. This point of view began with Ramona, included the Squaw Man's Nat-u-ritch, and carried through to the characters of The Arrow-Maker's exclusively Indian world.

With the use of this narrow range of character types, and within the playwriting conventions that developed during the century and a half covered by this survey, playwrights, as we have seen, showed Native Americans always as idealized or romanticized figures. By so doing, the unattractive realities of Indian-white relations did not have to be confronted, as was often the case in real life. The desirable, much-admired romance and exotic beauty of Indian life could be projected as white playwrights and audiences wished them to be: colorful and pleasing, titillating but not really dangerous. Only in the later days of Indian-play writing and production, in works such as Ramona and Strongheart, were realistic human emotions and logical reasoning processes attributed to Indian characters. And then, to our frustration, the influencial commercial theatre turned its back on the furthering of these creative, highly dramatic possibilities and made saleable a thin domestic melodrama, The Heart of Wetona, by disguising its cliché white characters as Indians. Almost another generation would pass before any further explications of Indian character would be essayed on the American stage.

In what seems to have been a seesaw of attitudes in theatrical presentations about Native Americans, there has, however, been a pattern. We have seen playwrights and public enchanted with the exotic beauty of Indians, sometimes showing admiration, respect, and even envy for their personal qualities and ways of life. We have also seen fear of Indians

expressed as outright violent hatred and satisfaction at their
destruction graphically realized on the stage. In the eighteenth century, when there was little question of the Indians'
being a serious obstacle to national progress and expansion,
they were most useful in the theatre as heroic ideals reflecting one of the most prominent philosophical concepts of the
time--that the best man was the Natural Man; for example,
an Indian--or as satirical (sometimes musical) commentators
on European and American life. In the nineteenth century
as the young nation began to stretch westward across the
central plains, although the heroic ideal and positive thinking
about Indians persisted through that period when Indian
plays were most popular, a growing fear of them came to be
translated into the form of Indian villains in violent melodramas. The fantasy was fulfilled by brave white characters who overcame categorically "Bad Injuns." Then, as the
westward movement succeeded, Indians were again seen less
seriously: any fear of them could be laughed away in burlesque and vaudeville. And finally, the overreactions of
government and westering pioneers, the overly brutal attempts at control that drew equally brutal retaliatory actions,
were the subject of objections voiced by rare playwrights
who showed us that Native Americans could also be honorable
human beings with a right to exist.

In the long history of Indian plays in the American
theatre--nearly as long as that of any other dramatic genre
--they have served not only to entertain but also to give
audiences impressions and information about Native Americans.
Sometimes the information was attractive, current, and useful; most often it was spurious, cut afresh from a white playwright's imagination or inaccurate sources of fact. Indian
plays took their place among other plays of American life as
a minor genre reflecting the widespread awareness of Indians
and attitudes toward them fashioned by the time in which they
were written and performed. The mirror was held up, not
to the natural reality of Indian life, but to the natural fears,
beliefs, and hopes of insecure white audiences who wanted
the cathartic thrill of seeing these emotions dramatized.

The attempt to portray Indians, fantastically or realistically, made use of a kind of mask of meaning which served
less to characterize the plays' subjects than to hide the white
audiences' fears that they might not, after all, be a chosen
race superior to that darker one whose innate sense of dignity,

power, and freedom made the whites feel their own insecurity the more. As the country and all its people advanced, the Indian presence came to seem less prominent, while, in a kind of inverse ratio, a new respect for that presence was growing, on the stage as in actual life. In the twentieth-century theatre, the mask began to slip away, revealing that Native Americans are not quite so darkly colored as had once been thought. The savage, noble or villainous, had lost his savagery and was revealed as an everyday human being after all.

NOTE

1. See Works by Arthur Farwell, Preston Ware Orem, and Charles Wakefield Cadman. Notes by Gilbert Chase. New World Record #213.

A CHRONOLOGICAL CHECKLIST OF PLAYS AND OTHER THEATRE WORKS FEATURING NATIVE AMERICAN CHARACTERS

1658 William Davenant. THE CRUELTY OF THE SPANIARDS IN PERU

1659 William Davenant. THE HISTORY OF SIR FRANCIS DRAKE

1664 Robert Howard and John Dryden. THE INDIAN QUEEN

1665 John Dryden. THE INDIAN EMPEROR

1689 Aphra Behn. THE WIDOW RANTER: OR, THE HISTORY OF BACON IN VIRGINIA

1704 John Dennis. LIBERTY ASSERTED

1721 L. F. de la Drèvetiére Delisle. ARLEQUIN SAUVAGE

1728 John Gay. POLLY (First performed 1777)

Francis Hawling. THE INDIAN EMPEROR

1735 Jean Philippe Rameau. LES INDES GALANTES

1736 Voltaire. ALZIRE; OU, LES AMERICAINS

1738 Anonymous. ART AND NATURE

1742 Anonymous. INKLE AND YARICO

1740–50(?) Anonymous. YARICO, A PASTORAL DRAMA

1753 Le Blanc de Villeneuve. LE PERE INDIEN

1753–90(?) Anonymous. THE LAST OF THE SERPENT TRIBE

1758 John Cleland. TOMBO CHIQUI

1759 George Alexander Stevens. THE FRENCH FLOGGED; OR, ENGLISH SAILORS IN AMERICA

1762 Arthur Murphy. ALZUMA (First performed 1773)

1764 Anonymous. THE PAXTON BOYS

(?) Chamfort. LE JEUNE INDIENNE

1766 Robert Rogers. PONTEACH; OR, THE SAVAGES OF AMERICA

1778 Henry Brooke. MONTEZUMA

1779 John Smith. A DIALOGUE BETWEEN AN INDIAN AND AN
ENGLISHMAN

1784 Alexander Maclaren. THE COUP-DE-MAIN

Johann Wilhelm Rose. POCAHONTAS

1785 Anonymous. ROBINSON CRUSOE; OR, HARLEQUIN FRIDAY

1786 Anonymous. THE PERUVIAN

1787 George Colman the Younger. INKLE AND YARICO

1790 John O'Keeffe. THE BASKET MAKER

William Richardson (attr.). THE INDIANS

John Scawen (attr.). NEW SPAIN; OR, LOVE IN MEXICO

1791 August von Kotzebue. DIE SONNENJUNGFRAU

1792 Anonymous. THE AMERICAN HEROINE; OR, INGRATITUDE
PUNISHED

Anonymous. NOOTKA SOUND

Thomas Morton. COLUMBUS; OR, A WORLD DISCOVERED

John O'Keeffe. THE CHEROKEE

1794 Anonymous. THE HUNTRESS; OR, TAMMANY'S FROLICS

Anne Kemble Hatton. TAMMANY; OR, THE INDIAN CHIEF

1795 James Bacon. THE AMERICAN INDIAN; OR, THE VIRTUES
OF NATURE

James Cobb. THE CHEROKEE

August von Kotzebue. DIE SPANIER IN PERU; ODER, ROLLAS
TOD

1797 Anonymous. HARLEQUIN AND QUIXOTTE; OR, THE MAGIC
      ARM

      John Burk. THE INDIAN WAR FEAST

      Mark Lonsdale (attr.). THE CATAWBA TRAVELLERS; OR
      KIEW NEIKA'S RETURN

1798 Anonymous. INKLE UND YARICO; ODER, ER WAR NICHT
      GANZ BARBAR

      Anonymous. ROBINSON CRUSOE; OR, THE GENIUS OF CO-
      LUMBIA (Revision of ROBINSON CRUSOE, 1785)

1799 James C. Cross. CORA; OR, THE VIRGIN OF THE SUN

      Thomas Dutton. PIZARRO; OR, THE DEATH OF ROLLA

      James Lawrence. THE VIRGIN OF THE SUN

      Matthew G. Lewis. ROLLA; OR, THE PERUVIAN HERO

      Archibald Maclaren. THE NEGRO SLAVES

      "A North Briton." PIZARRO

      Anne Plumptre. THE SPANIARDS IN PERU; OR, THE DEATH
      OF ROLLA

      Anne Plumptre. THE VIRGIN OF THE SUN

      Richard Brinsley Sheridan. PIZARRO

      Benjamin Thompson. PIZARRO; OR, THE DEATH OF ROLLA

      M. West. PIZARRO

1800 William Dunlap. PIZARRO IN PERU; OR, THE DEATH OF
      ROLLA

      William Dunlap. THE VIRGIN OF THE SUN

      John Fenwick. THE INDIAN

      Arthur Murphy. PERU REVENGED; OR, THE DEATH OF
      PIZARRO (Revision of ALZUMA, 1773)

      Charlotte Smith. PIZARRO

      Charlotte Smith. THE VIRGIN OF THE SUN

Benjamin Thompson. ROLLA; OR, THE VIRGIN OF THE SUN

1802   Joseph Croswell. A NEW WORLD PLANTED

1803   Anonymous. INDIAN CRUELTY; OR, THE DEATH OF MISS
McCREA

1808   James Nelson Barker. THE INDIAN PRINCESS; OR, LA BELLE
SAUVAGE

1809   Anonymous. HARLEQUIN PANATTATAH; OR, THE GENII OF
THE ALGONQUINS

1813   (?) Reynolds. THE VIRGIN OF THE SUN

1817   Anonymous. THE BOLD BUCCANEERS; OR, THE DISCOVERY
OF ROBINSON CRUSOE

James Nelson Barker. THE ARMOURER'S ESCAPE; OR, THREE
YEARS AT NOOTKA SOUND

1819   Anonymous. THE CARIB CHIEF

Anonymous. CATHERINE BROWN, THE CONVERTED CHERO-
KEE

Mordecai M. Noah. SHE WOULD BE A SOLDIER; OR, THE
PLAINS OF CHIPPEWA

1820   Felicia Dorothea Hemans. THE INDIAN'S REVENGE; SCENES
IN THE LIFE OF A MORAVIAN MISSIONARY

1821   Lewis Deffebach. OOLAITA; OR, THE INDIAN HEROINE

Joseph Doddridge. LOGAN, THE LAST OF THE RACE OF THE
SHIKELLEMUS, CHIEF OF THE CAYUGA NATION

1822   Anonymous. LA BELLE PERUVIENNE

Anonymous. PHILIP; OR, THE ABORIGINES

Anonymous. THE RIVAL INDIANS

1823   Anonymous. THE INDIAN HEROINE

Anonymous. THE PIONEERS

1825   Anonymous. THE VISION OF THE SUN

Henry J. Finn. MONTGOMERY; OR, THE FALLS OF MONT-
MORENCY

1826 George Pope Morris. BRIER CLIFF; OR, A PICTURE OF A
      FORMER TIME

1827 George Washington Parke Custis. THE INDIAN PROPHECY

1829 Anonymous. THE MANHATTOES

      Robert Montgomery Bird. KING PHILIP; OR, THE SAGAMORE

      James H. Kennicott. METACOMET

      Richard Penn Smith. WILLIAM PENN; OR, THE ELM TREE

      John Augustus Stone. METAMORA; OR, THE LAST OF THE
      WAMPANOAGS

1830 Anonymous. MIANTONIMOH; OR, THE WEPT OF WISH-TON-
      WISH

      Anonymous. NARRAMATTAH; OR, THE LOST FOUND

      Anonymous. THE WIGWAM; OR, TEMPLETON MANOR

      G. Blanchard. METAMORA; OR, THE INDIAN HUNTERS

      George W. P. Custis. THE PAWNEE CHIEF

      George W. P. Custis. POCAHONTAS; OR, THE SETTLERS
      OF VIRGINIA

      Henry Finn [and James Hackett]. THE INDIAN WIFE; OR,
      THE FALLS OF MONTMORENCY

      William H. C. Hosmer. THE FALL OF TECUMSEH

      James McHenry. THE MAID OF WYOMING

1830-50(?) Ebenezer Elliott. KERHONAH

1831 Nathaniel Deering. CARABASSET

      Anonymous. MIANTONIMOH

1832 Anonymous. WHITE EAGLE

      Robert Montgomery Bird. ORALLOOSSA, SON OF THE INCAS

      Joseph Stevens Jones. THE INDIAN MOTHER

1833 Caroline L. W. Hentz. LAMORAH; OR, THE WESTERN WILD

Louisa H. Medina. WACOUSTA; OR, THE CURSE

1834 Anonymous. BLACK HAWK

Anonymous. THE CHEROKEE CHIEF

Anonymous. OUTALLISSI

Anonymous. TUSCATOMBA

Joseph Stevens Jones. THE FIRE WARRIOR

Joseph Stevens Jones. PLYMOUTH ROCK

Louisa H. Medina. KAIRRISSAH

Jonas B. Phillips. ORANASKA; OR, THE CHIEF OF THE MO-HAWKS

1835 Anonymous. THE YEMASSEE

William Bayle Bernard. THE WEPT OF WISH-TON-WISH

1835(?) George Washington Harby. TUTOONA; OR, THE BATTLE OF SARATOGA

1836 Richard Emmons. TECUMSEH; OR, THE BATTLE OF THE THAMES

Joseph Stevens Jones. THE HUNTER IN THE FAR WEST

William Wheatley. SASSACUS; OR, THE INDIAN WIFE

1837 Anonymous. THE SNOW FIEND; OR, THE FAR, FAR WEST

1838 Anonymous. THE INDIAN GIRL

Anonymous. THE JESUIT'S COLONY; OR, INDIAN DOOM

Anonymous. THE STAR OF THE FOREST

Alexander Macomb. PONTIAC; OR, THE SIEGE OF DETROIT

Louisa H. Medina. NICK OF THE WOODS; OR, THE JIBBENAIN-OSAY

Robert Dale Owen. POCAHONTAS, A HISTORICAL DRAMA

1839 George Washington Harby. NICK OF THE WOODS; OR, THE SALT RIVER ROVER

J. T. Haines. NICK OF THE WOODS; OR, THE ALTAR OF REVENGE

1830-40(?) Anonymous. MIOUTOUMAH

Anonymous. ONTIATA; OR, THE INDIAN HEROINE

Anonymous. OROONOKA

Harold Duffee. ONYLDA, THE PEQUOT MAID

Lewis F. Thomas. OSCEOLA

1840 Anonymous. TIPPECANOE

Anonymous. MIANTONIMOH AND NARRAMATTAH

Joseph Stevens Jones. THE INDIAN HORDE; OR, THE TIGER OF WAR

Silas H. Steele. THE BATTLE OF TIPPECANOE

1841 Anonymous. CHIEF OF THE MOHEGANS; OR, THE DOG OF THE ISLAND

(?) Chatham. CONANCHEOTA

1841(?) John S. Sherbourne. OSCEOLA

1842 Anonymous. SHARRATAH; OR, THE LAST OF THE YEMAS-SEES

1843 Anonymous. THE RED MAN; OR, THE BLOOMINGDALE ROAD

Henry Rowe Schoolcraft. ALHALLA; OR, THE LORD OF TAL-LADEGA

1844 Nathaniel H. Bannister. PUTNAM, THE IRON SON OF '76

George Jones. TECUMSEH AND THE PROPHET OF THE WEST

1845 C. H. Saunders. TELULA; OR, THE STAR OF HOPE

1846 Anonymous. ONOLEETA

George Hielge. MONTEZUMA; OR, THE CONQUEST OF MEXICO

Walter M. Leman. PRAIRIE BIRD; OR, A CHILD OF THE DELAWARES

1847 John Brougham. METAMORA; OR, THE LAST OF THE POLLY-WOGS

1848 Charles Edward Anthon. THE SON OF THE WILDERNESS

Charlotte Barnes. THE FOREST PRINCESS; OR, TWO CEN-
TURIES AGO

Hariette Fanning Read. THE NEW WORLD

W. B. Dailey. SARATOGA: A DRAMATIC ROMANCE OF THE
REVOLUTION

1849 Anonymous. THE EAGLE EYE

Anonymous. THE LAST OF THE MOHICANS

1850(?) Anonymous. THE LIVE INDIAN

Anonymous. THE WEPT OF THE WISH-TON-WISH

Frank Lester Bingham. HENRY GRANDEN; OR, THE UNKNOWN
HEIR

1850 Nathaniel H. Bannister. OUA COUSTA; OR, THE LION OF
THE FOREST

1851 Anonymous. THE INDIAN QUEEN

R. Jones. WACOUSTA; OR, THE CURSE

1852 Anonymous. THE STAR OF THE WEST

George Henry Miles. DE SOTO; OR, THE HERO OF THE MIS-
SISSIPPI

1853 John H. Wilkins. CIVILIZATION; OR, THE HURON CHIEF

1855 Anonymous. MAGNOLIA; OR, THE CHILD OF THE FLOWER

1856 John Brougham. PO-CA-HON-TAS; OR, THE GENTLE SAVAGE

Henry Clay Moorehead. TAN-GO-RUA

Charles M. Walcot. HIAWATHA; OR, ARDENT SPIRITS AND
LAUGHING WATER

1857 Anonymous. WISSAHICKON; OR, THE HEROES OF 1776

Charles E. Bingham. THE OATMAN FAMILY

James Pilgrim. THE SILVER KNIFE; OR, THE HUNTERS OF
THE ROCKY MOUNTAINS

Henry Clay Preuss. FASHIONS AND FOLLIES OF WASHINGTON LIFE

Lewis F. Thomas. CORTEZ, THE CONQUEROR

1858 Thomas Dunn English. THE MORMONS; OR, LIFE AT SALT LAKE CITY

T. Law. THE MINUTE SPY

John Hovey Robinson. NICK WHIFFLES

1859 George Henry Miles. SEÑOR VALIENTE; OR, THE SOLDIER OF CHAPULTEPEC

1859 Dion Boucicault. THE OCTOROON

1860-70(?) Anonymous. IN QUOD; OR, COURTING THE WRONG LASS

1860(?) Delia Anne Heywood. KINDNESS SOFTENS EVEN SAVAGE HEARTS

1861 James Lawson. LIDDESDALE; OR, THE BORDER CHIEF

1862 Giuseppe Verdi and Francesco Maria Piave. LA FORZA DEL DESTINO

1864 Elizabeth A. Dana. IONA

1870 Antonio Carlos Gomes. IL GUARANY

James J. McCloskey. ACROSS THE CONTINENT; OR, SCENES FROM NEW YORK LIFE AND THE PACIFIC RAILROAD

J. C. Stewart. THE LAST OF THE MOHICANS

1871 Augustin Daly. HORIZON

Fred Meader. BUFFALO BILL, THE KING OF THE BORDER MEN

James O'Leary. ELLIE LAURA; OR, THE BORDER ORPHAN

1872 Ned Buntline (pseud. E. Z. C. Judson). THE SCOUTS OF THE PRAIRIE; OR, RED DEVILTRY AS IT IS

1873 Anonymous (attr. E. Z. C. Judson). THE LAST SHOT FOR CUSTER; OR, THE YELLOW HAND

Mary L. Cobb. HOME

Augustin Daly. ROUGHING IT

Thomas Blades De Walden. THE LIFE AND DEATH OF NATTY BUMPO

1874 Samuel H. M. Byers. POCAHONTAS, A MELODRAMA

1875 Charles White. THE BOGUS INDIAN

1876 Nathan Appleton. CENTENNIAL MOVEMENT, 1876

J. V. Arlington. THE RED RIGHT HAND; OR, BUFFALO BILL'S FIRST SCALP FOR CUSTER

W. Page McCarty. THE GOLDEN HORSESHOE

Charles White. THE REHEARSAL; OR, BARNEY'S OLD MAN

1877 Anonymous. MOUNTAIN MEADOW MASSACRE

Joseph I. C. Clarke. LUCK

1878 Prentiss Ingraham. THE KNIGHT OF THE PLAINS; OR, BUFFALO BILL'S BEST TRAIL

1879 A. S. Burk. MAY CODY; OR, LOST AND WON

1875-90(?) E. S. Brooks. A DREAM OF THE CENTURIES

Donn Piatt. BLENNERHASSETT'S ISLAND

1880 E. E. Rice. HIAWATHA, A LONG SONG OF THE LONGFELLOW

1882 Anonymous. TWENTY DAYS; OR, BUFFALO BILL'S PLEDGE

1883 [William F. Cody]. BUFFALO BILL'S WILD WEST, ROCKY MOUNTAIN AND PRAIRIE EXHIBITION

Anonymous. SIR HARRY VANE

1884 Robert Boodey Caverly. KING PHILIP

Robert Boodey Caverly. THE LAST NIGHT OF A NATION

Robert Boodey Caverly. MIANTONIMOH

Robert Boodey Caverly. THE REGICIDES

1884(?) Len Ellsworth Tilden. THE EMIGRANT'S DAUGHTER

1885 Robert Boodey Caverly. CHOCORUA IN THE MOUNTAIN

1886 Anonymous. THE PRAIRIE WAIF

Tony Denier. BUFFALO BILL AMONG THE INDIANS

Welland Hendricks. POCAHONTAS

James A. Herne. THE MINUTE MEN OF 1774-1775

Charles Mair. TECUMSEH

1887 Sarah Ann Curzon. LAURA SECORD, THE HEROINE OF 1812

Ina Dillaye. RAMONA

Alexander Hamilton. CANONICUS

Daniel S. Preston. COLUMBUS; OR, THE HERO OF THE NEW WORLD

1888 John Hunter Duvar. DE ROBERVAL

1889 Herr Cherrytree (pseud.). MORE TRUTH THAN POETRY

Herr Cherrytree. THE RENEGADE

Charles Townsend. BORDER LAND

1890 G. D. Cummings. THE HISTORY OF GERONIMO'S SUMMER CAMPAIGN OF 1885

1892 M. M. A. Hartnedy. CHRISTOPHER COLUMBUS

1893 David Belasco and Franklyn Fyles. THE GIRL I LEFT BEHIND ME

Nason Leavitt. THE FROGS OF WINDHAM

George Lansing Raymond. THE AZTEC GOD

George Lansing Raymond. COLUMBUS

Charles Townsend. THE GOLDEN GULCH

1894 A. A. Furman. PHILIP OF POKANOKET

1895 Scott Marble. THE GREAT TRAIN ROBBERY

1897 Daniel Garrison Brinton. MARIA CANDELARIA

1898 Frank Dumont. SOCIETY ACTING

Frank Dumont. THE GIRL FROM KLONDIKE; OR, WIDE AWAKE NELL

James Bovell Mackenzie. THAYANDENEGEA

1900 Frank W. Bacon. RAMONA

1905 David Belasco. THE GIRL OF THE GOLDEN WEST

William C. DeMille. STRONGHEART

Edwin Milton Royle. THE SQUAW MAN

1906 Arthur Nevin and Randolph Hartley. POIA

1907 Edward Harrigan. IN THE NORTH WOODS

Edwin O. Ropp. POCAHONTAS

1910 Joaquin Miller. AN OREGON IDYL

1911 Mary Austin. THE ARROW-MAKER

Victor Herbert and Joseph Redding. NATOMA

1912 Thomas Wood Stevens and Kenneth S. Goodman. THE MASQUE OF MONTEZUMA

Levin C. Tees. TATTERS, THE PET OF SQUATTER'S GULCH

1913 Marie E. J. Hobart. THE GREAT TRAIL

1916 George Scarborough [and David Belasco]. THE HEART OF WETONA

1917 Henry Hadley and David Stevens. AZORA

1918 Charles Wakefield Cadman and E. R. Eberhart. SHANEWIS

Philip Moeller. POKEY, OR THE BEAUTIFUL LEGEND OF THE AMOROUS INDIAN

1924 Rudolf Friml and Oscar Hammerstein II. ROSE MARIE

1927 Brian Hooker. WHITE EAGLE

1928 Walter Donaldson, William Anthony McGuire, and Gus Kahn. WHOOPEE

1930 Lynn Riggs. THE CHEROKEE NIGHT

1933   Virgil Geddes. POCAHONTAS AND THE ELDERS

1936   Maxwell Anderson. HIGH TOR

  Lew Christensen. POCAHONTAS

1937   Paul Green. THE LOST COLONY

1940   M. W. Robinson. POCAHONTAS

1946   Irving Berlin and Dorothy Fields. ANNIE GET YOUR GUN

  N. Mooney. POCAHONTAS

1950   Kermit Hunter. UNTO THESE HILLS

1951   John Patrick. LO AND BEHOLD

1952   Kermit Hunter. HORN IN THE WEST

1953   Thomas Patterson. THE ARACOMA STORY

1957   Paul Green. THE FOUNDERS

1963   Ken Kesey. ONE FLEW OVER THE CUCKOO'S NEST

1965   Paul Green. CROSS AND SWORD

1968   Arthur Kopit. INDIANS

1969   Kermit Hunter. TRAIL OF TEARS

1970   Paul Green. TRUMPET IN THE LAND

1972   Hanay Geiogamah. BODY INDIAN

1973   Anonymous. POCAHONTAS

  Hanay Geiogamah. FOGHORN

  Wayne Johnson and John Kauffman. THE INDIAN EXPERIENCE

  Christopher Hampton. SAVAGES

  James Magnuson. SQUANTO

  Sharon Pollock. WALSH

1974   Allan W. Eckert. TECUMSEH!

  Mark Medoff. DOING A GOOD ONE FOR THE RED MAN

Stuart Vaughan. GHOST DANCE

1975 Hanay Geiogamah. 49

Kermit Hunter. CONQUISTADOR

Kermit Hunter. BEYOND THE SUNDOWN

1976 Kermit Hutner. THE McINTOSH TRAIL

1978 Bogdanov, Philip. HIAWATHA

Lan. WINTER DANCERS

1980(?) Lance S. Belville. FOUR HEARTS AND THE LORDS OF THE NORTH

1980 Michael Smuin. A SONG FOR DEAD WARRIORS

Christopher Sergel. BLACK ELK LIVES

1981 Roger Sessions and G. A. Borgese. MONTEZUMA

1982 W. L. Munden. BLUE JACKET

Lanford Wilson. ANGELS FALL

BOOKS

Bataille, Gretchen M., and Charles P. P. Silet. The Pretend Indians. Images of Native Americans in the Movies. Ames: Iowa State University Press, 1980.

Bergquist, G. William. Three Centuries of English and American Drama. England: 1500-1800, United States: 1714-1830. New York: Hafner Publishing Company, 1963

Berkhofer, Robert F. The White Man's Indian: Images of the American Indian From Columbus to the Present. New York: Knopf, 1978.

Bird, Robert Montgomery. Nick of the Woods, or The Jibbenainosay. A Tale of Kentucky. Edited, with introduction, chronology, and bibliography by Cecil B. Williams. American Fiction Series, general editor, Harry Hayden Clark. New York: American Book Company, 1939.

Bissell, Benjamin. The American Indian in English Literature of the Eighteenth Century. Yale Studies in English, vol. LXVIII. New Haven, Conn.: Yale University Press, 1925.

Chateaubriand, François Auguste René, vicomte de. Travels in America. Translated by Richard Switzer. Lexington: University of Kentucky Press, 1969.

Clark, Barrett, general editor. America's Lost Plays. 21 vols. Princeton, N.J.: Princeton University Press, 1940-1941; reprint ed., Bloomington, Ind.: Indiana University Press, 1969.

Cochran, Thomas C., advisory ed.; Wayne Andrews, ed. Concise Dictionary of American History. New York: Charles Scribner's Sons, 1962.

Cooper, James Fenimore. The Wept of Wish-Ton-Wish. Columbus, Ohio: Charles E. Merrill, 1970.

Dippie, Brian W. The Vanishing American: White Attitudes and U. S. Indian Policy. Middletown, Conn.: Wesleyan University Press, 1980.

Drinnon, Richard. Facing West: The Metaphysics of Indian-Hating and Empire-Building. Minneapolis: University of Minnesota Press, 1980.

Drummond, Andrew H. American Opera Librettos. Metuchen, N.J.: Scarecrow Press, 1973.

Dunlap, William. A History of the American Theatre. New York: Burt Franklin, 1963.

Engle, Gary D. This Grotesque Essence: Plays from the American Minstrel Stage. Baton Rouge: Louisiana State University Press, 1978.

Fairchild, Hoxie Neale. The Noble Savage, A Study in Romantic Naturalism. New York: Columbia University Press, 1928; reprint ed., New York: Russell & Russell, 1961.

Fiedler, Leslie A. The Return of the Vanishing American. New York: Stein and Day, 1968.

Foreman, Carolyn Thomas. Indians Abroad. Norman: University of Oklahoma Press, 1943.

Friar, Ralph and Natasha. The Only Good Indian. New York: Drama Book Shop, 1972.

Fussell, Edwin. Frontier: American Literature and the American West. Princeton, N.J.: Princeton University Press, 1965.

Geiogamah, Hanay. New Native American Drama: Three Plays. Norman: University of Oklahoma Press, 1980.

Grimsted, David. Melodrama Unveiled, American Theatre and Culture 1800-1850. Chicago: University of Chicago Press, 1968.

Hazard, Lucy Lockwood. The Frontier in American Literature. New York: Frederick Ungar Publishing Co., 1961.

Hipsher, Edward Ellsworth. American Opera and Its Composers. Philadelphia: Theodore Presser, 1927; reprint ed., New York: Da Capo Press, 1978.

Hixson, Don L., and Don A. Hennessee. 19th Century American Drama, A Finding Guide. Metuchen, N.J.: Scarecrow Press, 1977.

Hutton, Laurence. Curiosities of the American Stage. New York: Harper and Brothers, 1891.

Ireland, Joseph Norton. Records of the New York Stage From 1750 to 1860. 2 vols. New York: Benjamin Blom, 1966.

Jacobs, Wilbur R. Dispossessing the American Indian: Indians and Whites on the Colonial Frontier. New York: Charles Scribner's Sons, 1972.

Jones, Gene. Where the Wind Blew Free: Tales of Young Westerners. New York: W. W. Norton, 1967.

Jonson, Ben. Complete Plays. 2 vols. Everyman's Library. London: J. M. Dent, 1963.

Keiser, Albert. The Indian in American Literature. New York: Octagon Books, 1970.

Ludlow, Noah M. Dramatic Life As I Found It. New York: Benjamin Blom, 1966.

Macminn, George R. Theatre of the Golden Era in California. Caldwell, Ida.: The Caxton Printers, 1941.

Mates, Julian. The American Musical Stage Before 1800. New Brunswick, N.J.: Rutgers University Press, 1962.

Melville, Herman. The Confidence-Man: His Masquerade. Hershel Parker, ed. Norton Critical Edition. New York: W. W. Norton, 1971.

Monaghan, Jay. The Great Rascal: The Life and Adventures of Ned Buntline. Boston: Little, Brown, 1952.

Moody, Richard. Dramas From the American Theatre 1767-1909. Cleveland and New York: World Publishing, 1966.

Moses, Montrose J. The Fabulous Forrest: The Record of an American Actor. New York: Benjamin Blom, 1969.

_____, ed. Representative Plays by American Dramatists. 3 vols. New York: E. P. Dutton, 1918; reprint ed., New York: Benjamin Blom, 1964.

Mossiker, Frances. Pocahontas, The Life and the Legend. New York: Alfred A. Knopf, 1976.

Murdoch, James E. The Stage, or Recollections of Actors and Acting From an Experience of Fifty Years. A Series of Dramatic Sketches. New York: Benjamin Blom, 1969.

O'Connor, John E. The Hollywood Indian: Stereotypes of Native Americans in Films. Trenton, N.J.: New Jersey State Museum, 1980.

Odell, George C. D. Annals of the New York Stage. 15 vols. New York: Columbia University Press, 1927-1949.

Parkman, Francis. The Conspiracy of Pontiac. New York: Collier Books, 1962.

Pearce, Roy Harvey. The Savages of America. A Study of the Indian and the Idea of Civilization. Baltimore: The Johns Hopkins Press, 1953.

Quinn, Arthur Hobson. A History of the American Drama from the Beginnings to the Civil War. 2 vols. In one. New York: F. S. Crofts, 1936.

_____. A History of the American Drama from the Civil War to Present Day. 2 vols. in one. New York: F. S. Crofts, 1936.

_____. Representative American Plays. New York: Appleton-Century-Crofts, 1953.

Rees, James. The Dramatic Authors of America. Philadelphia: G. B. Zieber, 1845.

Roberts, Kenneth. Northwest Passage. New York: Doubleday, Doran, 1937.

Rogers, Robert. Ponteach; or, The Savages of America. With an Introduction and Biography of the Author by Allan Nevins. Chicago: The Caxton Club, 1917.

Rosenfeld, Sybil. The Theatre of the London Fairs in the Eighteenth Century. Cambridge: At the University Press, 1960.

Rourke, Constance. American Humor. A Study of the National Character. New York: Doubleday, 1931; reprint ed., New York: Doubleday Anchor Books, 1953.

Rusk, Ralph Leslie. The Literature of the Middle Western Frontier. 2 vols. New York: Columbia University Press, 1925.

Seilhamer, George O. History of the American Theatre Before the Revolution. 3 vols. New York: Greenwood Press, 1968.

Sell, Henry Blackman, and Victor Weybright. Buffalo Bill and the Wild West. New York: Oxford University Press, 1955.

Simms, William Gilmore. The Yemassee. Edited, with Introduction, Chronology, and Bibliography by Alexander Cowie. New York: Hafner Publishing, 1962.

Smith, James L. Victorian Melodramas: Seven English, French, and American Melodramas. London: Dent, 1976.

Sonneck, Oscar G. Early Opera in America. New York: G. Schirmer, 1915.

Spiller, Robert, et al., editors. Literary History of the United States. 3rd ed., revised. New York: Macmillan, 1963.

Trigger, Bruce G., volume editor. Handbook of North American Indians: Northeast. (Volume 15.) Washington, D.C.: Smithsonian Institution, 1978.

Tyler, Moses Coit. A History of American Literature 1607-1765. New York: Collier Books, 1962.

Van Every, Dale. Disinherited: The Lost Birthright of the American Indian. Morrow Paperback Editions. New York: William Morrow, 1966.

Wells, Henry W., ed. Three Centuries of Drama: American. 2 vols. New York: Readex Microprint, 1967.

Young, William C. Documents of American Theatre History: Famous American Playhouses 1716-1899. 2 vols. Chicago: American Library Association, 1973.

Zollah, Elemire. The Writer and the Shaman: A Morphology of the American Indian. Translated by Ramond Rosenthal. New York: Harcourt Brace Jovanovich, 1973.

DISSERTATIONS

Cox, Paul Ronald. "The Characterization of the American Indian in American Indian Plays 1800-1860 as a Reflection of the American Romantic Movement." Ph.D. dissertation, New York University, 1970.

Fenton, Frank L. "The San Francisco Theatre, 1849-1859." Ph.D. dissertation, Stanford University, 1942.

Fishman, Josephine. "The Dramatization of the Novels of James Fenimore Cooper." M.A. thesis, Stanford University, 1951.

Green, Reyna Diane. "The Only Good Indian." Ph.D. dissertation, University of Indiana, 1973.

Johnson, Albert Edward. "American Dramatizations of American Literary Material from 1850-1900." Ph.D. dissertation, Cornell University, 1948.

Marchiafava, Bruce Thomas. "The Influence of Patriotism in the American Drama and Theatre, 1773-1830." Ph.D. dissertation, Northwestern University, 1969.

Shames, Priscilla. "The Long Hope: A Study of American Indian

Stereotypes in American Popular Fiction, 1890-1910." Ph.D. dissertation, University of California at Los Angeles, 1969.

Sitton, Fred E. "The Indian Play in American Drama, 1750-1900." Ph.D. dissertation, Northwestern University, 1962.

Switzer, Marjorie Elizabeth. "The Development of Indian Plays on the American Stage with Special Reference to the Pocahontas Story." M.A. thesis, University of Chicago, 1929.

ARTICLES

Amacher, Richard E. "Behind the Curtain with the Noble Savage: Stage Management of Indian Plays 1825-1860." Theatre Survey, vol. 7, no. 2 (Nov. 1966): 101-14.

Bank, Rosemarie K. "Melodrama as a Social Document: Social Factors in the American Frontier Play." Theatre Studies 22 (1975-1976): 42-48.

Brown, K. M. "A Native American Theatre Ensemble." Journal of American Indian Education 13 (Oct. 1973): 1-6.

Drummond, A. M., and Richard Moody. "Indian Treaties: The First American Dramas." Quarterly Journal of Speech XXXIX (1953): 15-24.

Hartwell, A. A. "The Life, Deeds, and Teachings of Tammany, the Famous Indian Chief." New York Folklore Quarterly, vol. 5, no. 1 (Spring 1949): 25-30.

Locke, Robinson. The Robinson Locke Collection of Scrapbooks. Series 5, volume 53. Lincoln Center Library for the Performing Arts. New York Public Library.

McCutcheon. "The First English Plays in New Orleans." American Literature 11 (May 1939): 174.

"The Redskin in the Drama, Early Representations of the American Indian in the Theatre." New York Dramatic Mirror. 20 (July 1907): 1.

Rich, Louis M. "The American Indian Plays." Quarterly Journal of Speech XXX (1944): 212.

Shank, Theodore, Jr. "Theatre for the Majority: Its Influence on a 19th-Century American Theatre." ETJ 11 (1959): 188-189.

PHONOGRAPH RECORDS

John Bray. <u>The Indian Princess</u>. Federal Music Society Opera
Company, John Baldon, conductor. New World Records #232.

<u>Music of the Federal Era</u>. Federal Music Society, John Baldon,
conductor. New World Records #299.

<u>Works by Arthur Farwell, Preston Ware Orem and Charles Wakefield
Cadman</u>. The New World Singers, John Miner, conductor. New
World Records #213.

INTERVIEWS

Discussion of Indian plays and research with Hanay Geiogamah at
the American Indian Community House, New York, September 22,
1983.